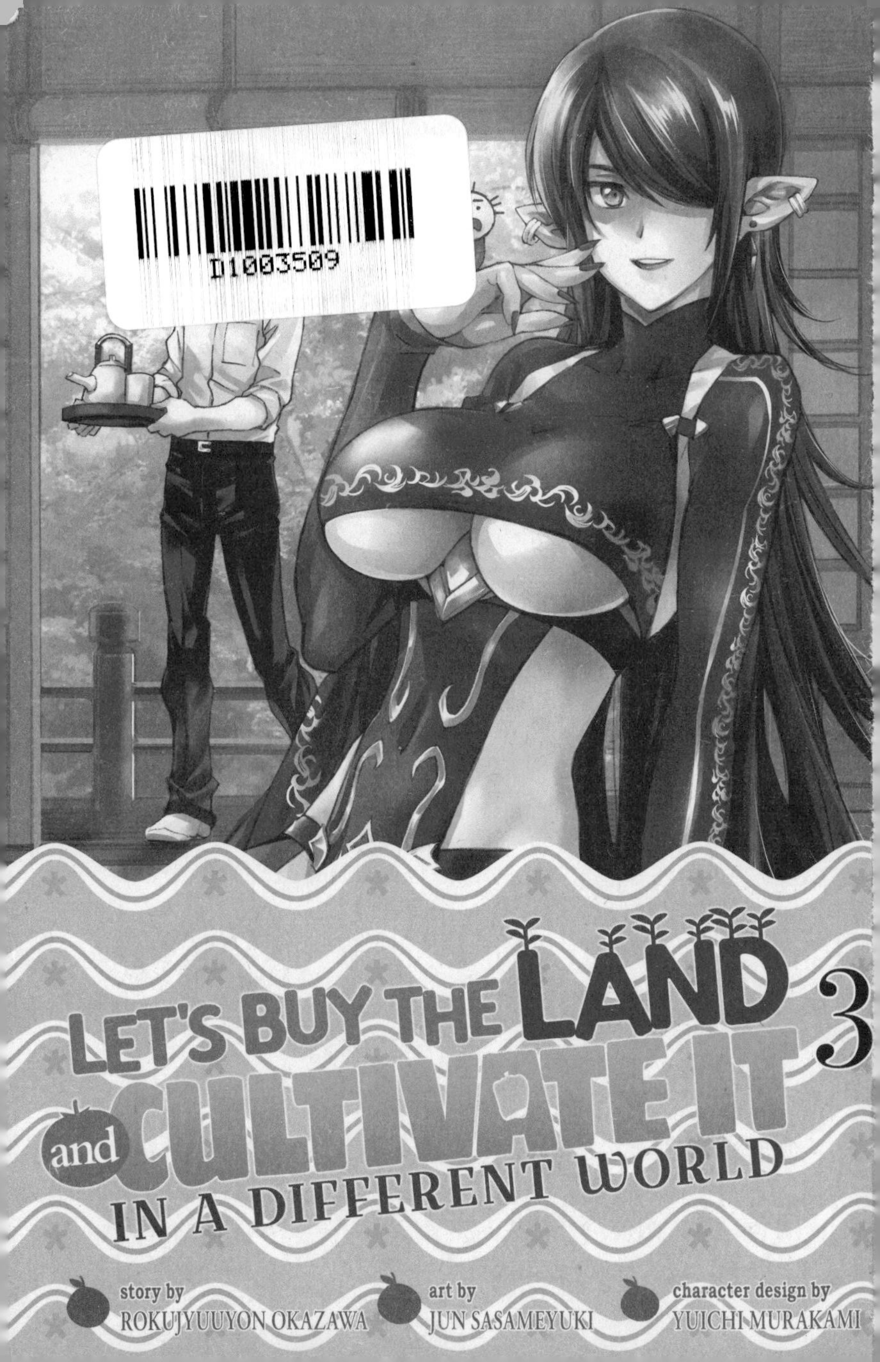

LET'S BUY THE LAND and CULTIVATE IT IN A DIFFERENT WORLD 3

story by
ROKUJYUUYON OKAZAWA

art by
JUN SASAMEYUKI

character design by
YUICHI MURAKAMI

Characters

Kidan

Originally named Itonami Norio, Kidan was a run-of-the-mill office worker until the day he was suddenly summoned to another world. Though initially exiled for not being gifted with a skill, he actually possessed a literally god-given power called the Supreme Wielder, which makes him the master of any tool he holds in his hands.

Plattie

Hails from the Merfolk Kingdom. She's a prideful mermaid who looks down on land-dwellers and their treatment of the seas. But ever since being fished up by Kidan, she's committed herself to being his wife. She's also famous for making magical potions and contributes greatly to Kidan's efforts in developing the land.

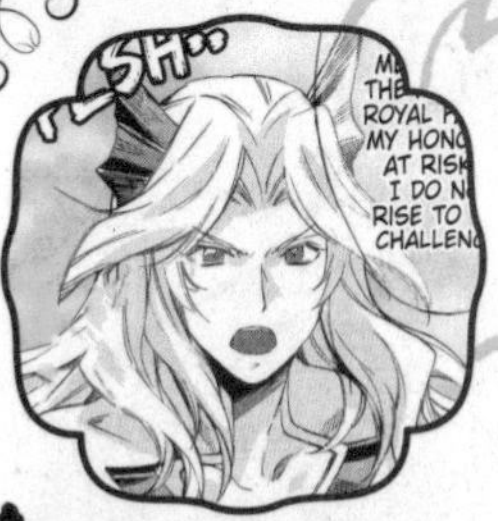

Arowana

The Crown Prince of the Merfolk Kingdom. He originally intervened to take his sister home, but came to recognize Kidan as the Chosen One, and entrusted his sister with him.

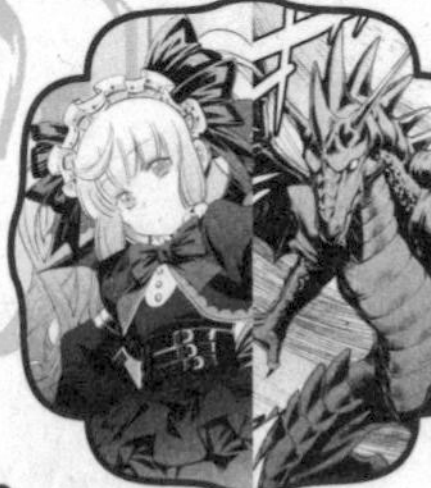

Veel

The Grinzell Dragon. Currently training herself as the heir to the Geyser Dragon, but is always loafing around at the farm.

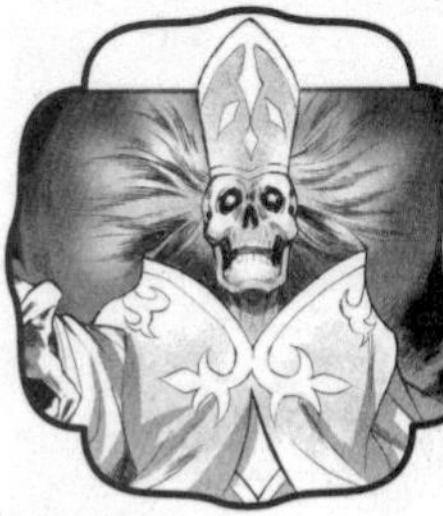

Sensei

The Ruler of the Undead, the Unliving King. The master of a nearby dungeon and Kidan's neighbor.

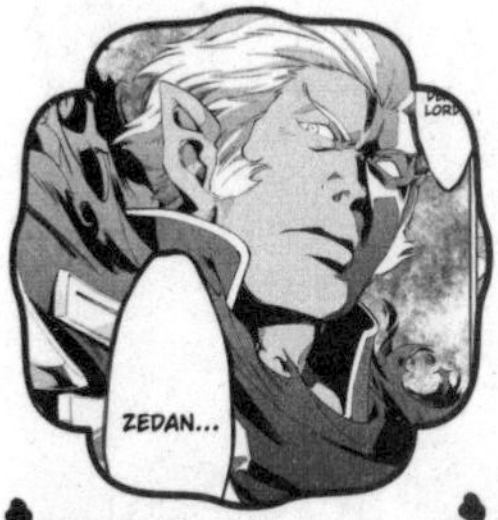
ZEDAN...

Zedan

The Demon Lord. Upon returning from battle, he found that Astareth had been removed from her position as one of the Four Heavenly Kings.

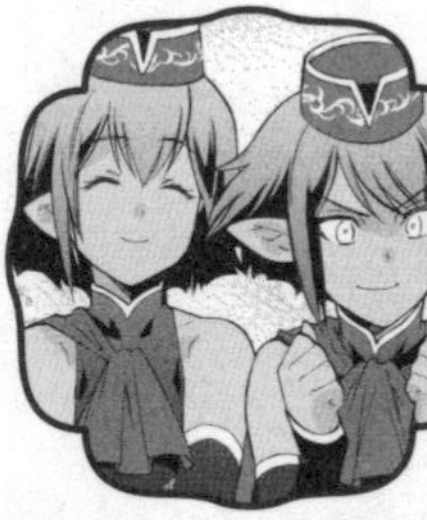

Belena and Bati

Aides to Astareth. They are her loyal followers and left the Land of Demons with her.

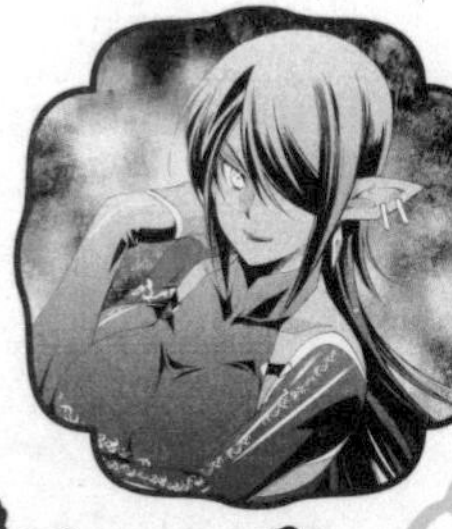

Astareth

Astareth of Chaos, one of the Four Heavenly Kings of the Demon Lord. After losing the battle at the farm, she was kicked out of the Land of the Demons.

Story

Though he was among a group of humans summoned to another world, Kidan was swiftly tossed aside for not possessing a skill like the others. Unfazed, he decided to dedicate himself to this second chance at life by buying and cultivating a plot of land on the wild frontier, along with his new wife, Plattie, and their neighbors, Sensei and Veel. Plattie's brother, the Mermaid Prince Arowana, had originally intended to bring her back home, but grew to understand their relationship. When demon forces attacked, Kidan and his crew held their ground effortlessly. This defeat caused the leader of the attack, Astareth, to be banished from the Land of Demons, forcing her to seek refuge on the farm.

Contents

CHAPTER 13

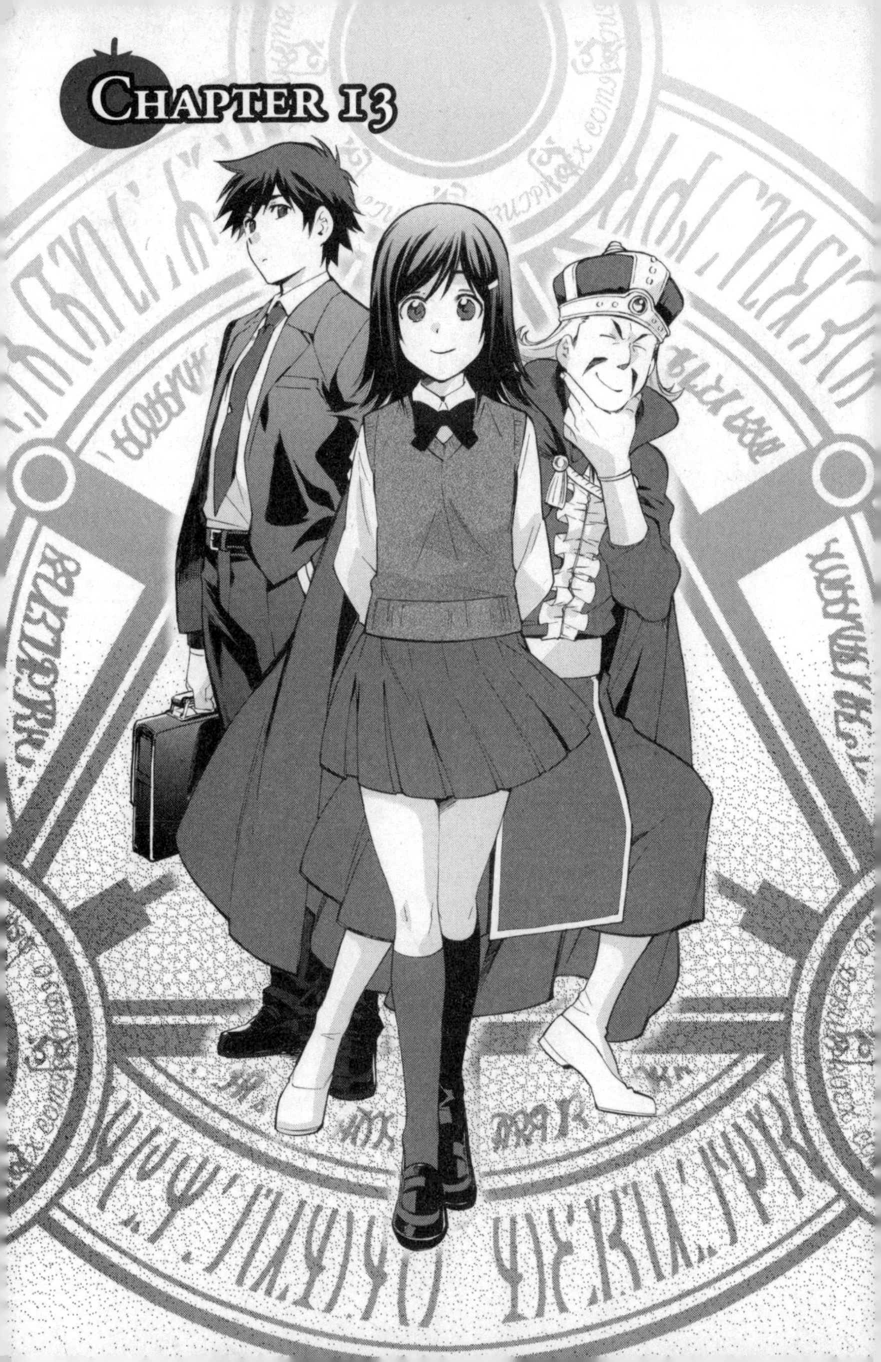

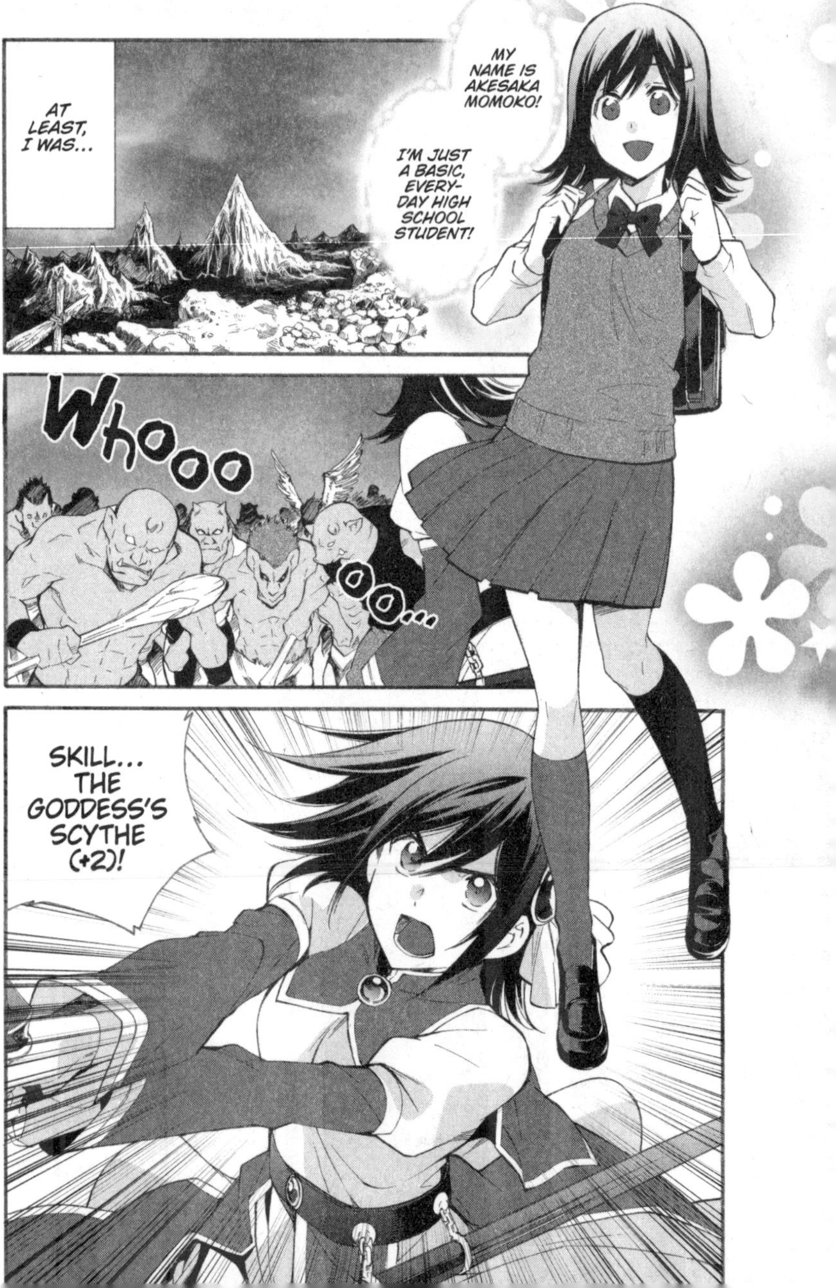
MY NAME IS AKESAKA MOMOKO!
I'M JUST A BASIC, EVERY-DAY HIGH SCHOOL STUDENT!
AT LEAST, I WAS...
Whoooooo...
SKILL... THE GODDESS'S SCYTHE (+2)!

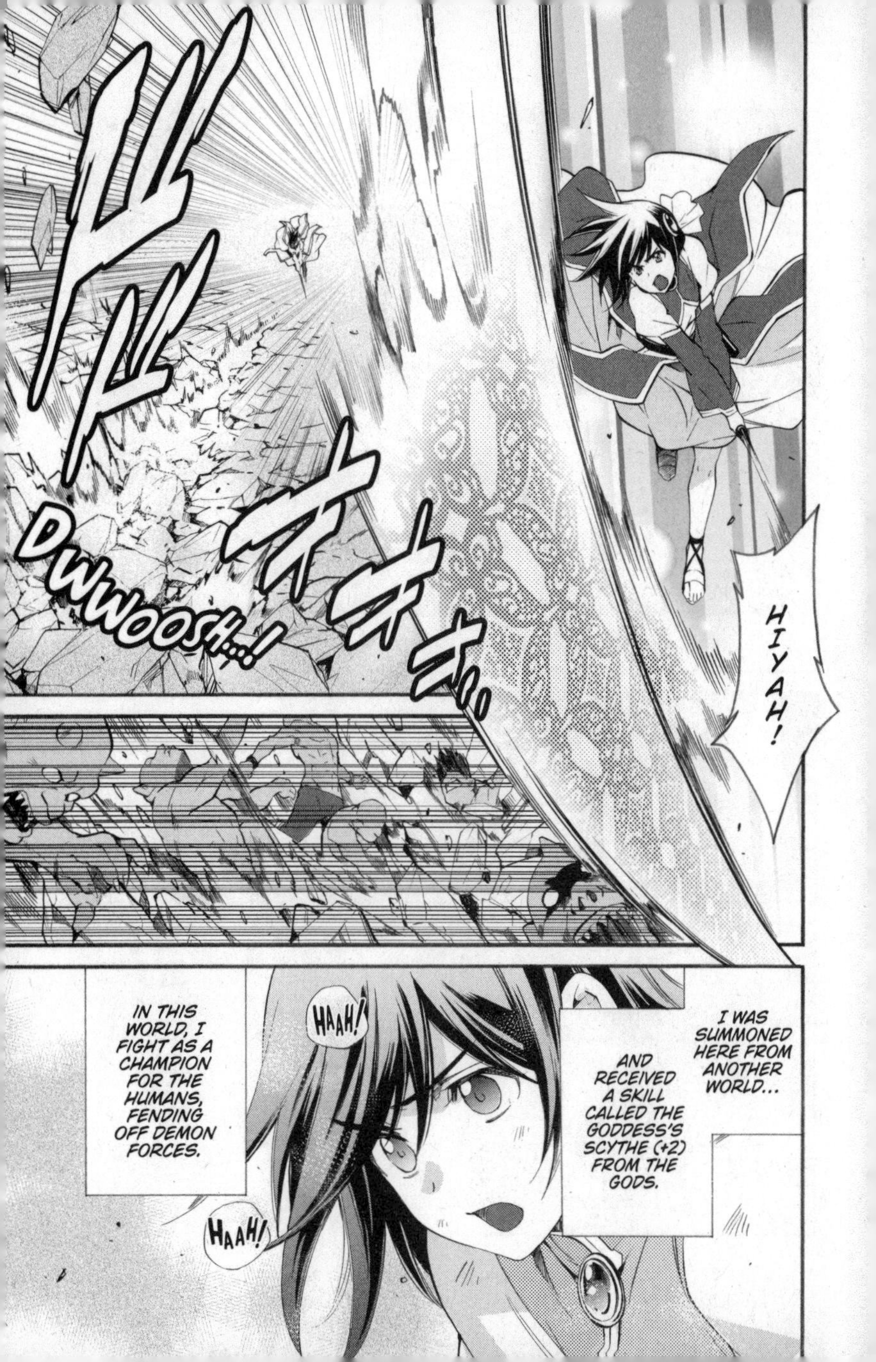
HIYAH!
DWWOOSH...!
I WAS SUMMONED HERE FROM ANOTHER WORLD...
AND RECEIVED A SKILL CALLED THE GODDESS'S SCYTHE (+2) FROM THE GODS.
HAAH!
IN THIS WORLD, I FIGHT AS A CHAMPION FOR THE HUMANS, FENDING OFF DEMON FORCES.
HAAH!

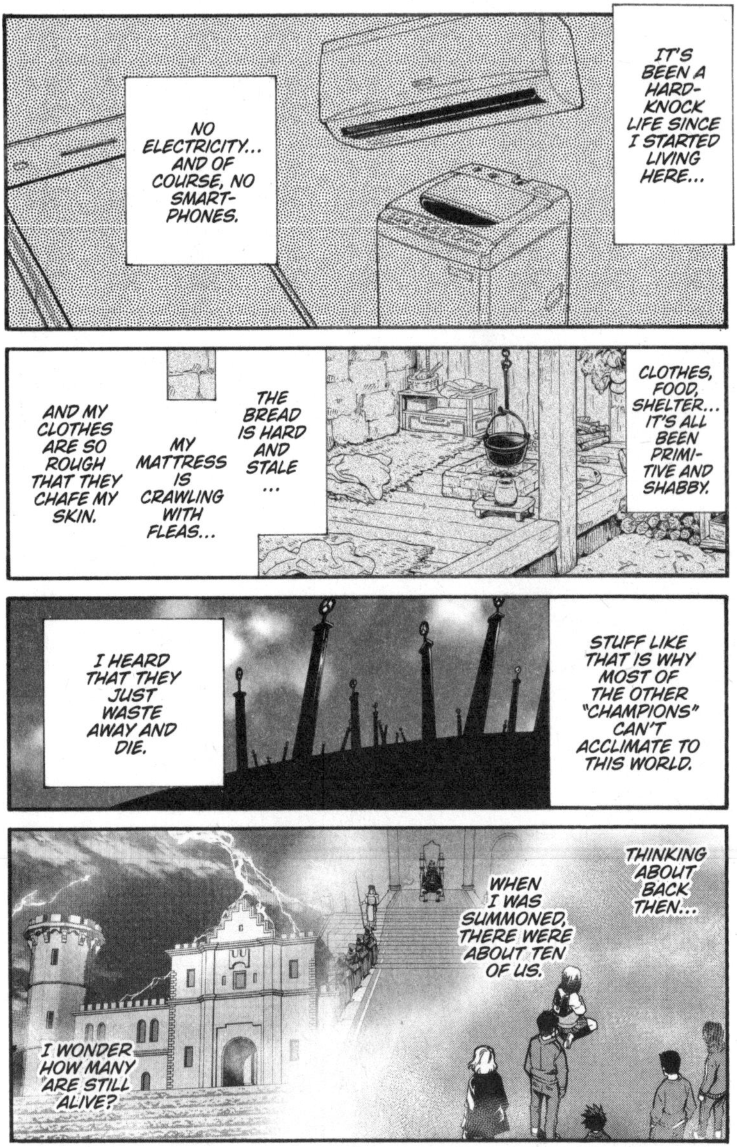
IT'S BEEN A HARD-KNOCK LIFE SINCE I STARTED LIVING HERE...
NO ELECTRICITY... AND OF COURSE, NO SMARTPHONES.
CLOTHES, FOOD, SHELTER... IT'S ALL BEEN PRIMITIVE AND SHABBY.
THE BREAD IS HARD AND STALE ...
MY MATTRESS IS CRAWLING WITH FLEAS...
AND MY CLOTHES ARE SO ROUGH THAT THEY CHAFE MY SKIN.
STUFF LIKE THAT IS WHY MOST OF THE OTHER "CHAMPIONS" CAN'T ACCLIMATE TO THIS WORLD.
I HEARD THAT THEY JUST WASTE AWAY AND DIE.
THINKING ABOUT BACK THEN...
WHEN I WAS SUMMONED, THERE WERE ABOUT TEN OF US.
I WONDER HOW MANY ARE STILL ALIVE?

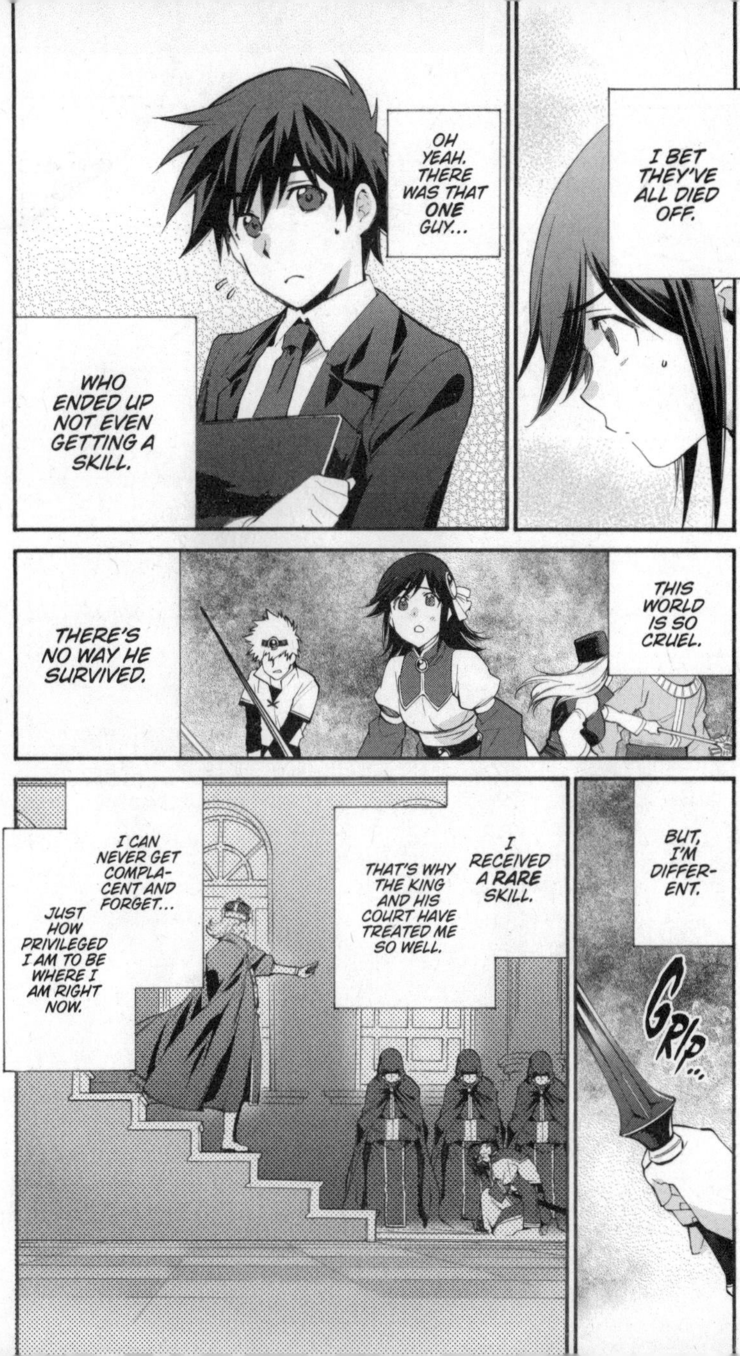

I BET THEY'VE ALL DIED OFF.
OH YEAH. THERE WAS THAT ONE GUY...
WHO ENDED UP NOT EVEN GETTING A SKILL.
THIS WORLD IS SO CRUEL.
THERE'S NO WAY HE SURVIVED.
BUT, I'M DIFFER-ENT.
GRIP...
I RECEIVED A RARE SKILL.
THAT'S WHY THE KING AND HIS COURT HAVE TREATED ME SO WELL.
I CAN NEVER GET COMPLA-CENT AND FORGET...
JUST HOW PRIVILEGED I AM TO BE WHERE I AM RIGHT NOW.

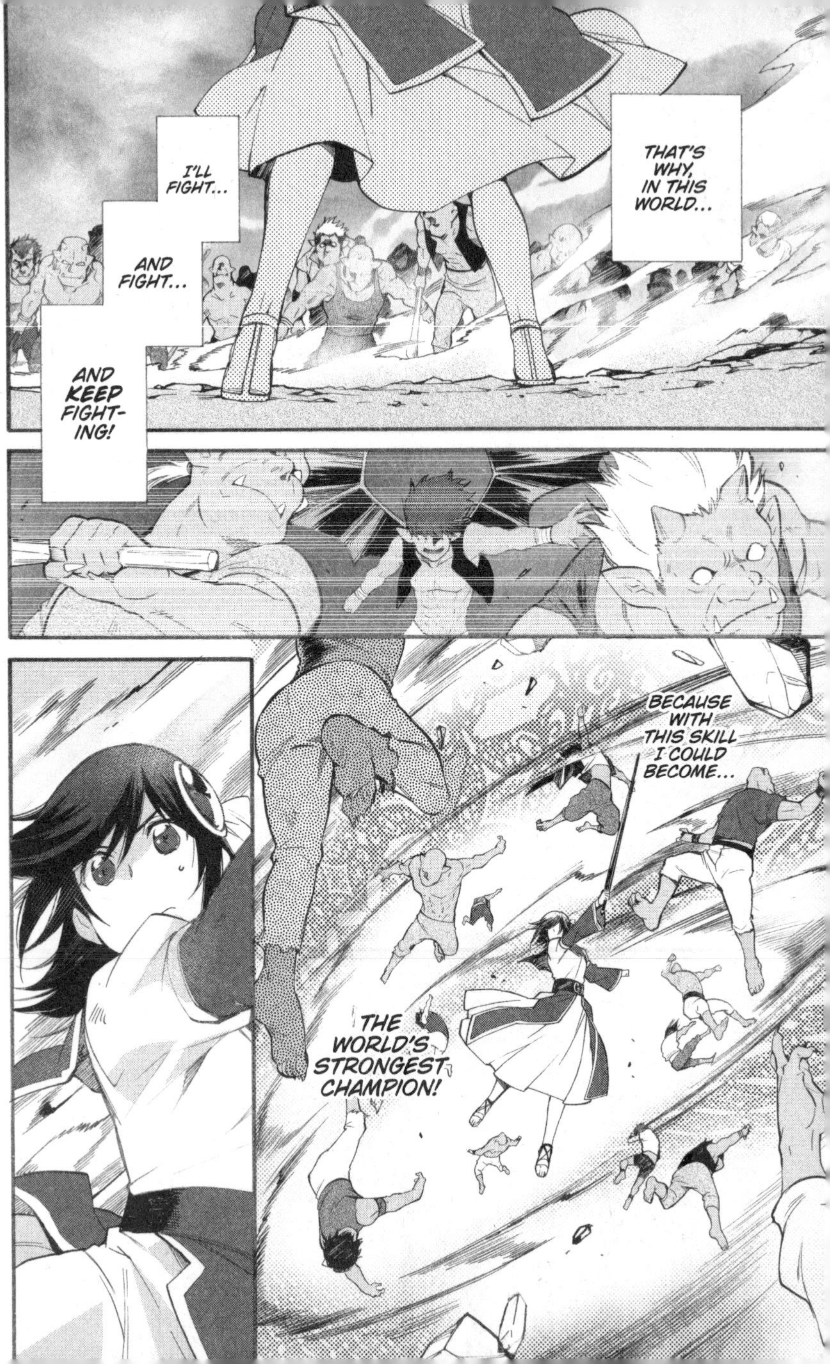
THAT'S WHY, IN THIS WORLD...
I'LL FIGHT...
AND FIGHT...
AND KEEP FIGHTING!
BECAUSE WITH THIS SKILL I COULD BECOME...
THE WORLD'S STRONGEST CHAMPION!

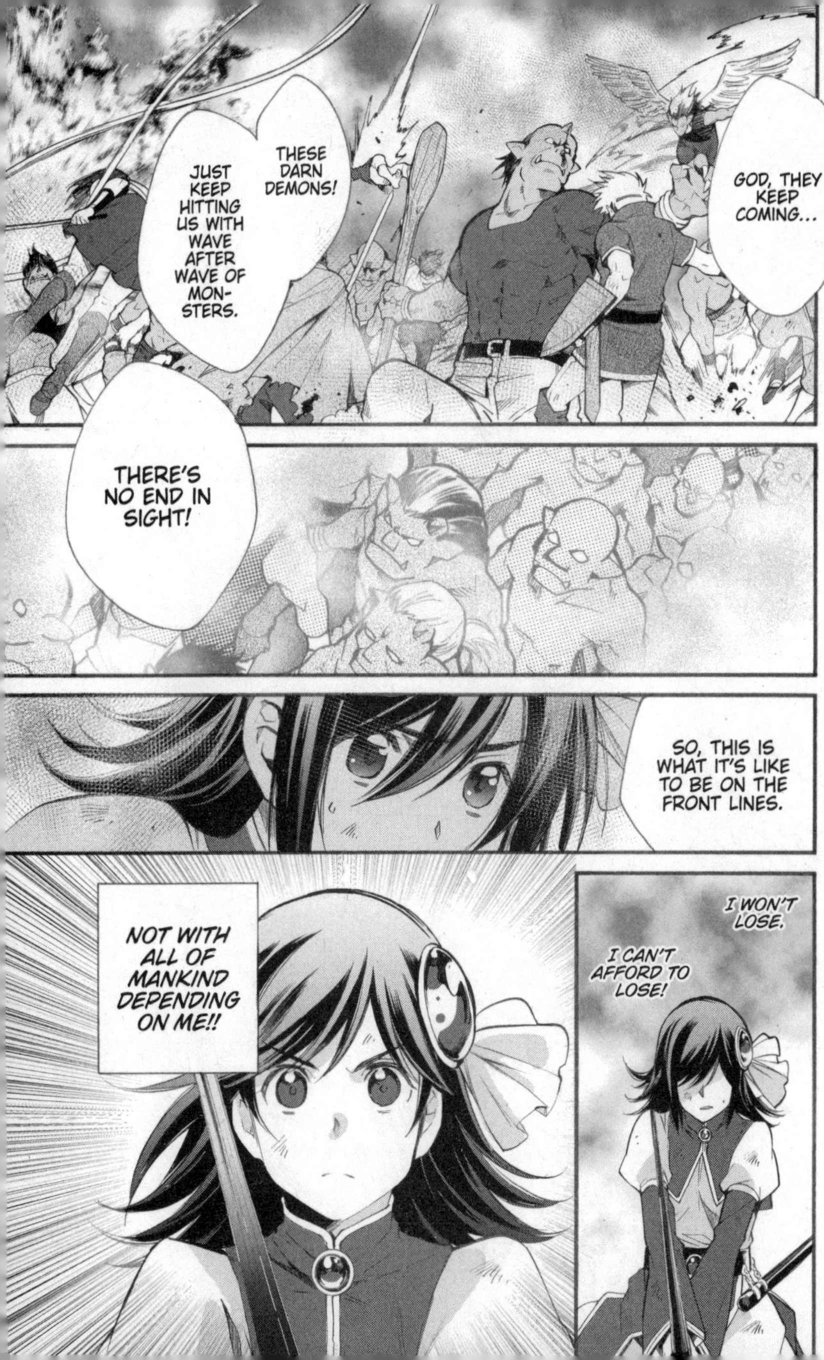
GOD, THEY KEEP COMING...
THESE DARN DEMONS!
JUST KEEP HITTING US WITH WAVE AFTER WAVE OF MON-STERS.
THERE'S NO END IN SIGHT!
SO, THIS IS WHAT IT'S LIKE TO BE ON THE FRONT LINES.
I WON'T LOSE.
I CAN'T AFFORD TO LOSE!
NOT WITH ALL OF MANKIND DEPENDING ON ME!!

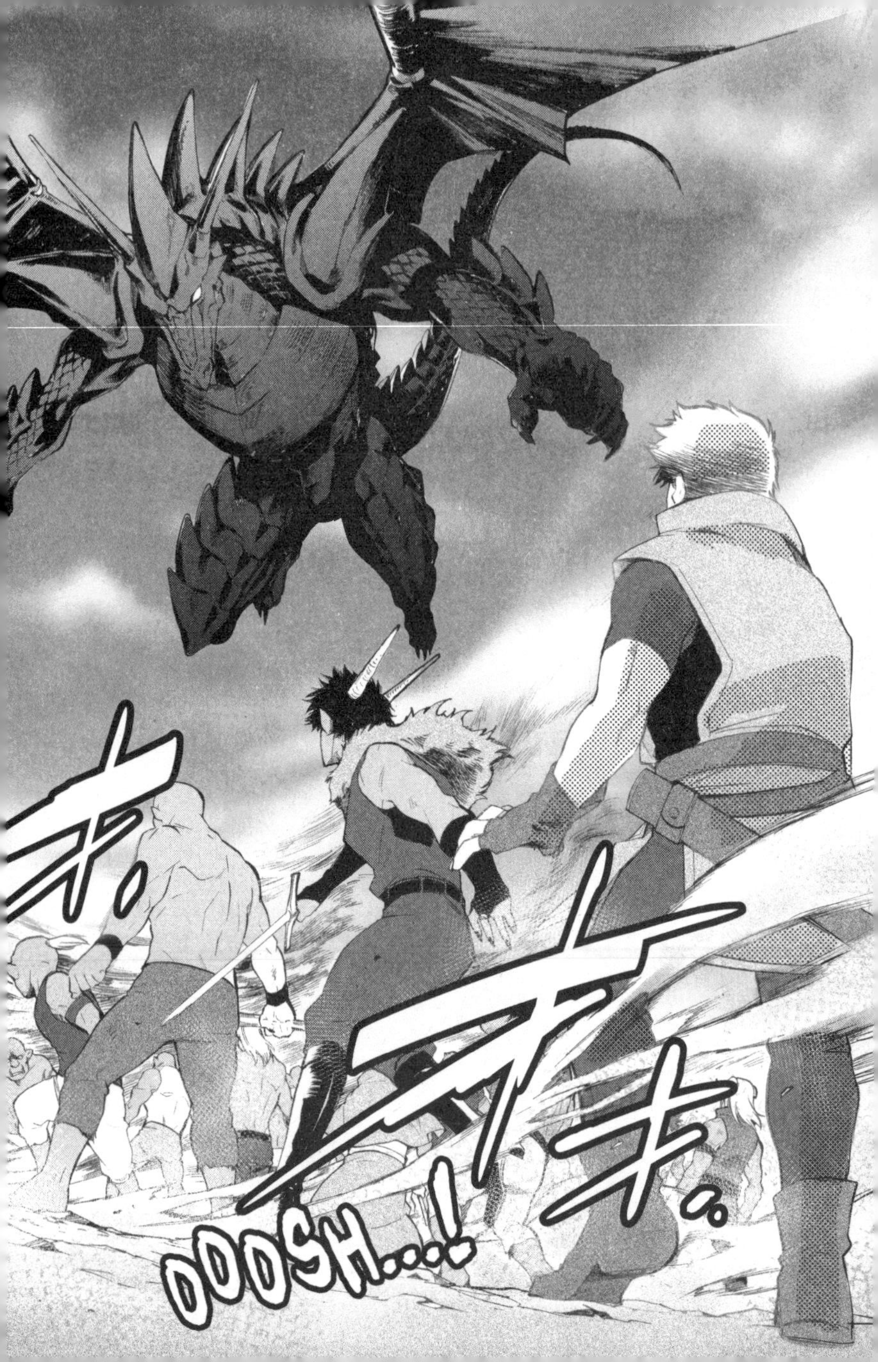
OOOSH...!

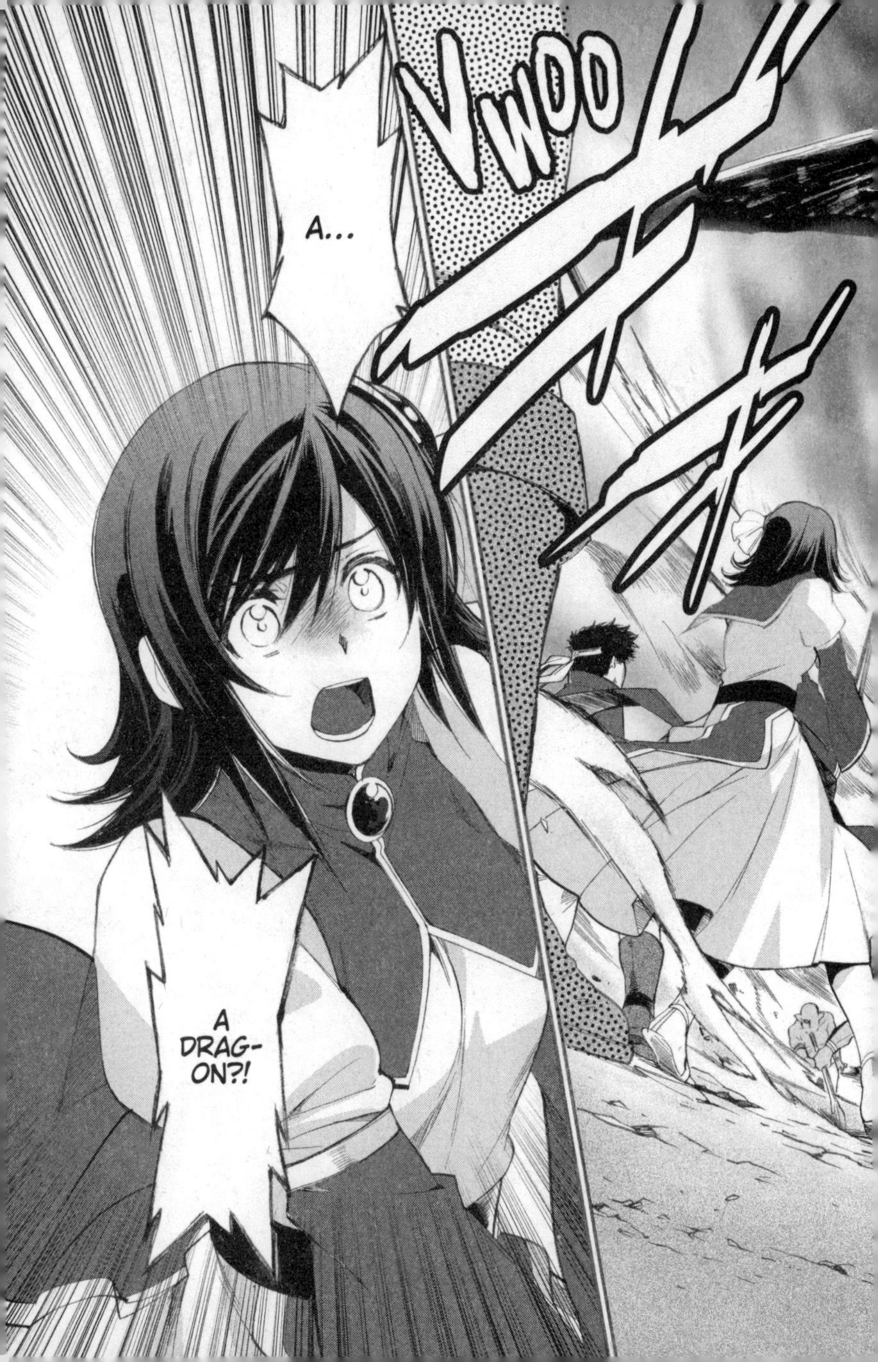
VWOOM
A...
A DRAG-ON?!

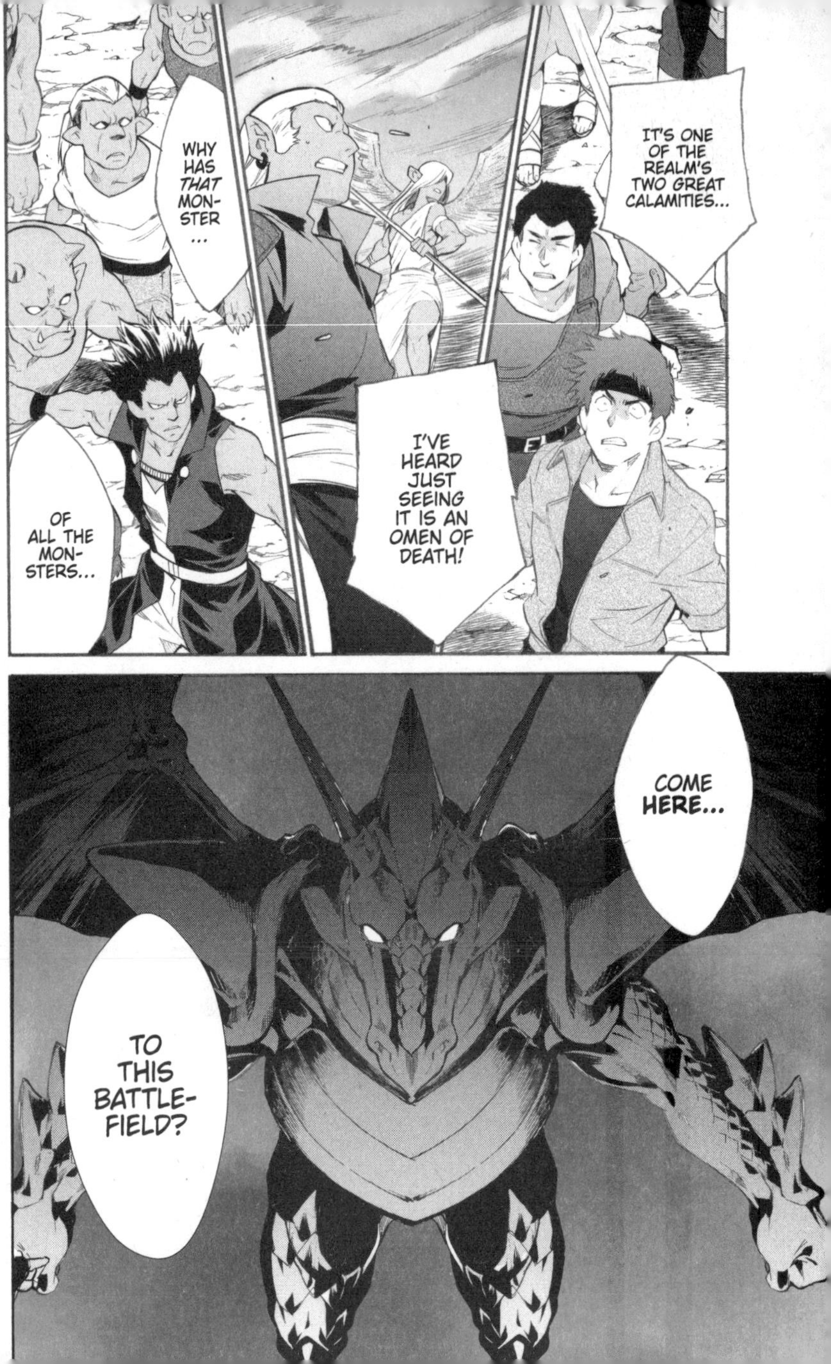
IT'S ONE OF THE REALM'S TWO GREAT CALAMITIES...
I'VE HEARD JUST SEEING IT IS AN OMEN OF DEATH!
WHY HAS *THAT* MON-STER...
OF ALL THE MON-STERS...
COME **HERE...**
TO THIS BATTLE-FIELD?

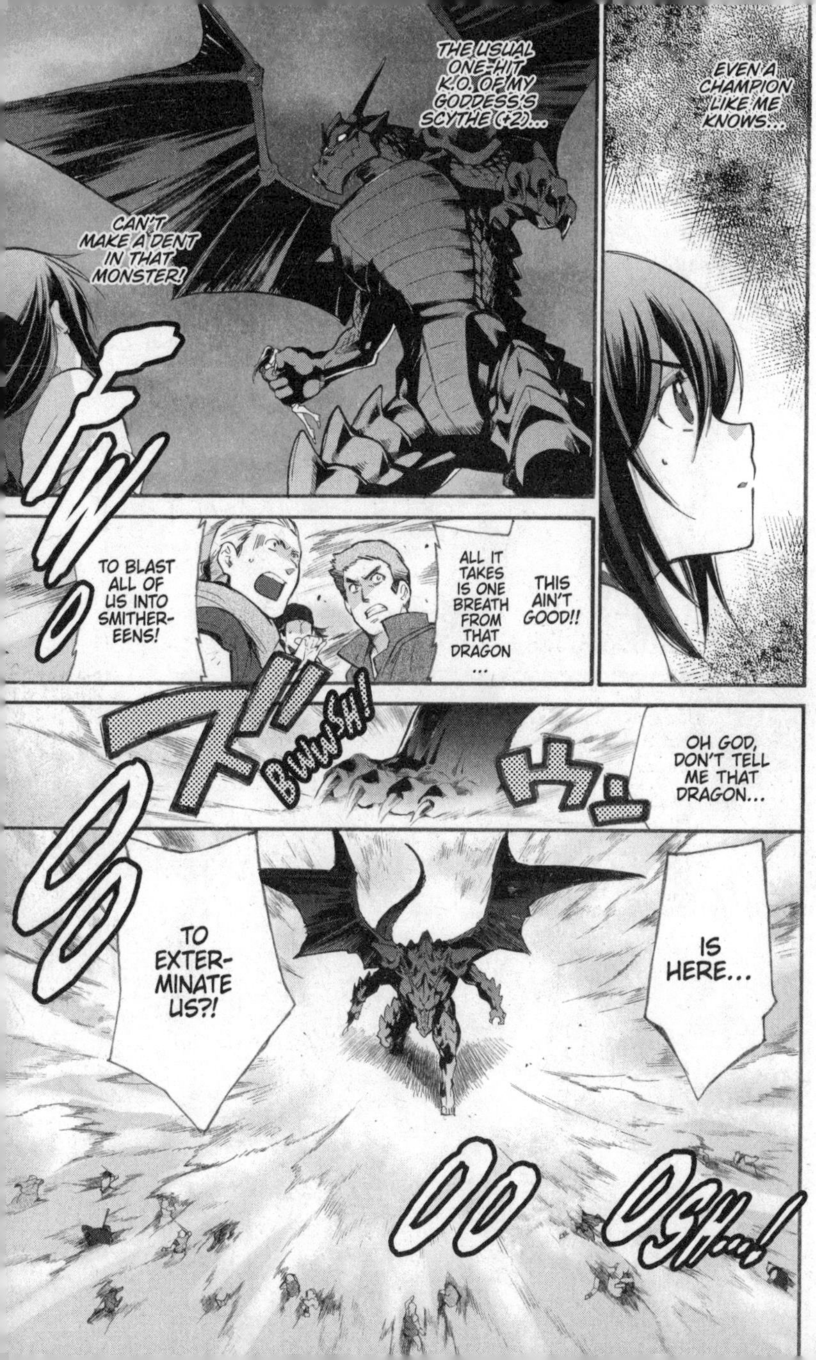
EVEN A CHAMPION LIKE ME KNOWS...
THE USUAL ONE-HIT K.O. OF MY GODDESS'S SCYTHE (+2)...
CAN'T MAKE A DENT IN THAT MONSTER!
THIS AIN'T GOOD!!
ALL IT TAKES IS ONE BREATH FROM THAT DRAGON...
TO BLAST ALL OF US INTO SMITHEREENS!
OH GOD, DON'T TELL ME THAT DRAGON...
BWUUSH!
IS HERE...
TO EXTERMINATE US?!

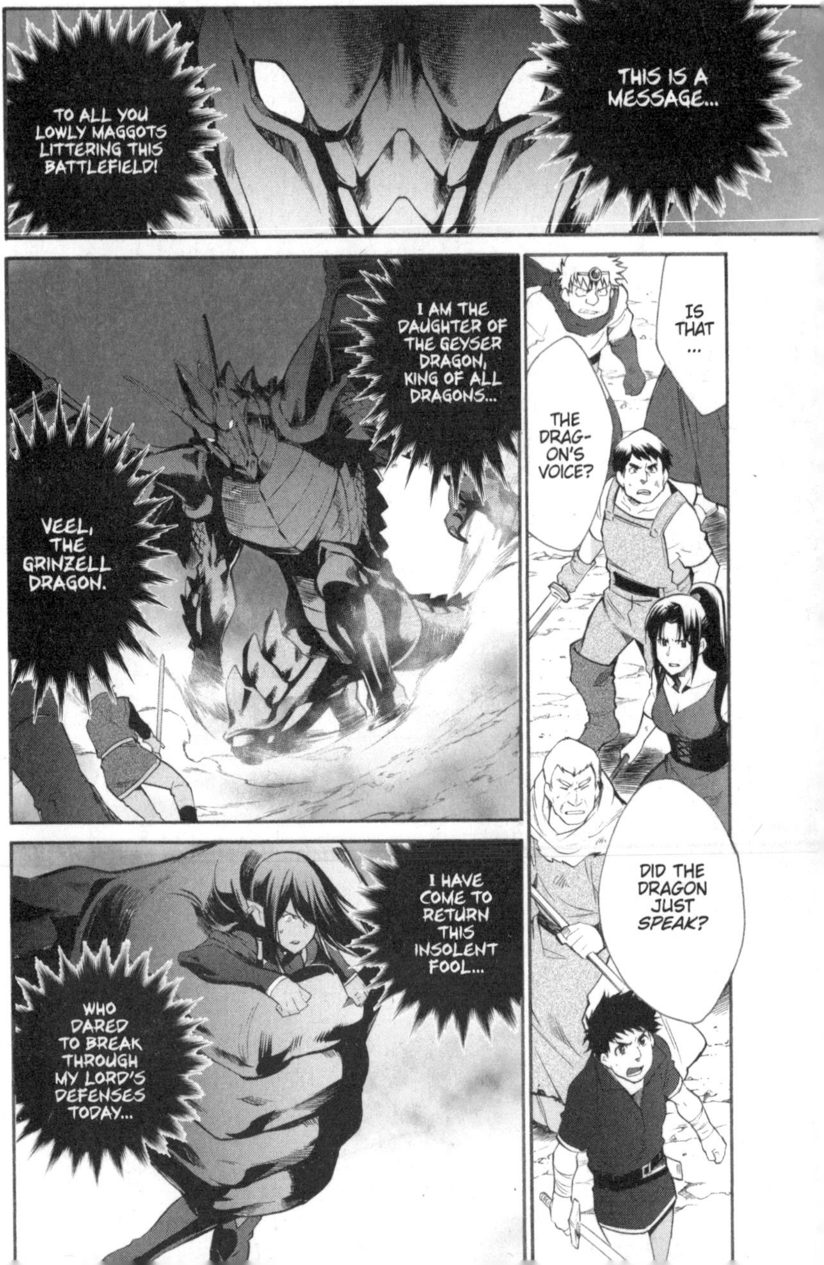
THIS IS A MESSAGE...
TO ALL YOU LOWLY MAGGOTS LITTERING THIS BATTLEFIELD!
IS THAT ...
THE DRAG-ON'S VOICE?
DID THE DRAGON JUST SPEAK?
I AM THE DAUGHTER OF THE GEYSER DRAGON, KING OF ALL DRAGONS...
VEEL, THE GRINZELL DRAGON.
I HAVE COME TO RETURN THIS INSOLENT FOOL...
WHO DARED TO BREAK THROUGH MY LORD'S DEFENSES TODAY...

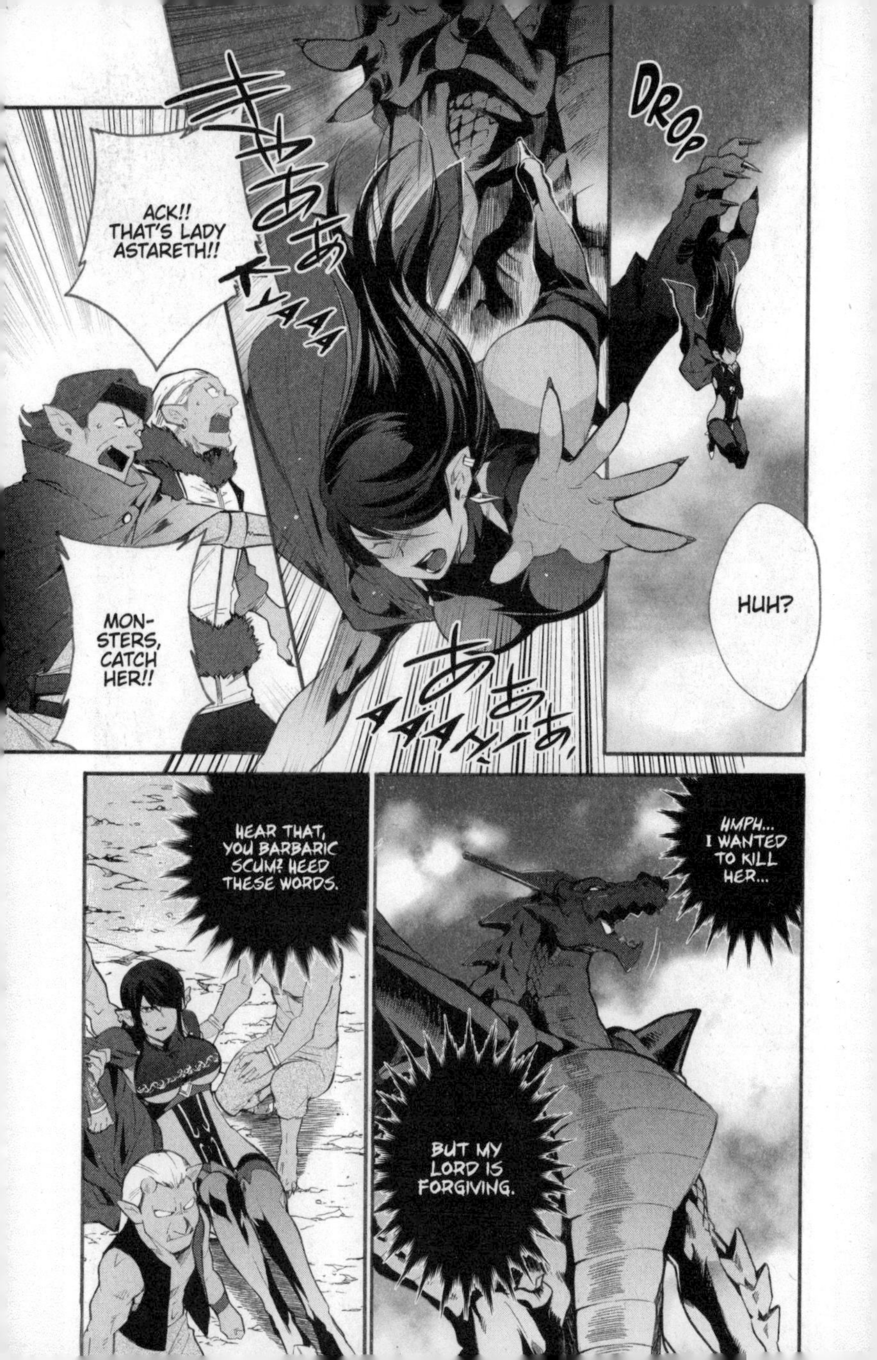
DROP
HUH?
きゃああ
KYAAAA
あああ
AAAAH
ACK!! THAT'S LADY ASTARETH!!
MONSTERS, CATCH HER!!
HMPH... I WANTED TO KILL HER...
BUT MY LORD IS FORGIVING.
HEAR THAT, YOU BARBARIC SCUM? HEED THESE WORDS.

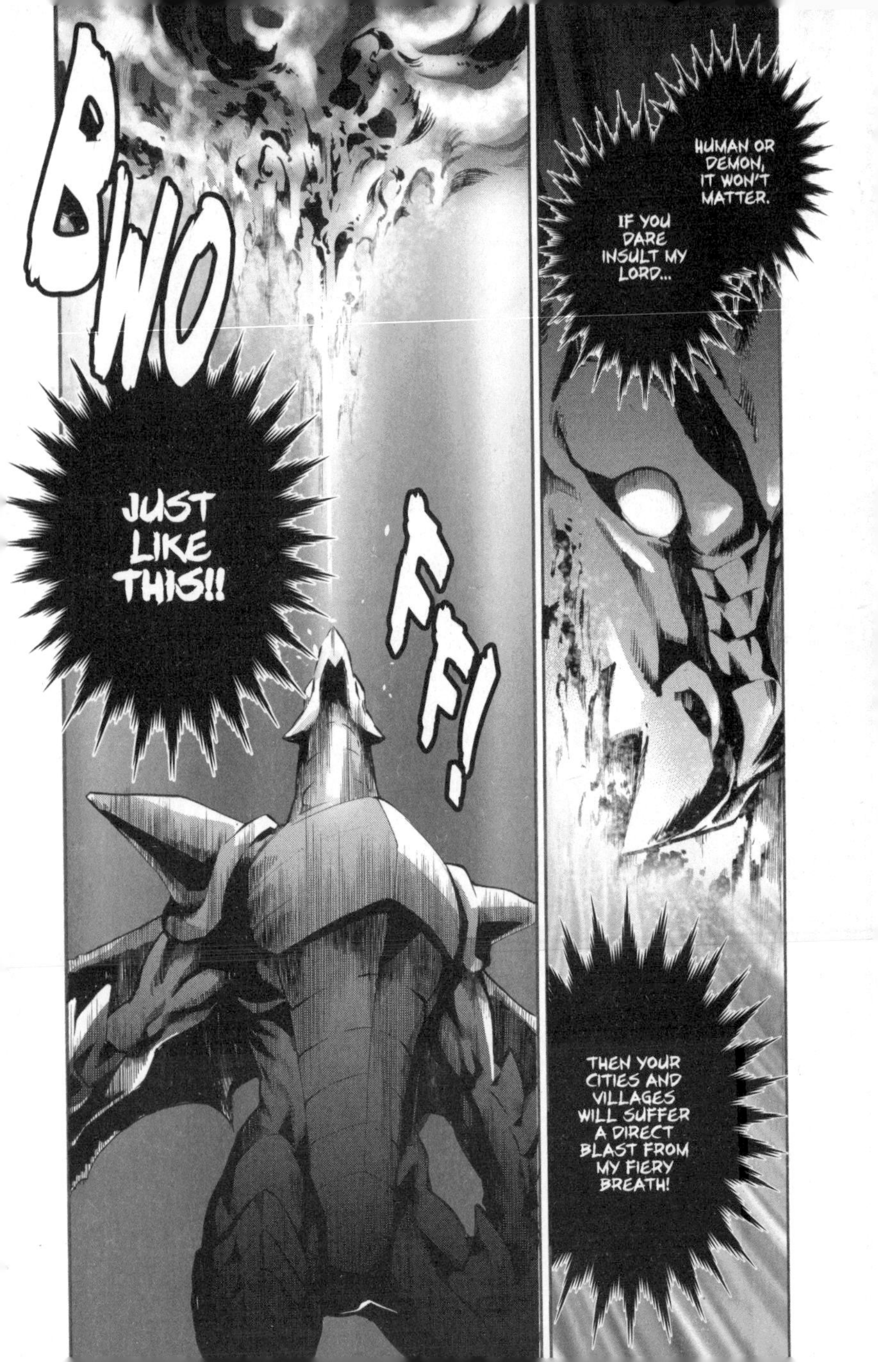
HUMAN OR DEMON, IT WON'T MATTER.
IF YOU DARE INSULT MY LORD...
THEN YOUR CITIES AND VILLAGES WILL SUFFER A DIRECT BLAST FROM MY FIERY BREATH!
BWHO
JUST LIKE THIS!!
FF!

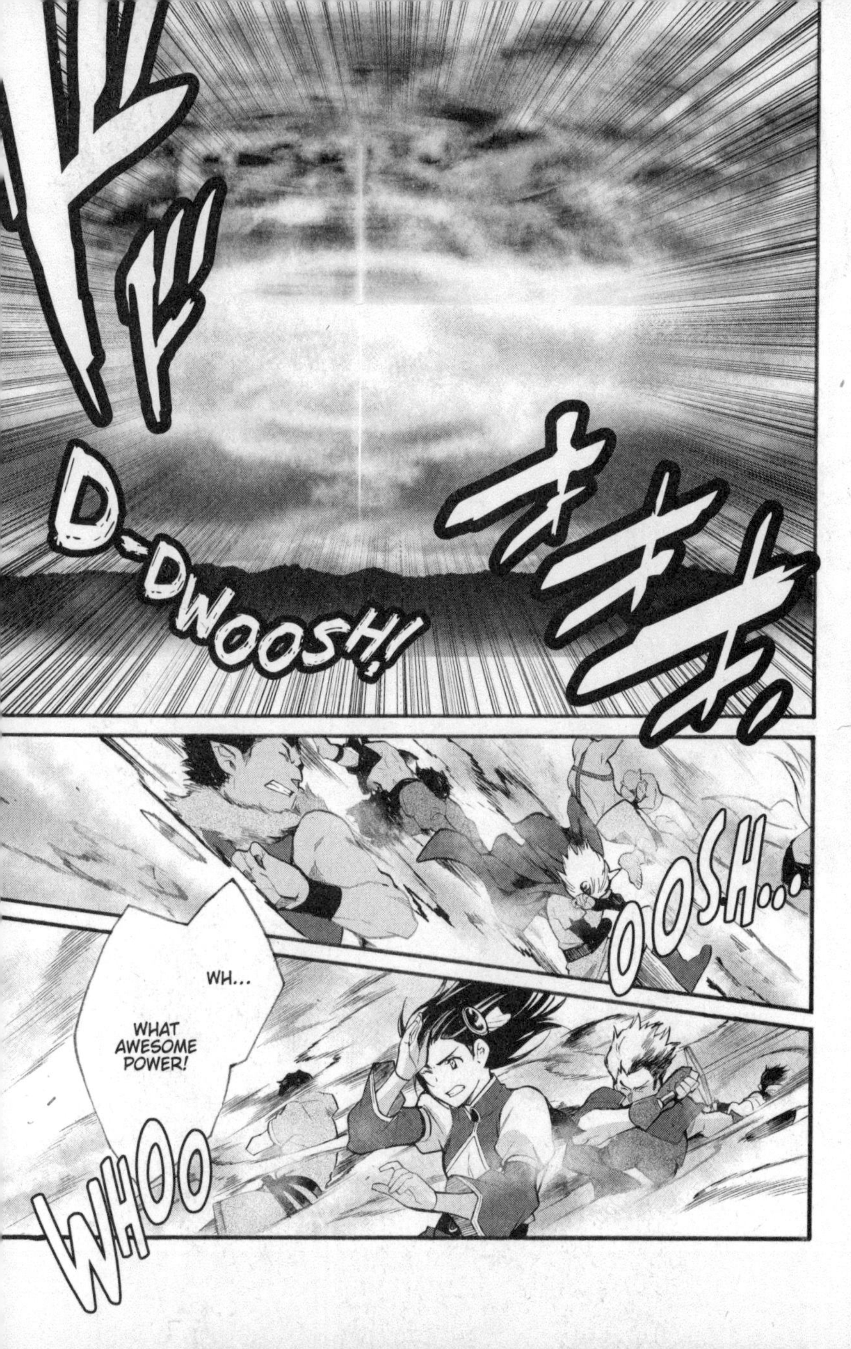
D-DWOOSH!
OOSH...
WH...
WHAT AWESOME POWER!
WHOO

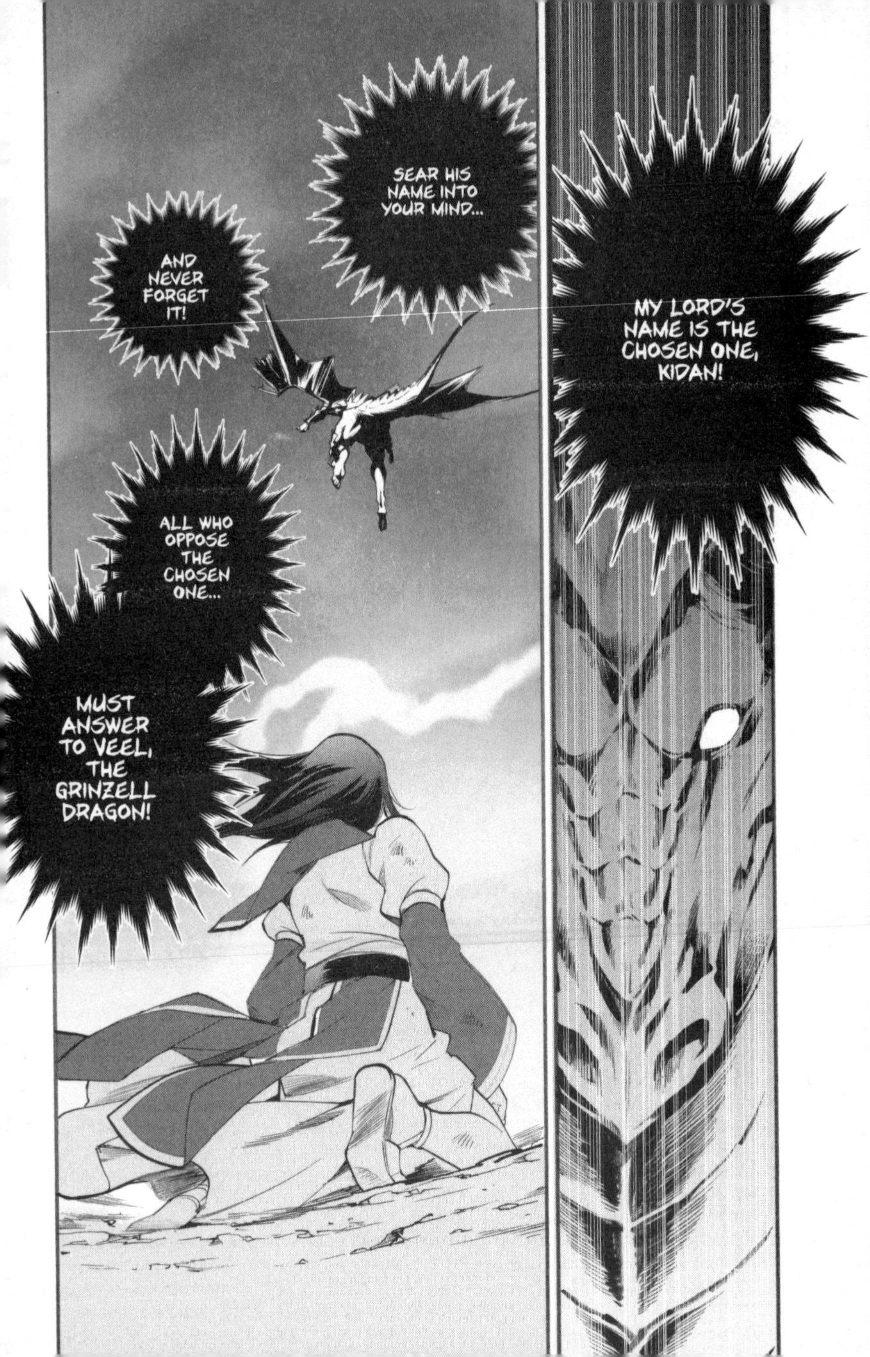
MY LORD'S NAME IS THE CHOSEN ONE, KIDAN!
SEAR HIS NAME INTO YOUR MIND...
AND NEVER FORGET IT!
ALL WHO OPPOSE THE CHOSEN ONE...
MUST ANSWER TO VEEL, THE GRINZELL DRAGON!

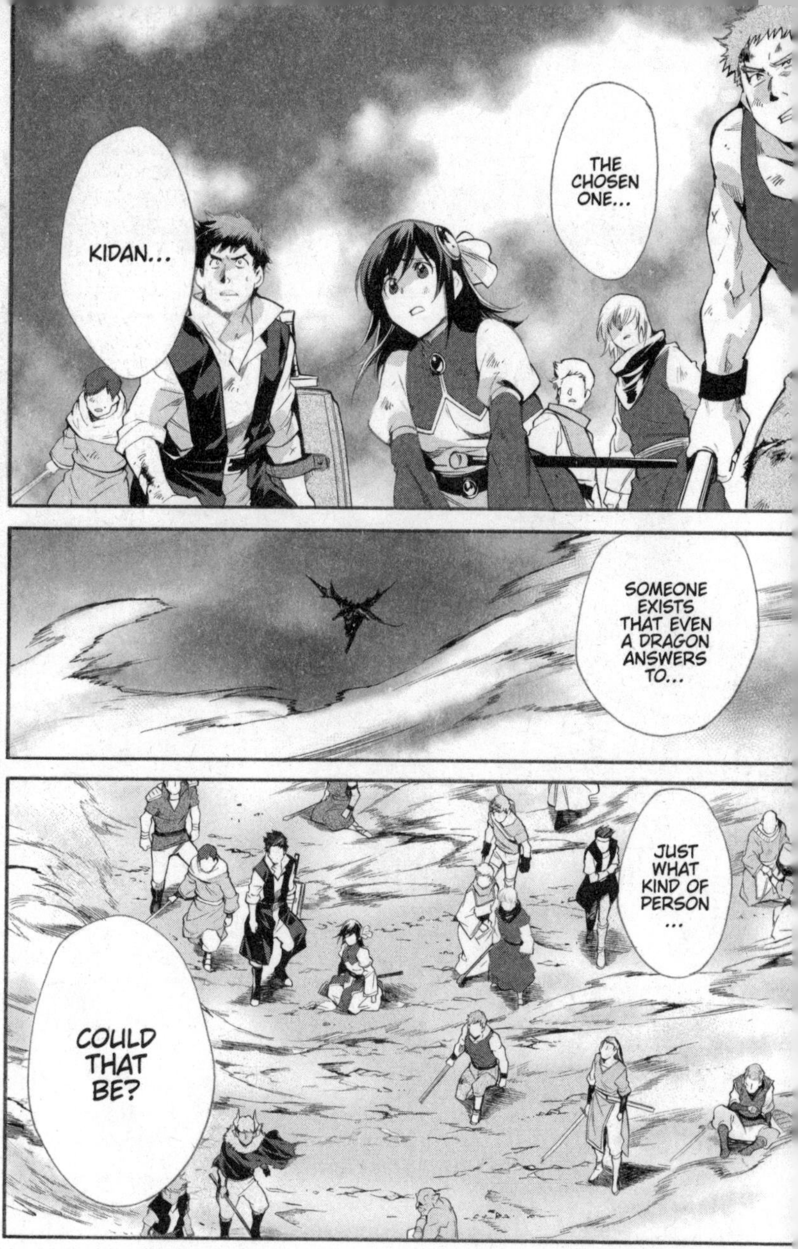
THE CHOSEN ONE...
KIDAN...
SOMEONE EXISTS THAT EVEN A DRAGON ANSWERS TO...
JUST WHAT KIND OF PERSON ...
COULD THAT BE?

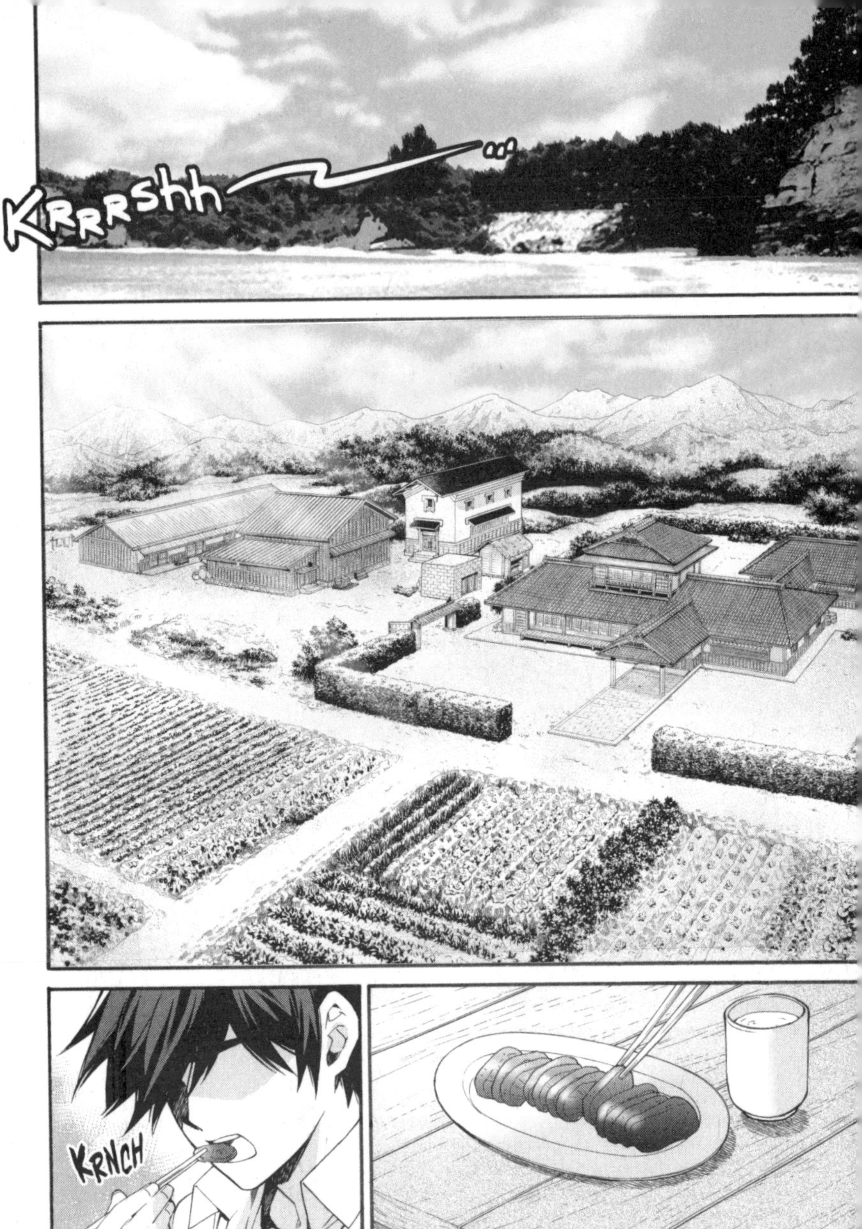
Krrrshh
KRNCH

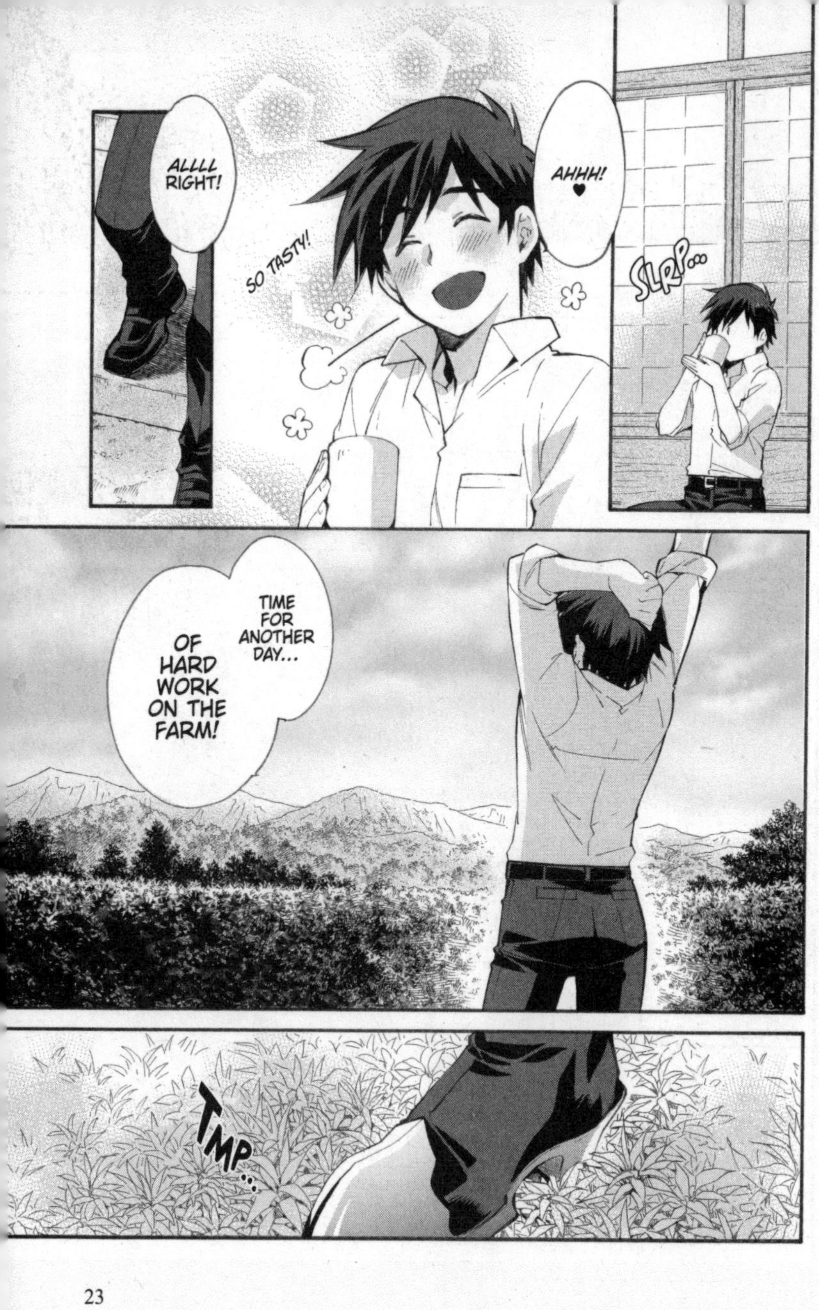
SLRP...
AHHH! ♥
SO TASTY!
ALLLL RIGHT!
TIME FOR ANOTHER DAY...
OF HARD WORK ON THE FARM!
TMP...

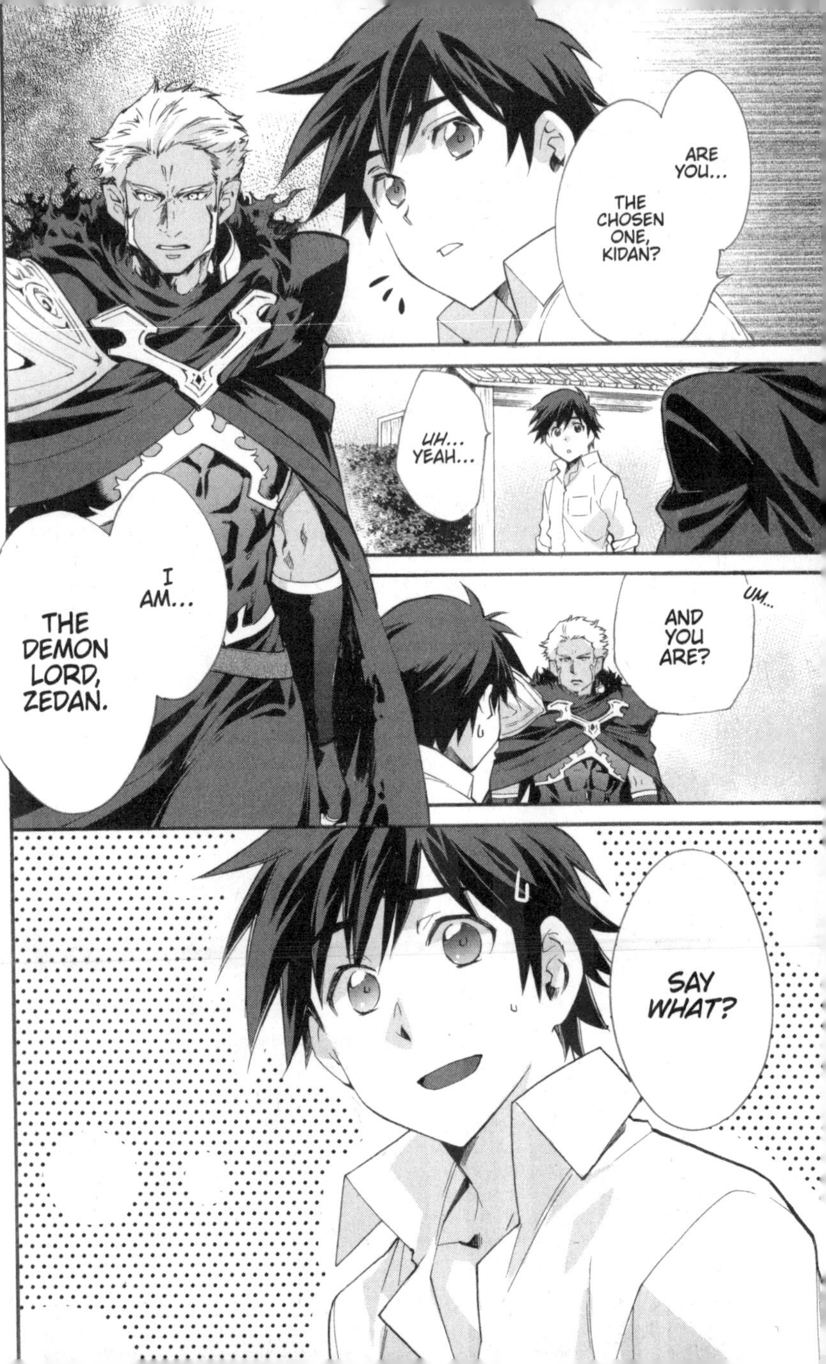
ARE YOU... THE CHOSEN ONE, KIDAN?
UH... YEAH...
UM... AND YOU ARE?
I AM... THE DEMON LORD, ZEDAN.
SAY WHAT?

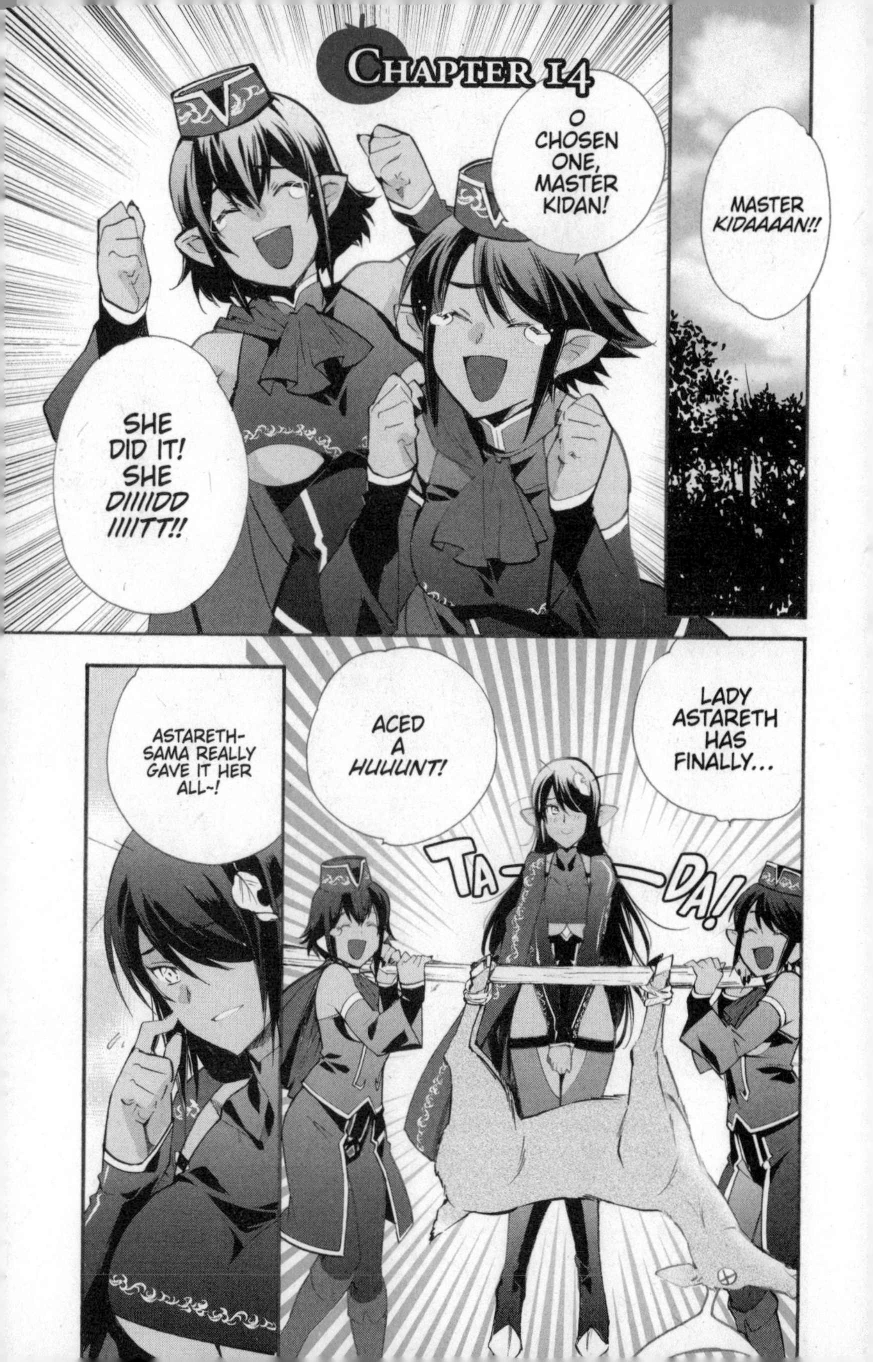
MASTER KIDAAAAN!!
CHAPTER 14
O CHOSEN ONE, MASTER KIDAN!
SHE DID IT! SHE DIIIIDD IIIITT!!
LADY ASTARETH HAS FINALLY...
ACED A HUUUNT!
TA—DA!
ASTARETH-SAMA REALLY GAVE IT HER ALL~!

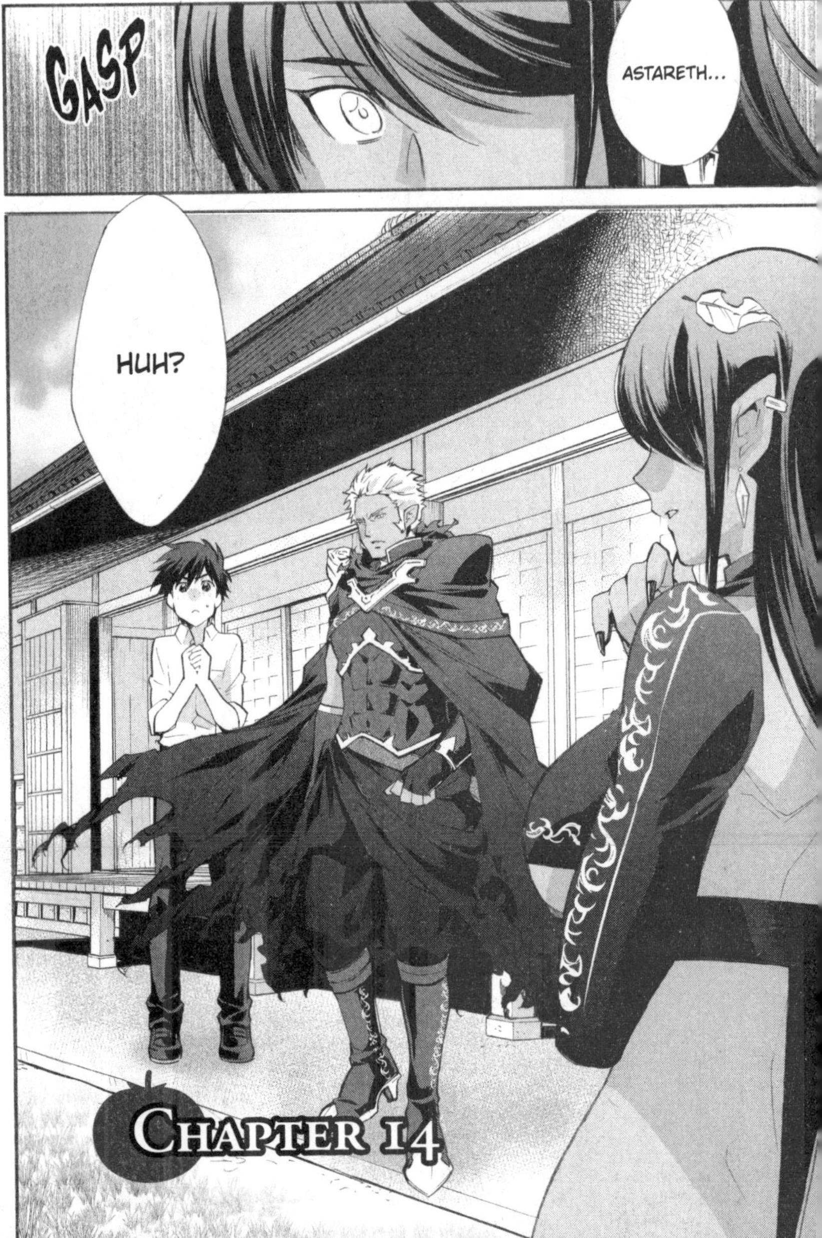
ASTARETH...
GASP
HUH?
CHAPTER 14

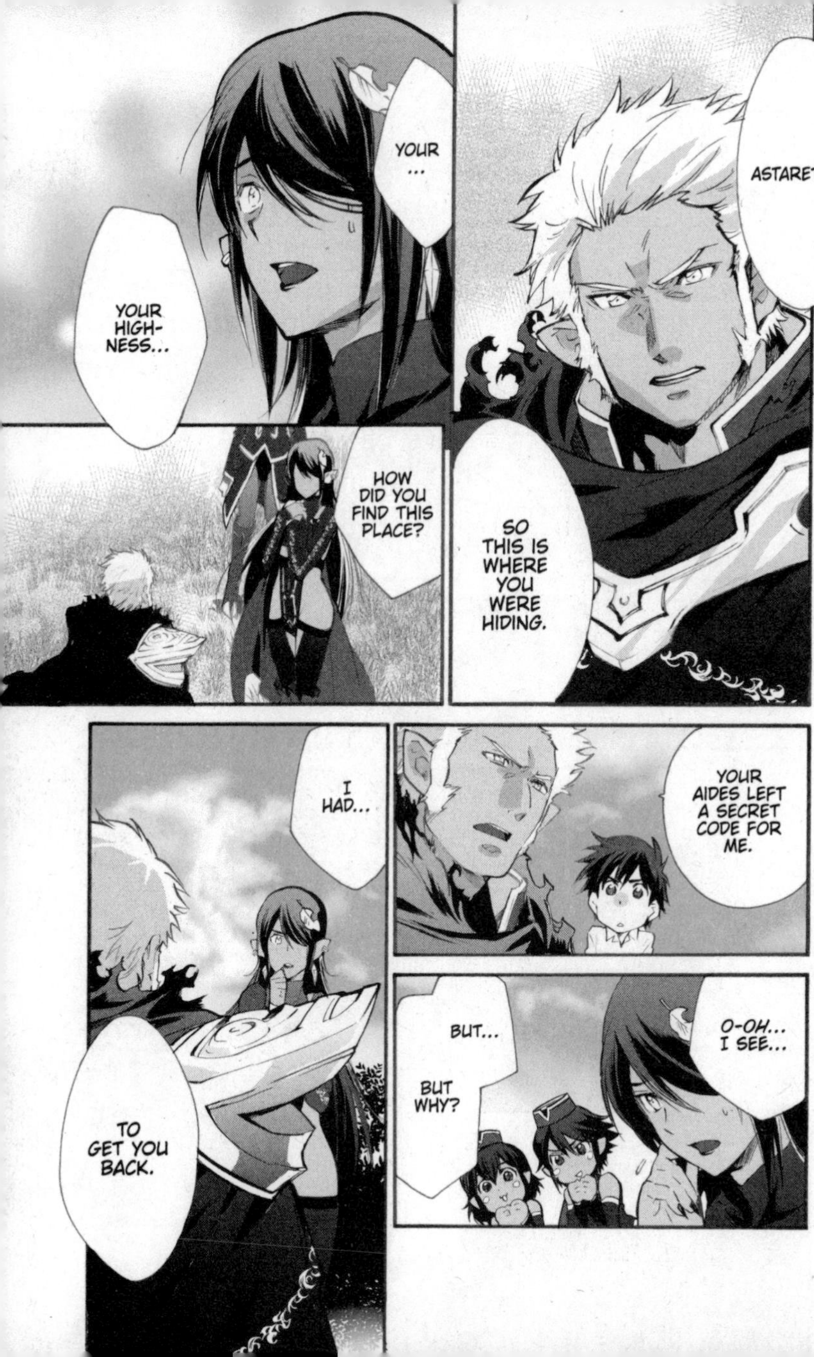
ASTARETH...
SO THIS IS WHERE YOU WERE HIDING.
YOUR ...
YOUR HIGHNESS...
HOW DID YOU FIND THIS PLACE?
YOUR AIDES LEFT A SECRET CODE FOR ME.
O-OH... I SEE...
BUT...
BUT WHY?
I HAD...
TO GET YOU BACK.

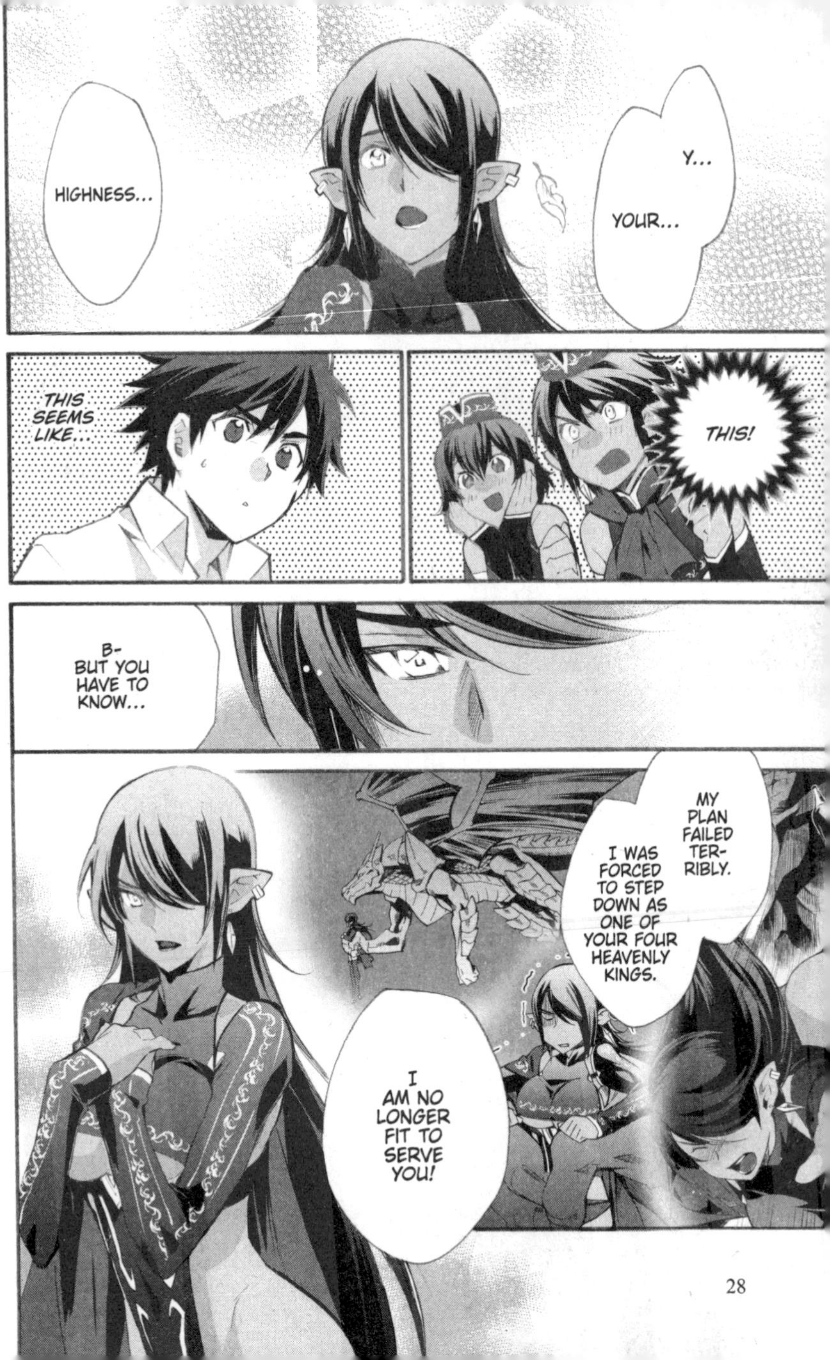
Y... YOUR...
HIGHNESS...
THIS!
THIS SEEMS LIKE...
B- BUT YOU HAVE TO KNOW...
MY PLAN FAILED TER- RIBLY.
I WAS FORCED TO STEP DOWN AS ONE OF YOUR FOUR HEAVENLY KINGS.
I AM NO LONGER FIT TO SERVE YOU!

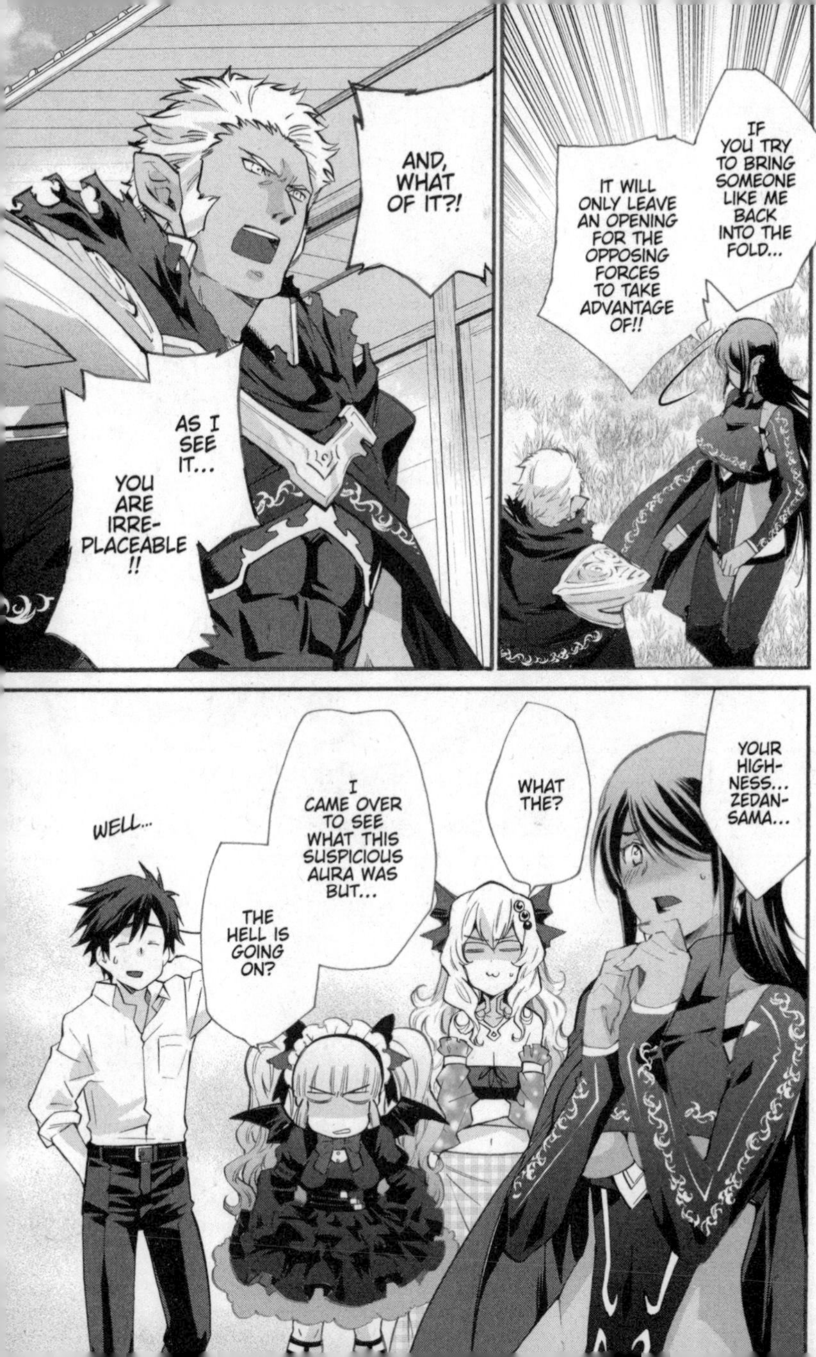
IF YOU TRY TO BRING SOMEONE LIKE ME BACK INTO THE FOLD...
IT WILL ONLY LEAVE AN OPENING FOR THE OPPOSING FORCES TO TAKE ADVANTAGE OF!!
AND, WHAT OF IT?!
AS I SEE IT...
YOU ARE IRRE-PLACEABLE!!
YOUR HIGH-NESS... ZEDAN-SAMA...
WHAT THE?
I CAME OVER TO SEE WHAT THIS SUSPICIOUS AURA WAS BUT...
THE HELL IS GOING ON?
WELL...

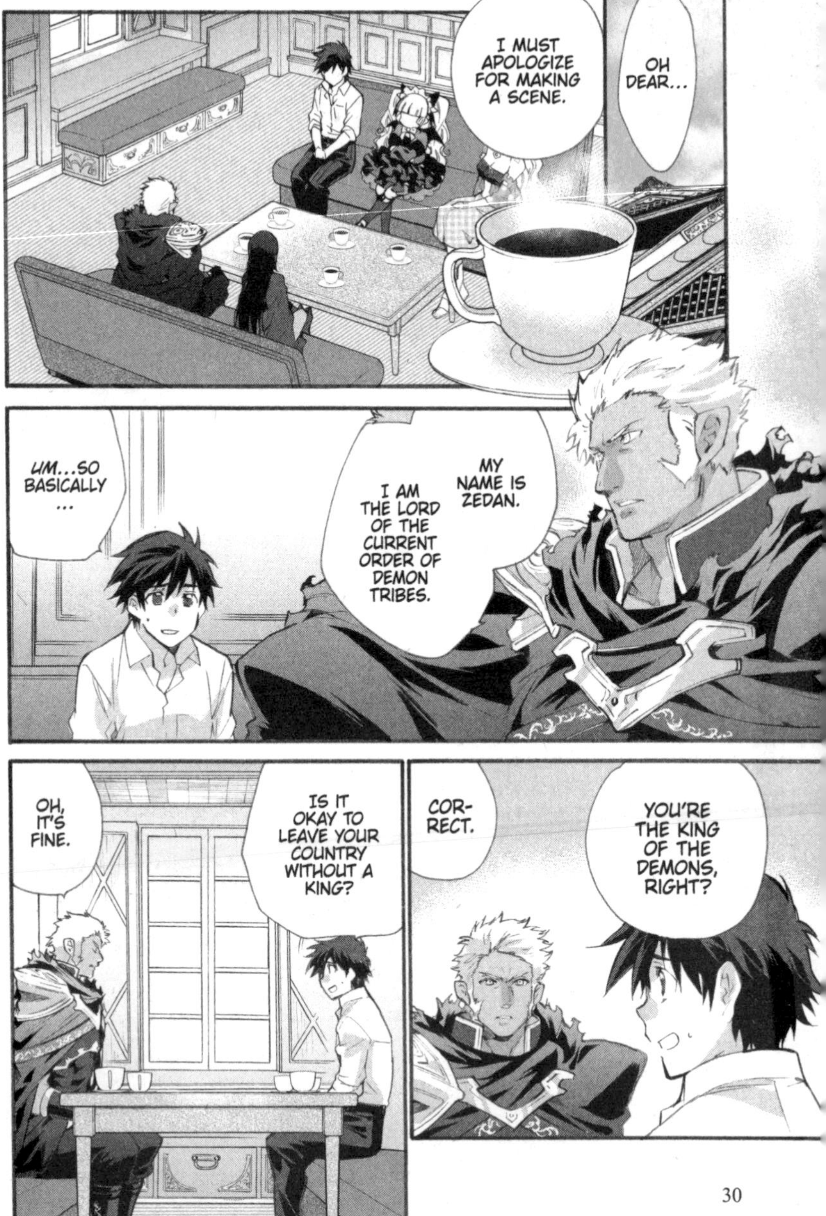
OH DEAR…
I MUST APOLOGIZE FOR MAKING A SCENE.
MY NAME IS ZEDAN.
I AM THE LORD OF THE CURRENT ORDER OF DEMON TRIBES.
UM…SO BASICALLY…
YOU'RE THE KING OF THE DEMONS, RIGHT?
COR-RECT.
IS IT OKAY TO LEAVE YOUR COUNTRY WITHOUT A KING?
OH, IT'S FINE.

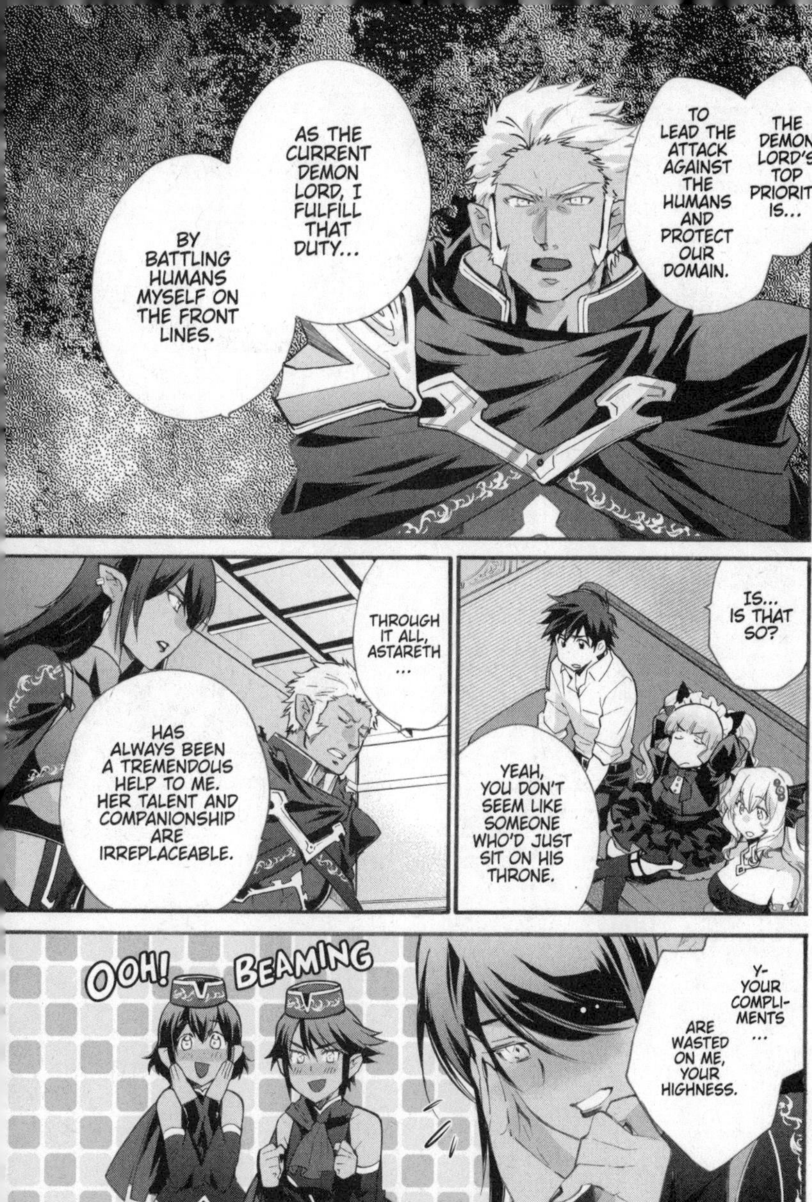
THE DEMON LORD'S TOP PRIORITY IS...
TO LEAD THE ATTACK AGAINST THE HUMANS AND PROTECT OUR DOMAIN.
AS THE CURRENT DEMON LORD, I FULFILL THAT DUTY...
BY BATTLING HUMANS MYSELF ON THE FRONT LINES.
IS... IS THAT SO?
YEAH, YOU DON'T SEEM LIKE SOMEONE WHO'D JUST SIT ON HIS THRONE.
THROUGH IT ALL, ASTARETH...
HAS ALWAYS BEEN A TREMENDOUS HELP TO ME. HER TALENT AND COMPANIONSHIP ARE IRREPLACEABLE.
Y-YOUR COMPLIMENTS...
ARE WASTED ON ME, YOUR HIGHNESS.
BEAMING
OOH!

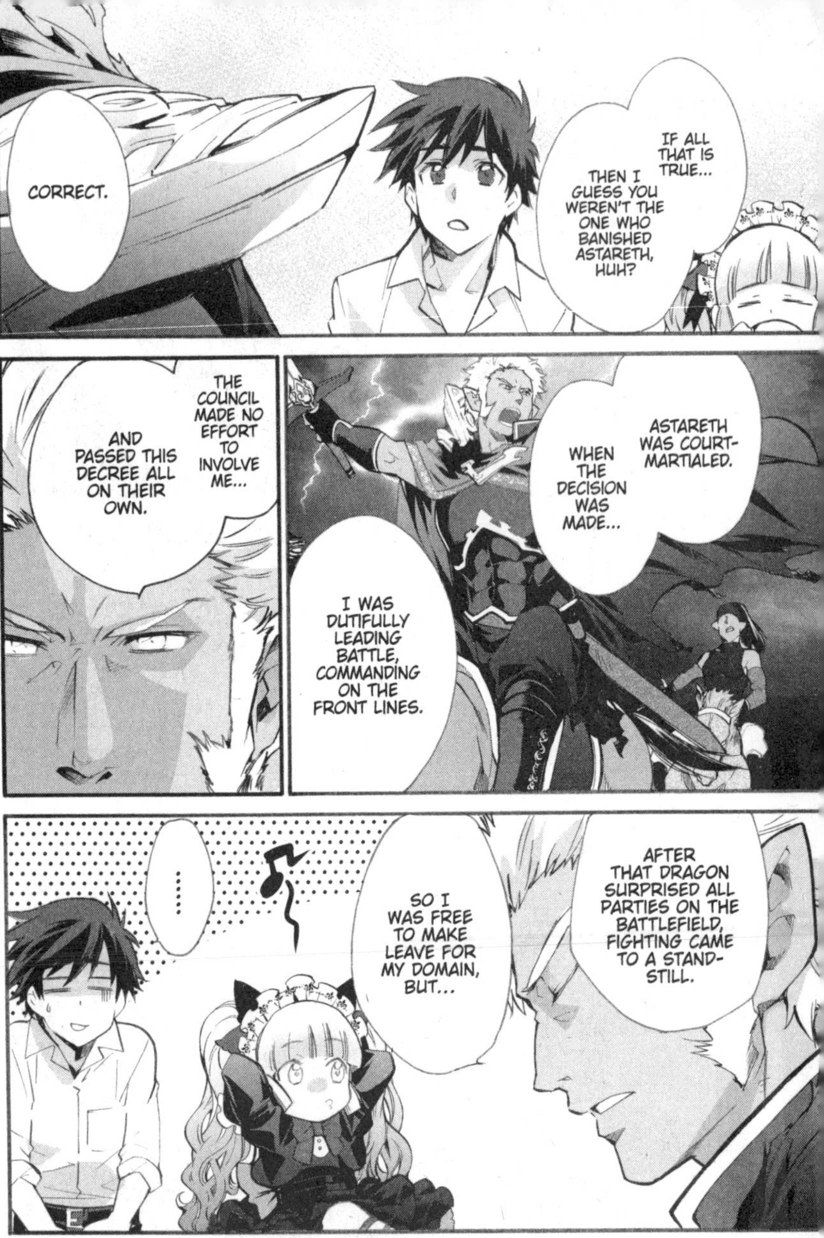
IF ALL THAT IS TRUE...
THEN I GUESS YOU WEREN'T THE ONE WHO BANISHED ASTARETH, HUH?
CORRECT.
ASTARETH WAS COURT-MARTIALED.
WHEN THE DECISION WAS MADE...
I WAS DUTIFULLY LEADING BATTLE, COMMANDING ON THE FRONT LINES.
THE COUNCIL MADE NO EFFORT TO INVOLVE ME...
AND PASSED THIS DECREE ALL ON THEIR OWN.
AFTER THAT DRAGON SURPRISED ALL PARTIES ON THE BATTLEFIELD, FIGHTING CAME TO A STAND-STILL.
SO I WAS FREE TO MAKE LEAVE FOR MY DOMAIN, BUT...
......

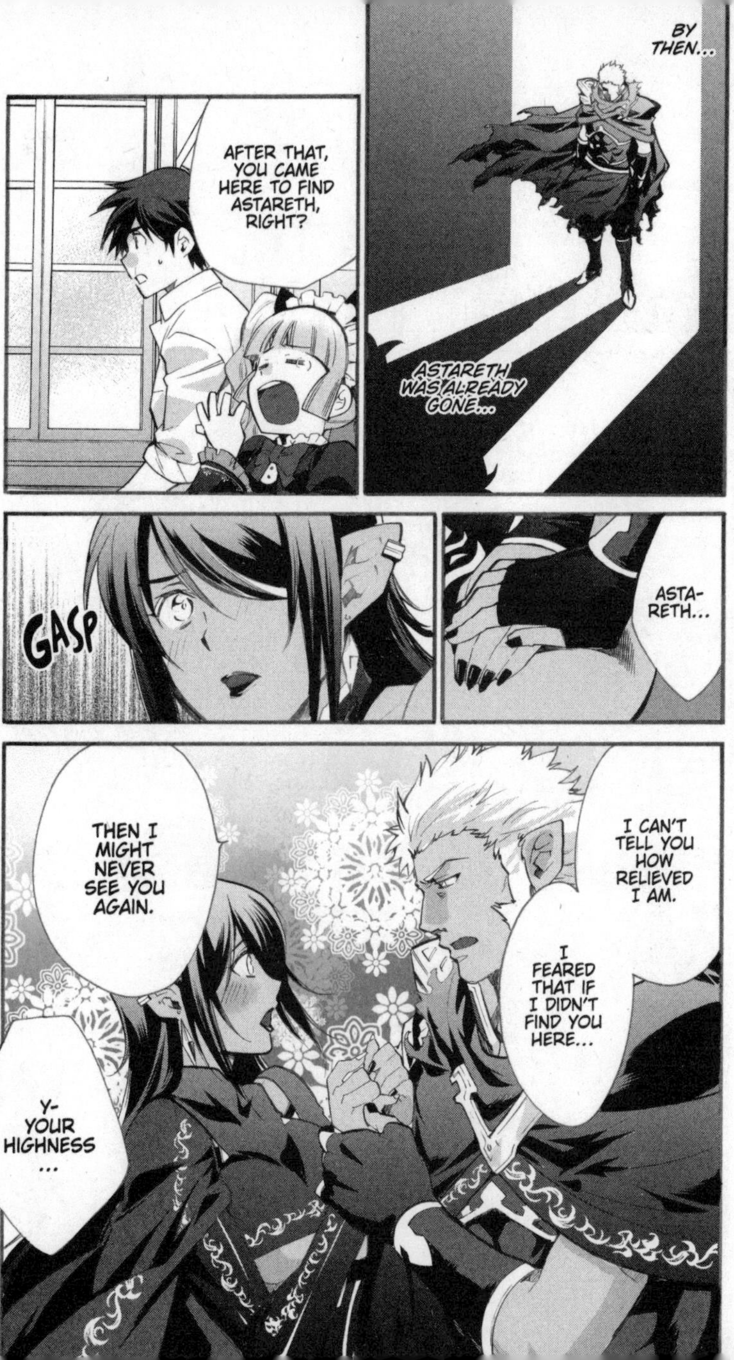
BY THEN...
ASTARETH WAS ALREADY GONE...
AFTER THAT, YOU CAME HERE TO FIND ASTARETH, RIGHT?
ASTA-RETH...
GASP
I CAN'T TELL YOU HOW RELIEVED I AM.
I FEARED THAT IF I DIDN'T FIND YOU HERE...
THEN I MIGHT NEVER SEE YOU AGAIN.
Y-YOUR HIGHNESS...

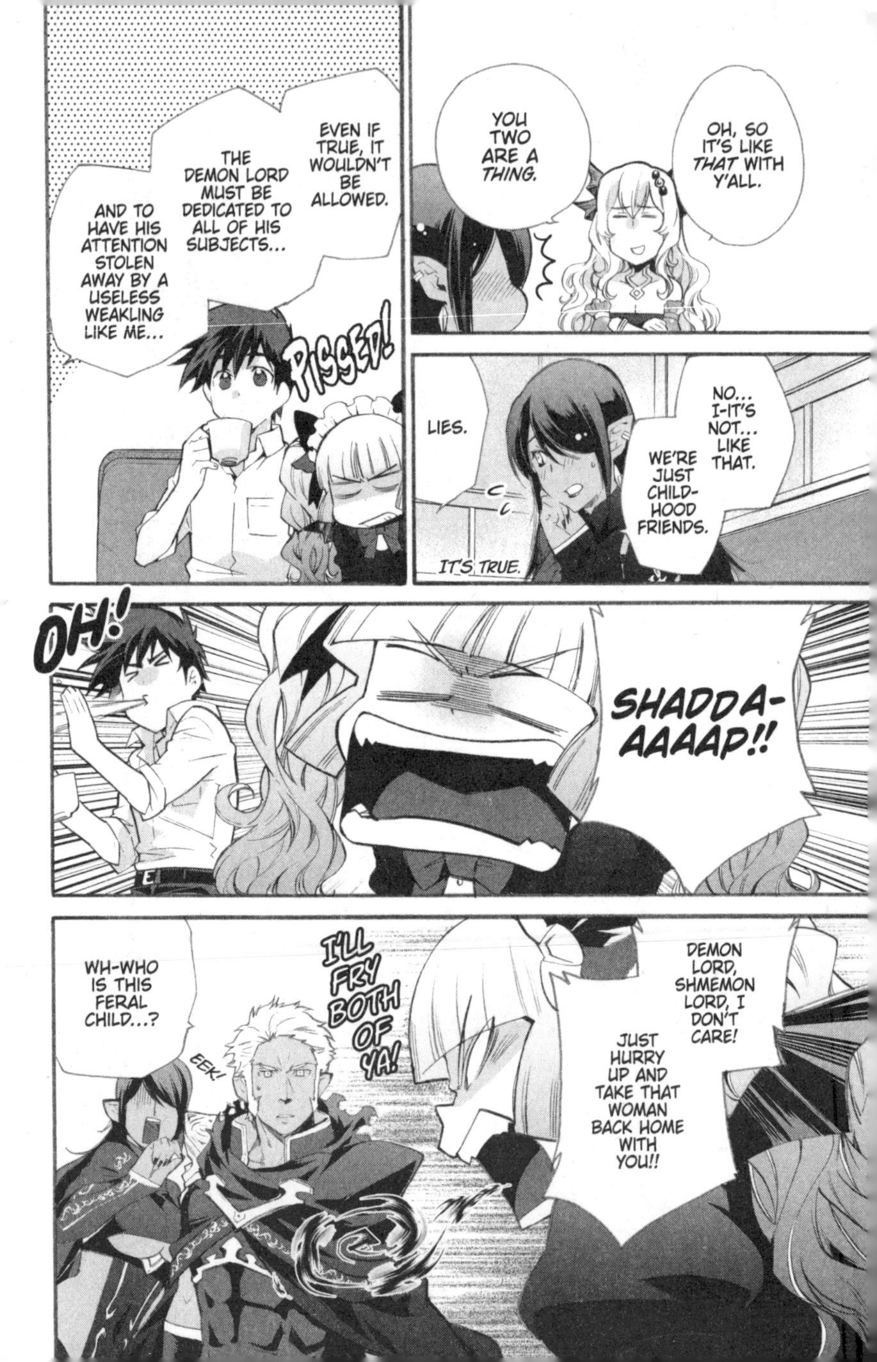
OH, SO IT'S LIKE *THAT* WITH Y'ALL.
YOU TWO ARE A *THING.*
NO... I-IT'S NOT... LIKE THAT.
WE'RE JUST CHILD-HOOD FRIENDS.
LIES.
IT'S TRUE.
EVEN IF TRUE, IT WOULDN'T BE ALLOWED.
THE DEMON LORD MUST BE DEDICATED TO ALL OF HIS SUBJECTS...
AND TO HAVE HIS ATTENTION STOLEN AWAY BY A USELESS WEAKLING LIKE ME...
PISSED!
SHADDA-AAAAP!!
OH!
DEMON LORD, SHMEMON LORD, I DON'T CARE!
JUST HURRY UP AND TAKE THAT WOMAN BACK HOME WITH YOU!!
I'LL FRY BOTH OF YA!
WH-WHO IS THIS FERAL CHILD...?
EEK!

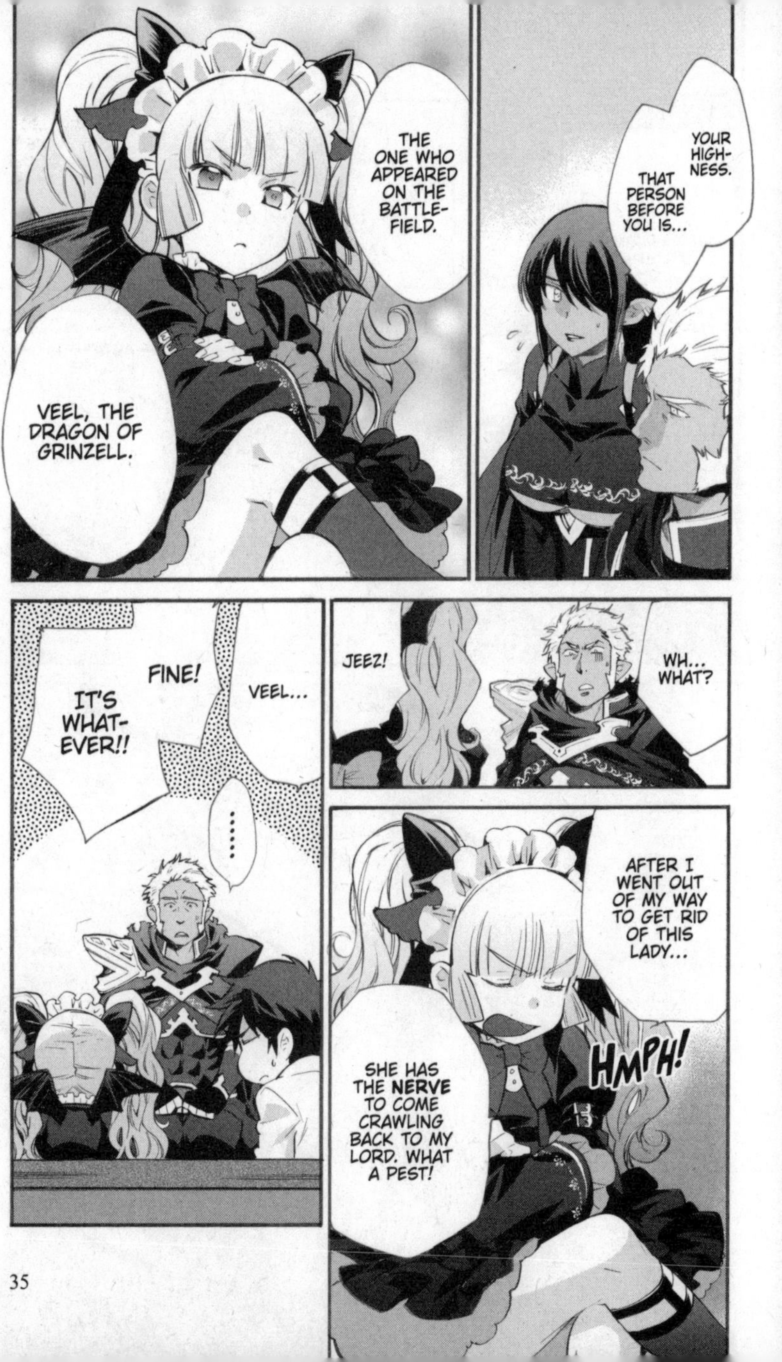
YOUR HIGHNESS.
THAT PERSON BEFORE YOU IS...
THE ONE WHO APPEARED ON THE BATTLEFIELD.
VEEL, THE DRAGON OF GRINZELL.
WH... WHAT?
JEEZ!
AFTER I WENT OUT OF MY WAY TO GET RID OF THIS LADY...
HMPH!
SHE HAS THE **NERVE** TO COME CRAWLING BACK TO MY LORD. WHAT A PEST!
VEEL...
FINE!
IT'S WHATEVER!!
......

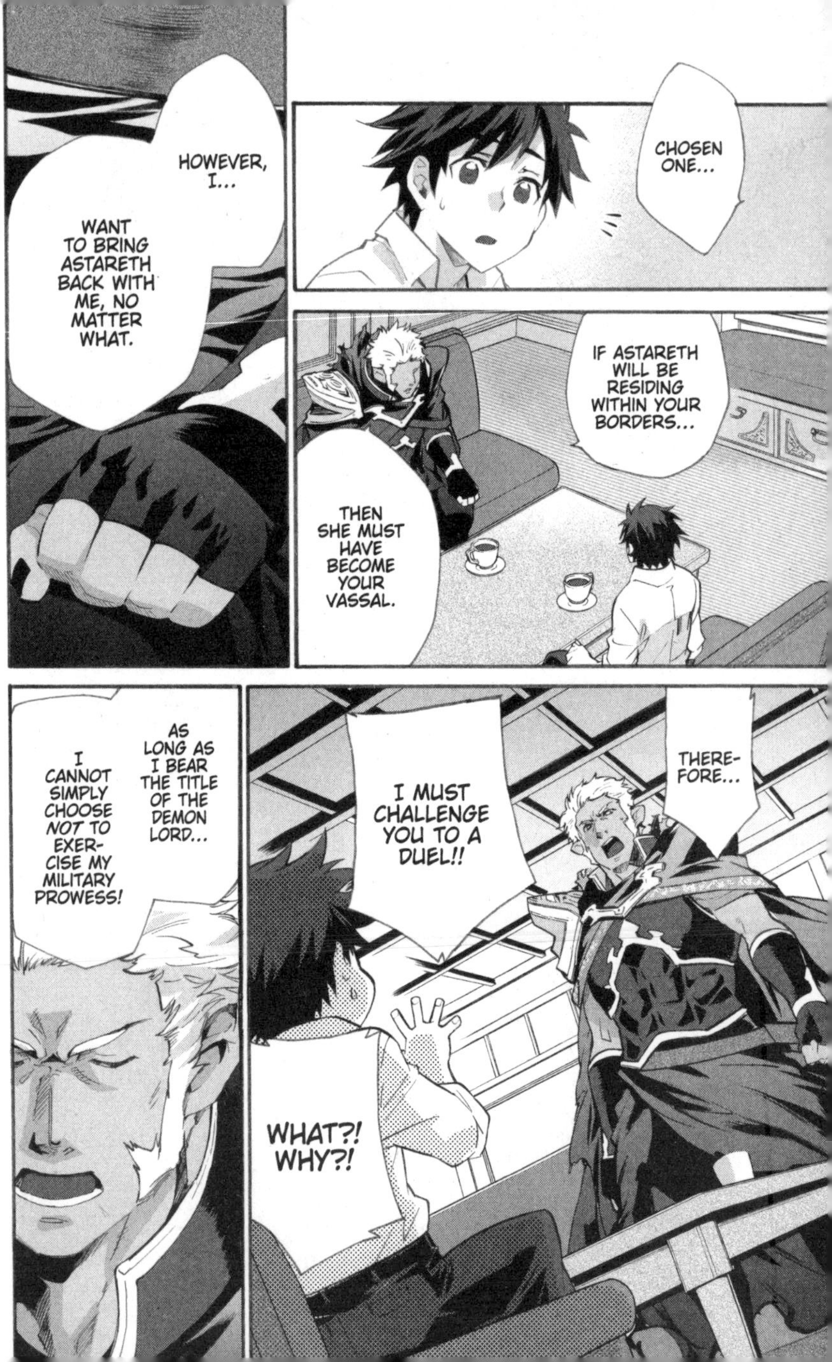
CHOSEN ONE...
IF ASTARETH WILL BE RESIDING WITHIN YOUR BORDERS...
THEN SHE MUST HAVE BECOME YOUR VASSAL.
HOWEVER, I...
WANT TO BRING ASTARETH BACK WITH ME, NO MATTER WHAT.
THEREFORE...
I MUST CHALLENGE YOU TO A DUEL!!
WHAT?! WHY?!
AS LONG AS I BEAR THE TITLE OF THE DEMON LORD...
I CANNOT SIMPLY CHOOSE *NOT* TO EXERCISE MY MILITARY PROWESS!

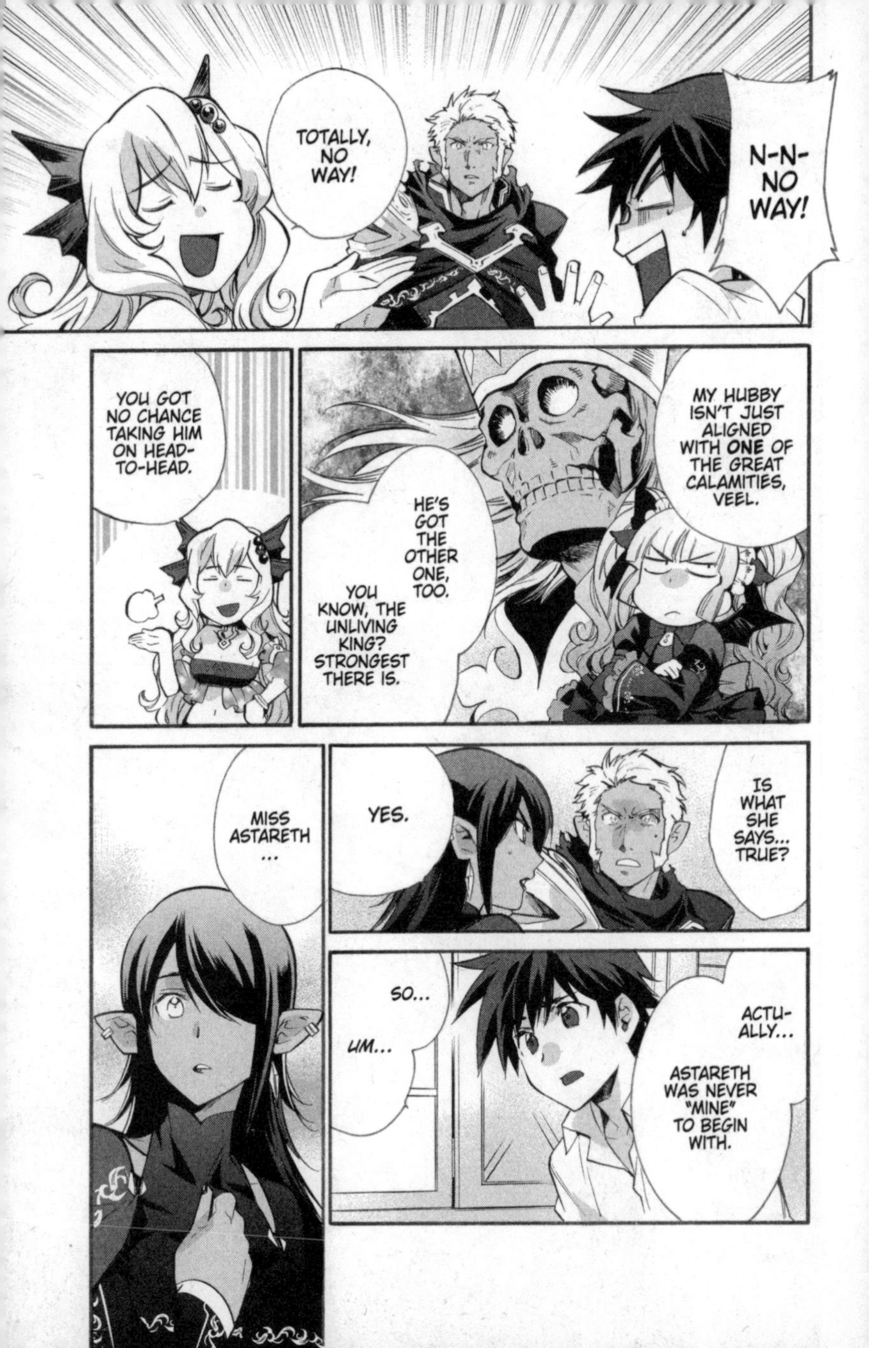
N-N-NO WAY!
TOTALLY, NO WAY!
MY HUBBY ISN'T JUST ALIGNED WITH ONE OF THE GREAT CALAMITIES, VEEL.
HE'S GOT THE OTHER ONE, TOO.
YOU KNOW, THE UNLIVING KING? STRONGEST THERE IS.
YOU GOT NO CHANCE TAKING HIM ON HEAD-TO-HEAD.
IS WHAT SHE SAYS... TRUE?
YES.
ACTU-ALLY...
ASTARETH WAS NEVER "MINE" TO BEGIN WITH.
SO...
UM...
MISS ASTARETH...

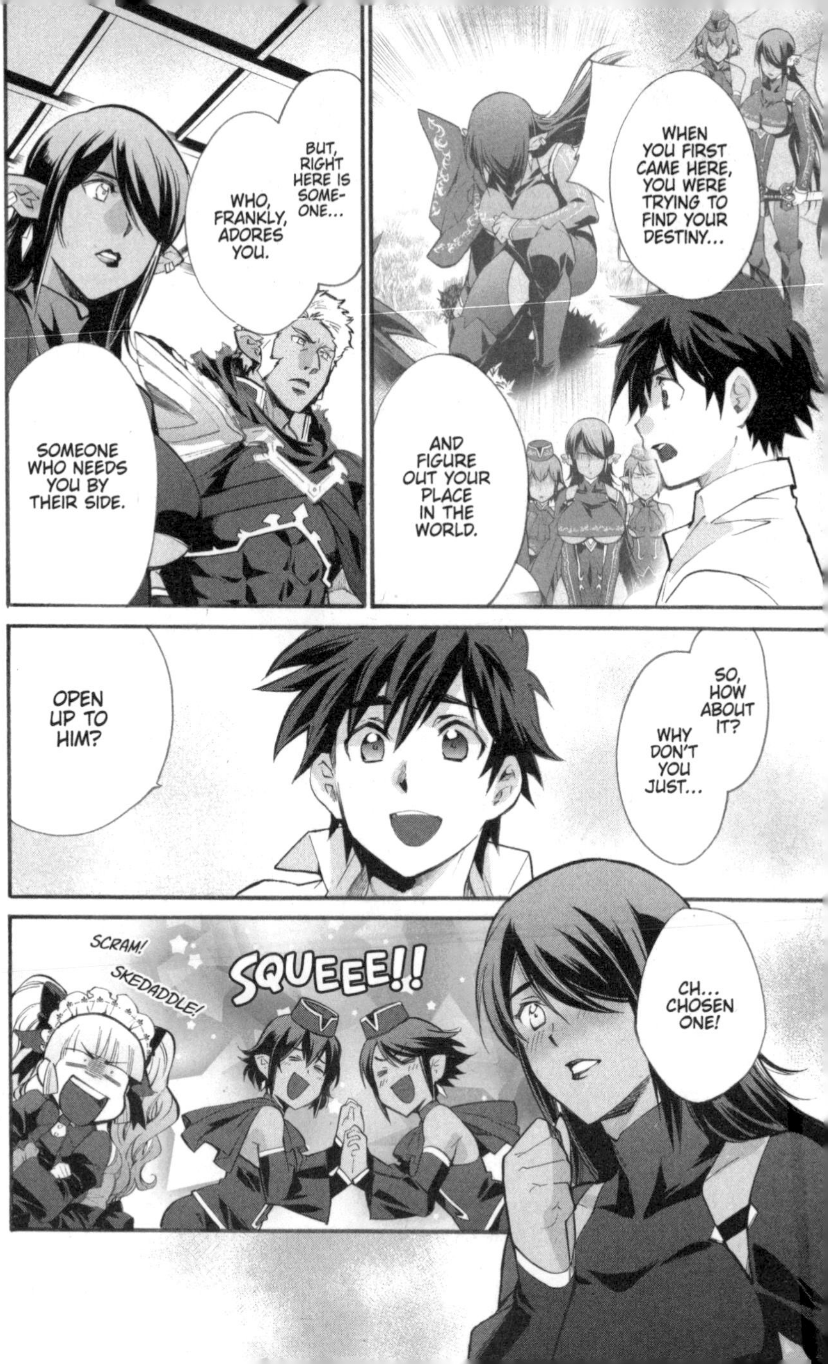
WHEN YOU FIRST CAME HERE, YOU WERE TRYING TO FIND YOUR DESTINY...
AND FIGURE OUT YOUR PLACE IN THE WORLD.
BUT, RIGHT HERE IS SOME-ONE...
WHO, FRANKLY, ADORES YOU.
SOMEONE WHO NEEDS YOU BY THEIR SIDE.
SO, HOW ABOUT IT?
WHY DON'T YOU JUST...
OPEN UP TO HIM?
CH... CHOSEN ONE!
SQUEEEE!!
SKEDADDLE!
SCRAM!

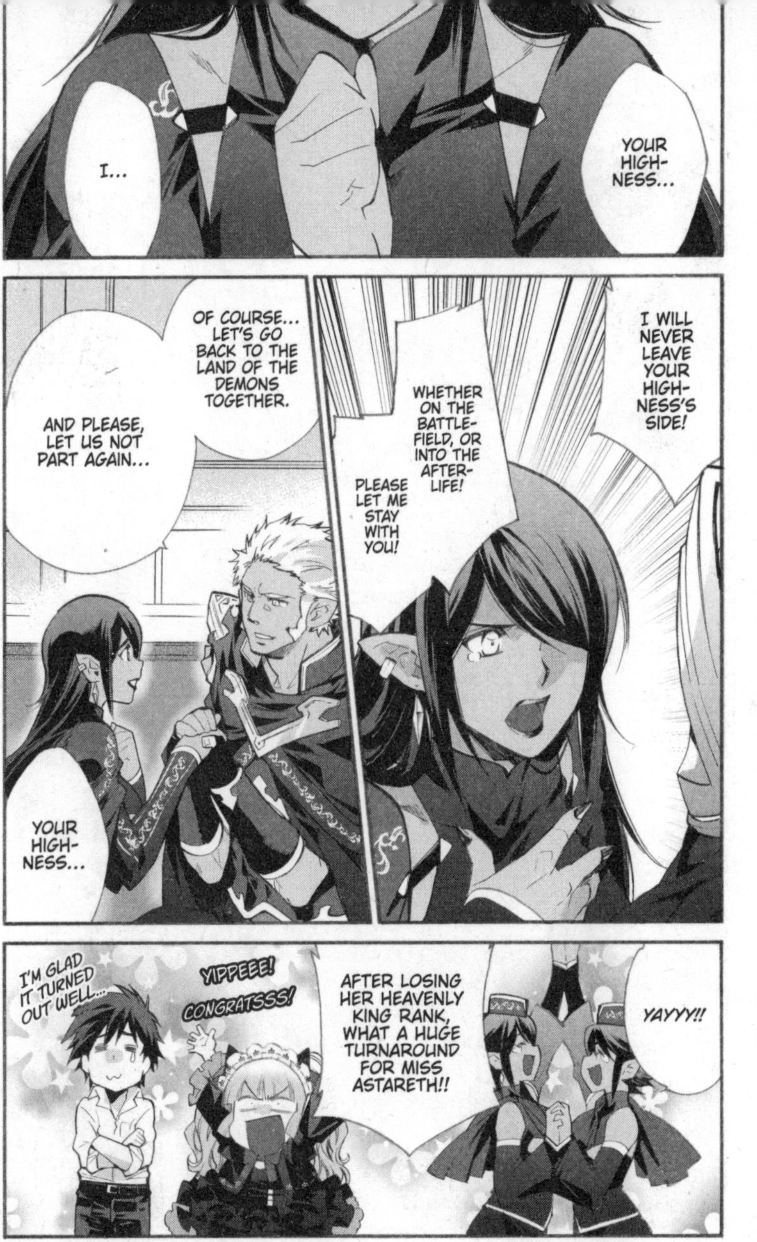
YOUR HIGHNESS...
I...
I WILL NEVER LEAVE YOUR HIGHNESS'S SIDE!
WHETHER ON THE BATTLEFIELD, OR INTO THE AFTERLIFE!
PLEASE LET ME STAY WITH YOU!
OF COURSE... LET'S GO BACK TO THE LAND OF THE DEMONS TOGETHER.
AND PLEASE, LET US NOT PART AGAIN...
YOUR HIGHNESS...
YAYYY!!
AFTER LOSING HER HEAVENLY KING RANK, WHAT A HUGE TURNAROUND FOR MISS ASTARETH!!
CONGRATSSS!
YIPPEEE!
I'M GLAD IT TURNED OUT WELL...

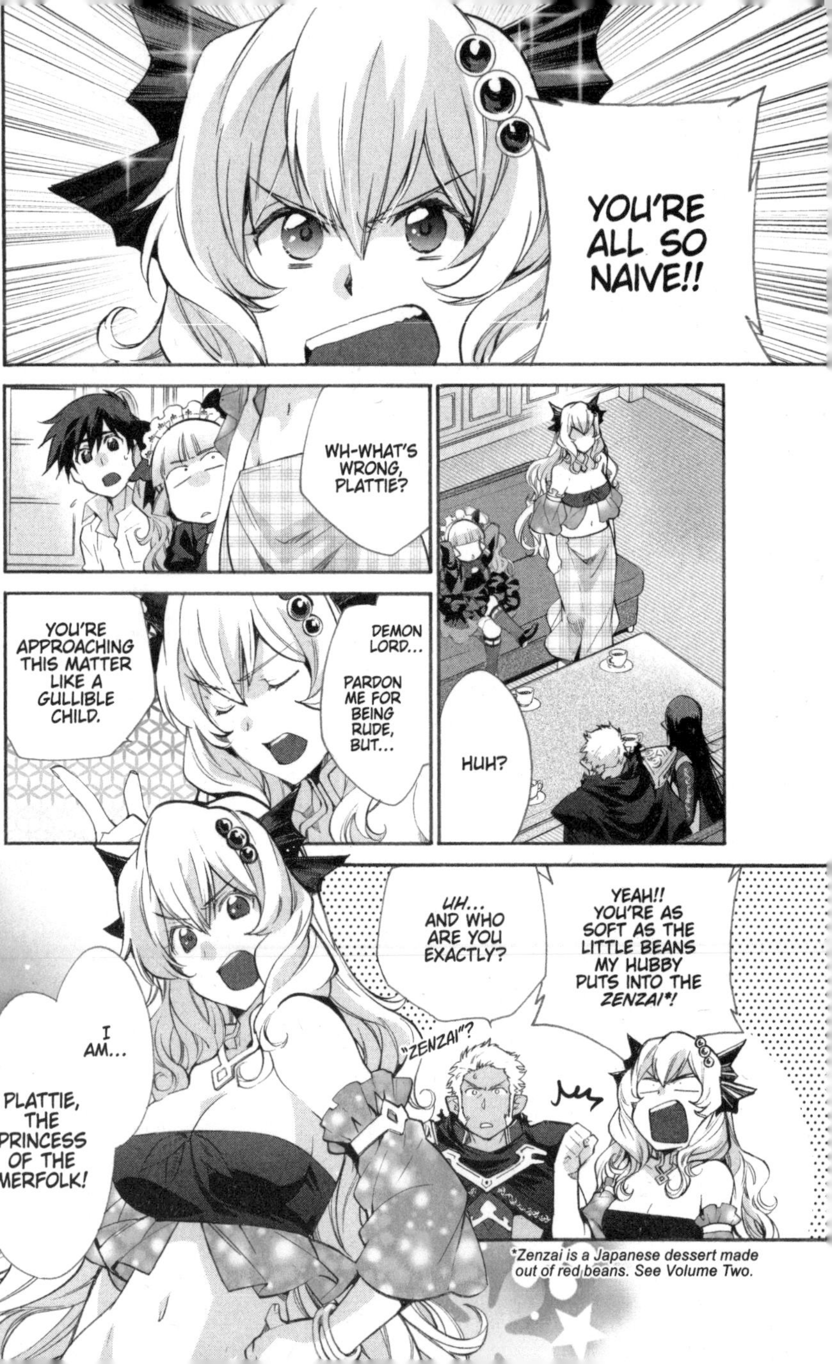
YOU'RE ALL SO NAIVE!!
HUH?
WH-WHAT'S WRONG, PLATTIE?
DEMON LORD...
PARDON ME FOR BEING RUDE, BUT...
YOU'RE APPROACHING THIS MATTER LIKE A GULLIBLE CHILD.
YEAH!! YOU'RE AS SOFT AS THE LITTLE BEANS MY HUBBY PUTS INTO THE *ZENZAI**!
UH... AND WHO ARE YOU EXACTLY?
"ZENZAI"?
I AM...
PLATTIE, THE PRINCESS OF THE MERFOLK!

**Zenzai is a Japanese dessert made out of red beans. See Volume Two.*

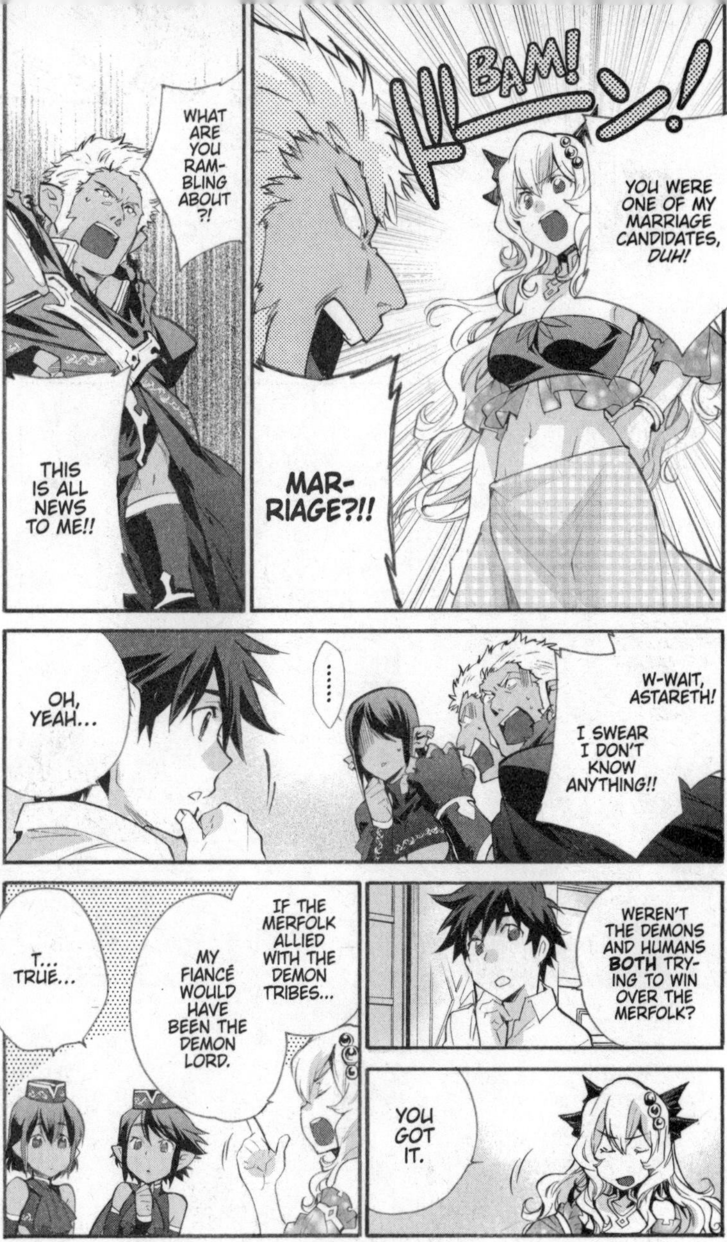
BAM!
YOU WERE ONE OF MY MARRIAGE CANDIDATES, DUH!
MAR-RIAGE?!!
WHAT ARE YOU RAMBLING ABOUT?!
THIS IS ALL NEWS TO ME!!
W-WAIT, ASTARETH!
I SWEAR I DON'T KNOW ANYTHING!!
......
OH, YEAH...
WEREN'T THE DEMONS AND HUMANS **BOTH** TRYING TO WIN OVER THE MERFOLK?
YOU GOT IT.
IF THE MERFOLK ALLIED WITH THE DEMON TRIBES...
MY FIANCÉ WOULD HAVE BEEN THE DEMON LORD.
T... TRUE...

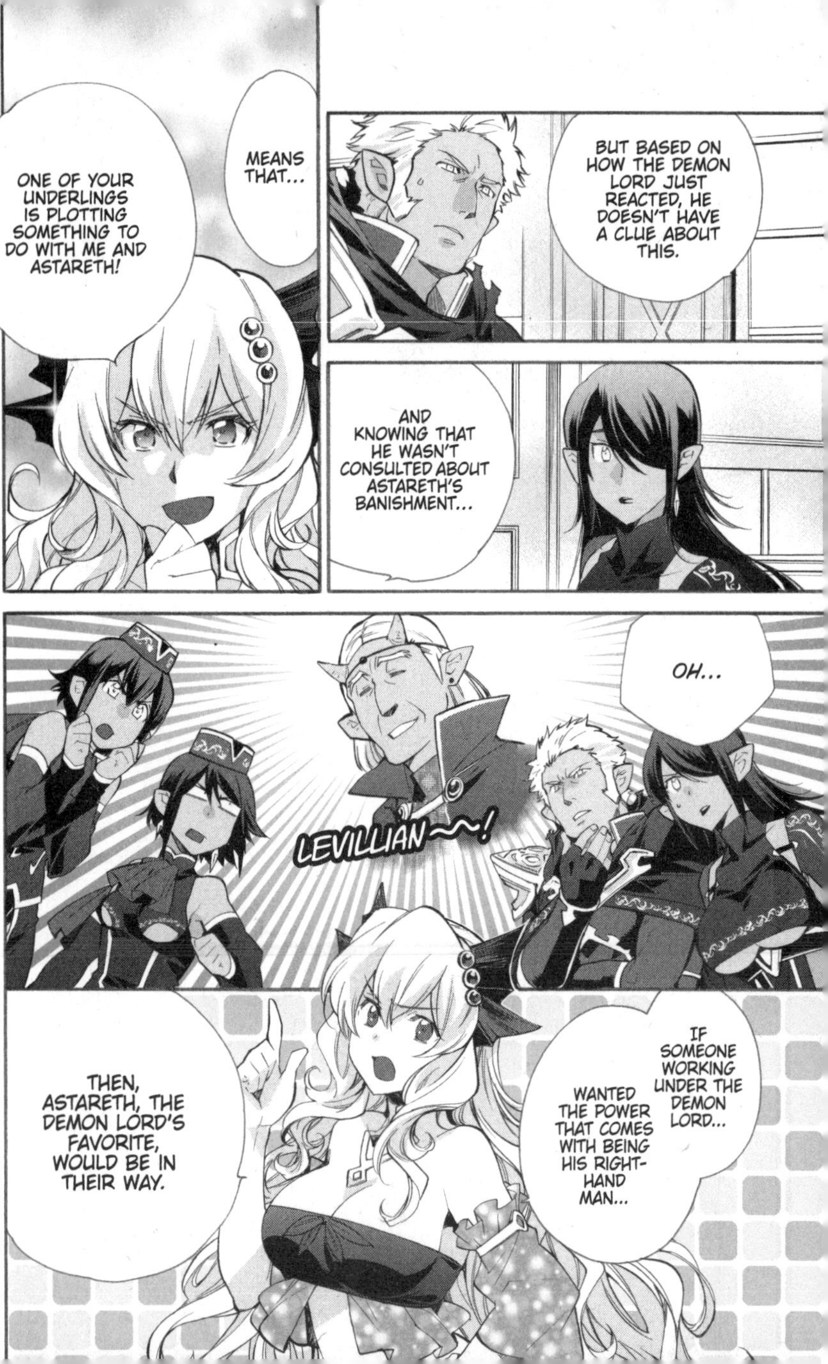
BUT BASED ON HOW THE DEMON LORD JUST REACTED, HE DOESN'T HAVE A CLUE ABOUT THIS.
AND KNOWING THAT HE WASN'T CONSULTED ABOUT ASTARETH'S BANISHMENT...
MEANS THAT...
ONE OF YOUR UNDERLINGS IS PLOTTING SOMETHING TO DO WITH ME AND ASTARETH!
OH...
LEVILLIAN~~!
IF SOMEONE WORKING UNDER THE DEMON LORD...
WANTED THE POWER THAT COMES WITH BEING HIS RIGHT-HAND MAN...
THEN, ASTARETH, THE DEMON LORD'S FAVORITE, WOULD BE IN THEIR WAY.

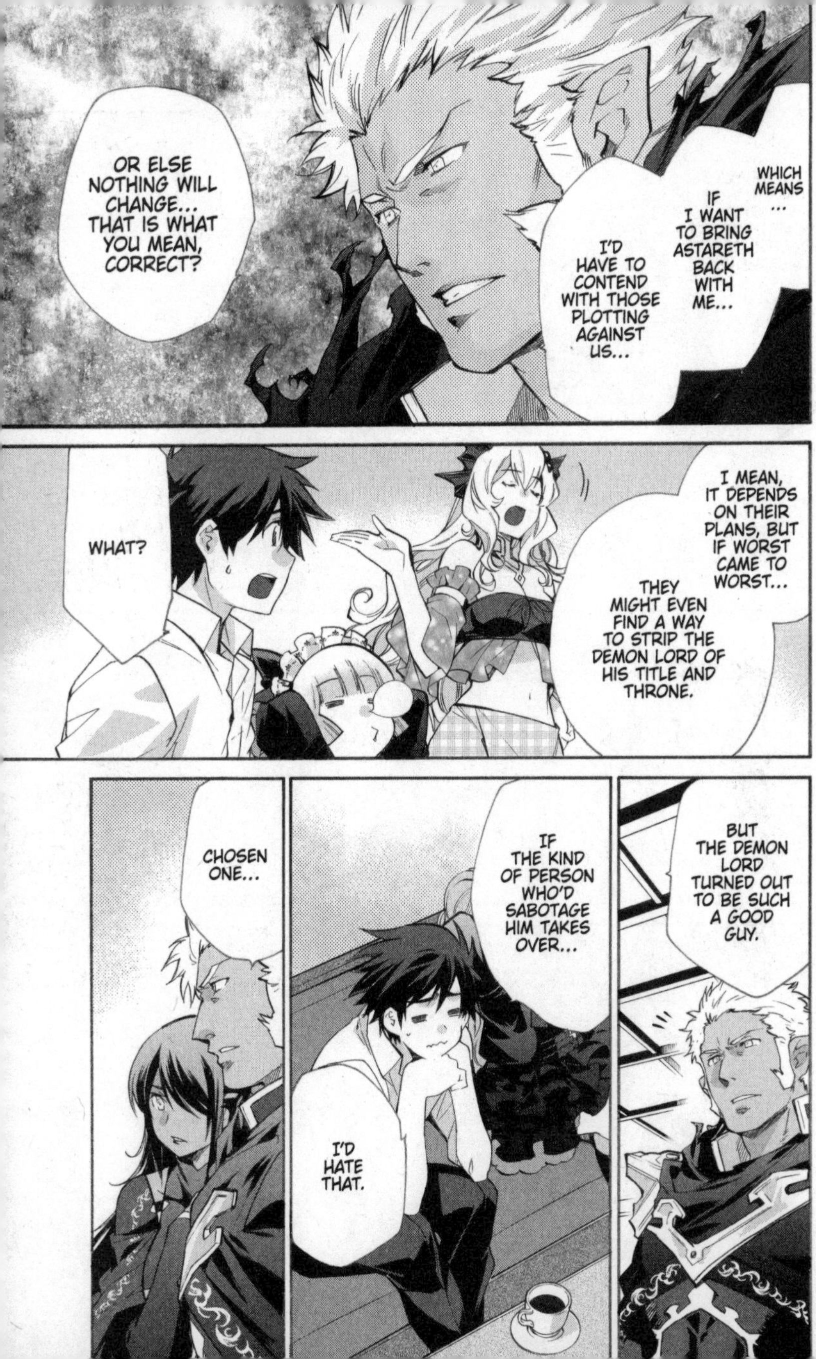
WHICH MEANS ...
IF I WANT TO BRING ASTARETH BACK WITH ME...
I'D HAVE TO CONTEND WITH THOSE PLOTTING AGAINST US...
OR ELSE NOTHING WILL CHANGE... THAT IS WHAT YOU MEAN, CORRECT?
I MEAN, IT DEPENDS ON THEIR PLANS, BUT IF WORST CAME TO WORST...
THEY MIGHT EVEN FIND A WAY TO STRIP THE DEMON LORD OF HIS TITLE AND THRONE.
WHAT?
BUT THE DEMON LORD TURNED OUT TO BE SUCH A GOOD GUY.
IF THE KIND OF PERSON WHO'D SABOTAGE HIM TAKES OVER...
I'D HATE THAT.
CHOSEN ONE...

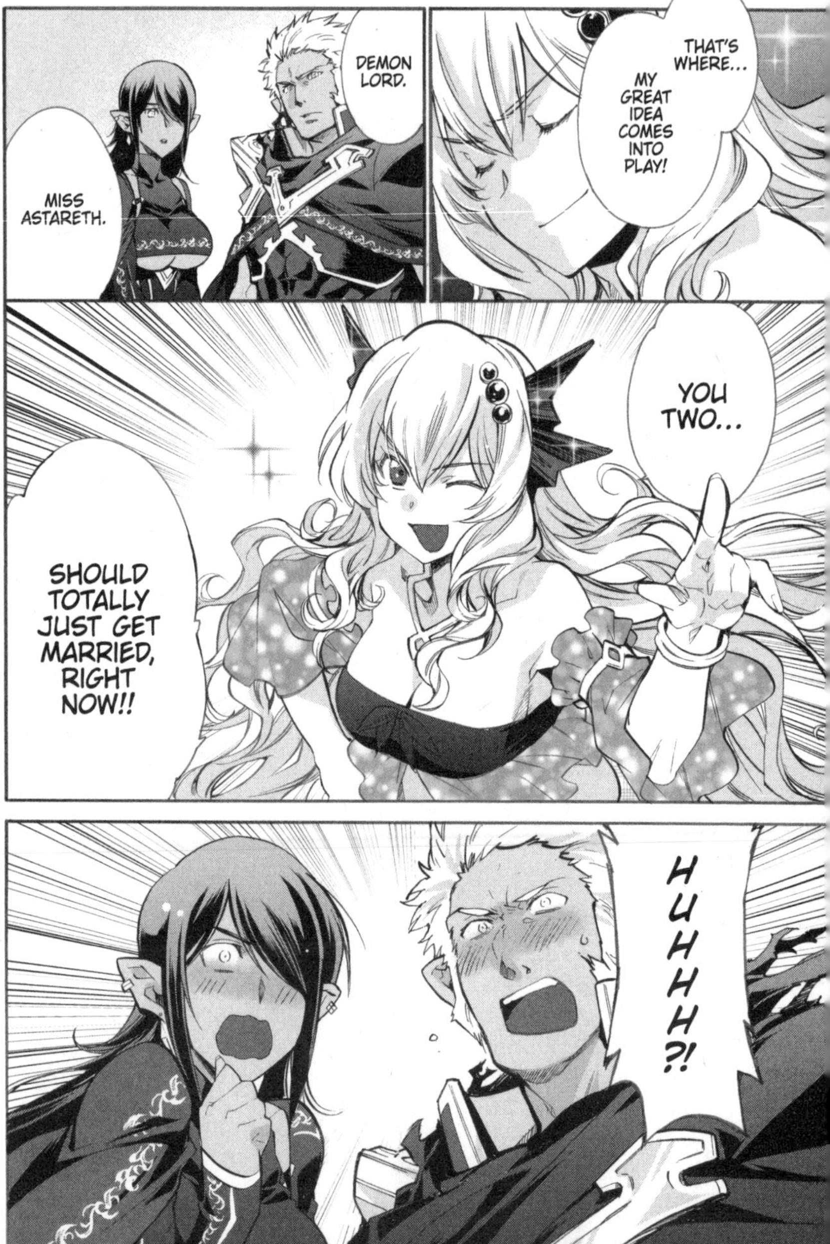
THAT'S WHERE...
MY GREAT IDEA COMES INTO PLAY!
DEMON LORD.
MISS ASTARETH.
YOU TWO...
SHOULD TOTALLY JUST GET MARRIED, RIGHT NOW!!
HUHHHH?!

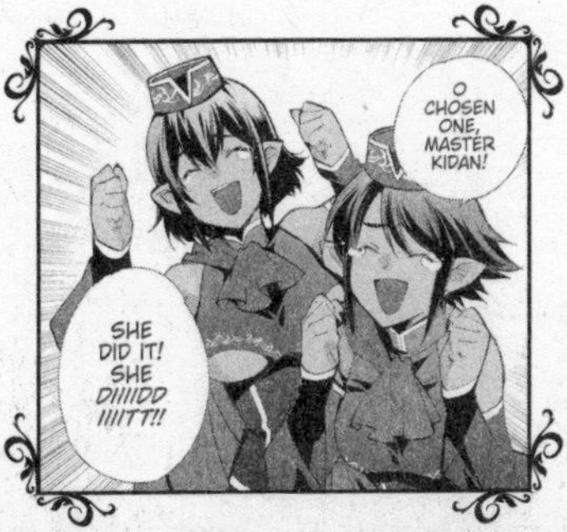
O CHOSEN ONE, MASTER KIDAN!
SHE DID IT! SHE DIIIIDD IIIITT!!

LET'S BUY THE LAND and CULTIVATE IT IN A DIFFERENT WORLD

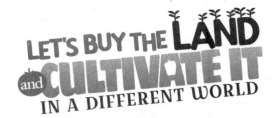

Chapter 15

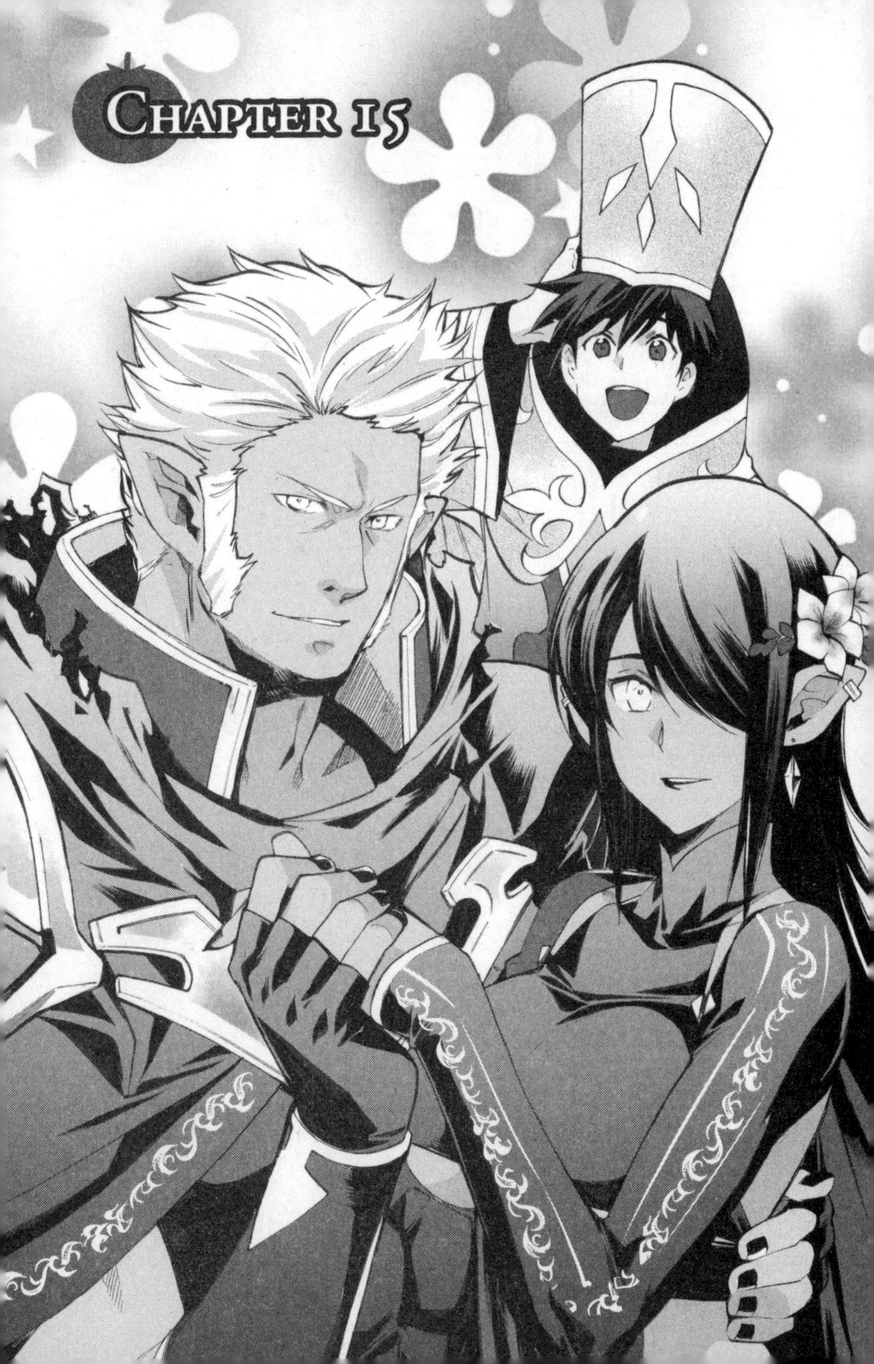

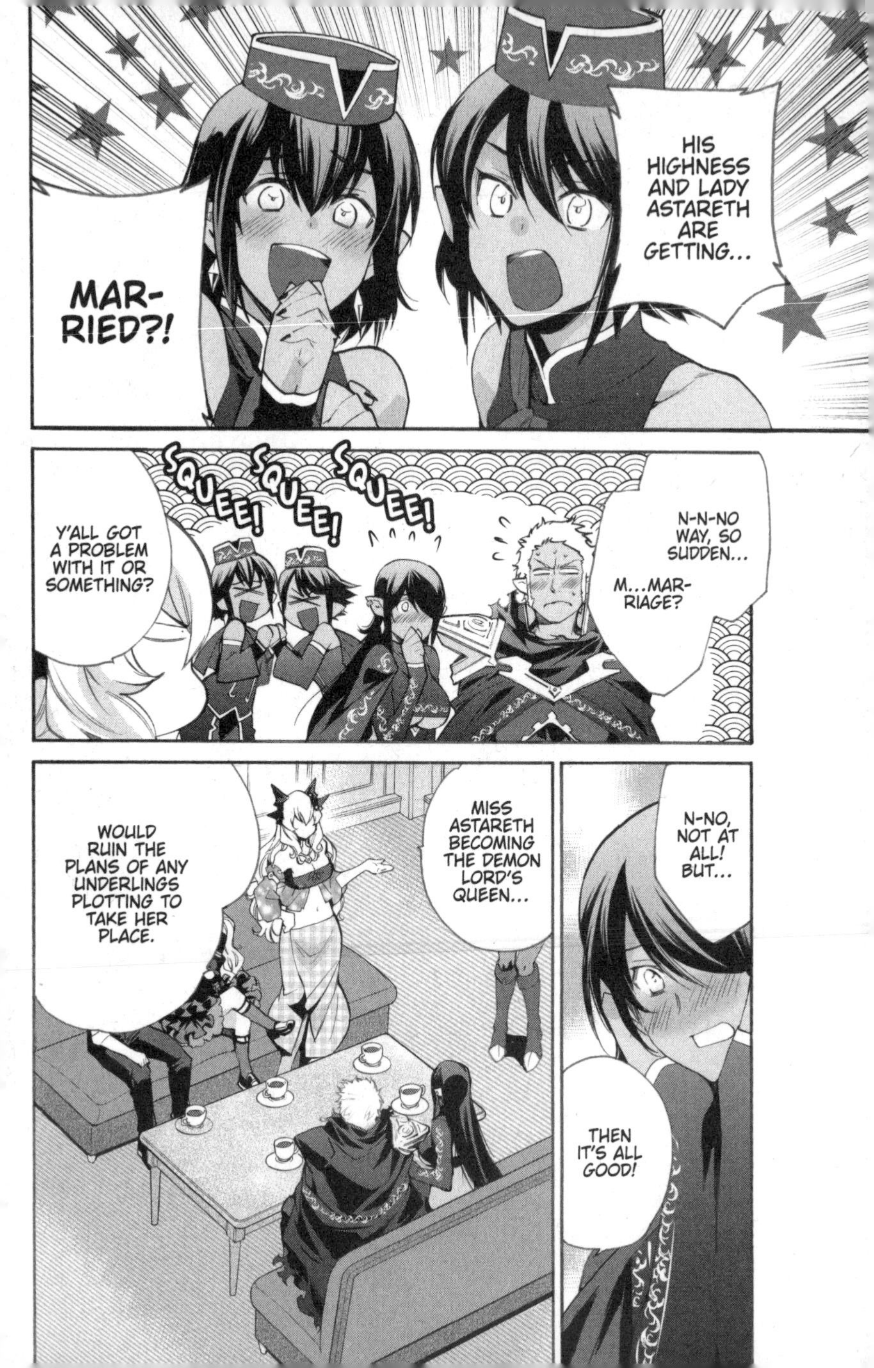
HIS HIGHNESS AND LADY ASTARETH ARE GETTING...
MAR-RIED?!
N-N-NO WAY, SO SUDDEN...
M...MAR-RIAGE?
SQUEE! SQUEE! SQUEE!
Y'ALL GOT A PROBLEM WITH IT OR SOMETHING?
N-NO, NOT AT ALL! BUT...
THEN IT'S ALL GOOD!
MISS ASTARETH BECOMING THE DEMON LORD'S QUEEN...
WOULD RUIN THE PLANS OF ANY UNDERLINGS PLOTTING TO TAKE HER PLACE.

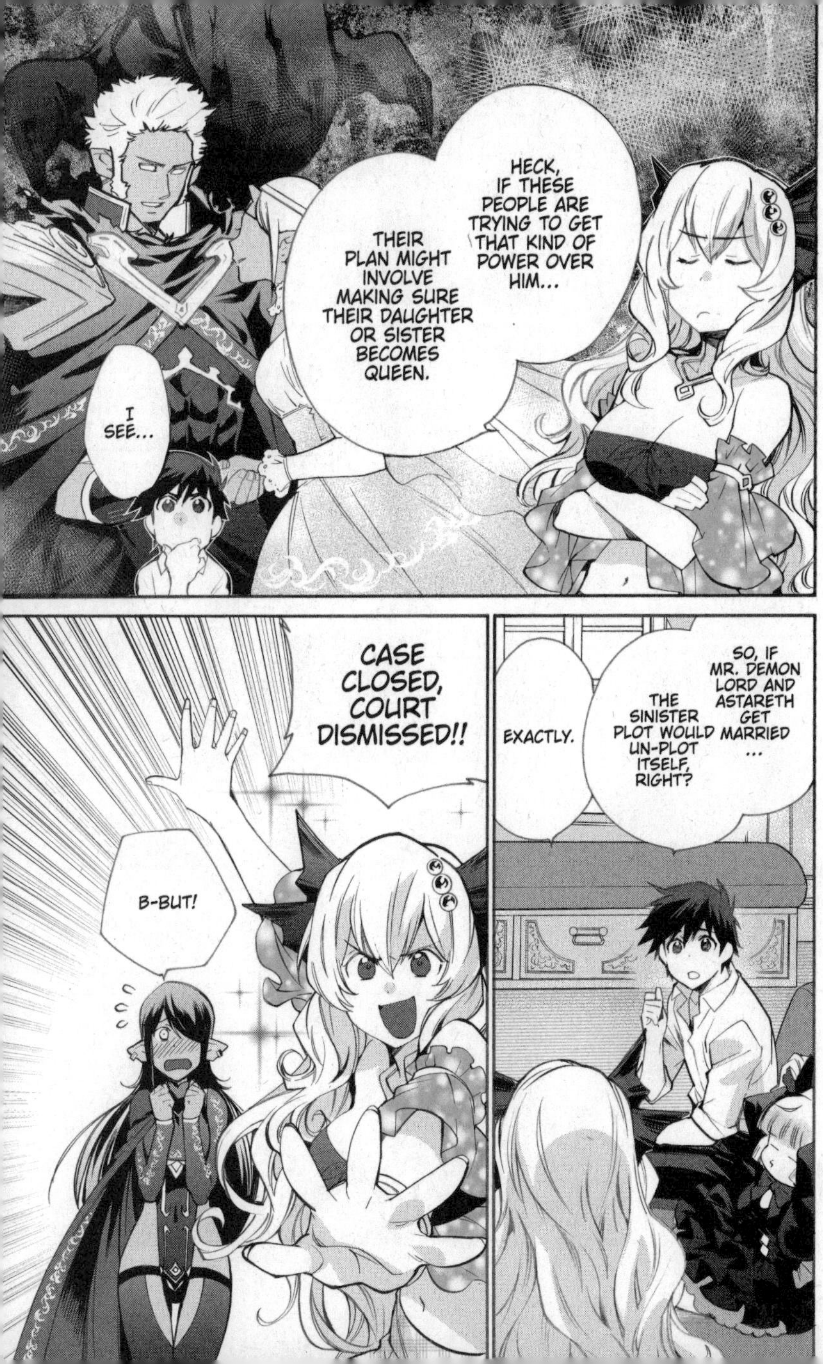
HECK, IF THESE PEOPLE ARE TRYING TO GET THAT KIND OF POWER OVER HIM...
THEIR PLAN MIGHT INVOLVE MAKING SURE THEIR DAUGHTER OR SISTER BECOMES QUEEN.
I SEE...
SO, IF MR. DEMON LORD AND ASTARETH GET MARRIED...
THE SINISTER PLOT WOULD UN-PLOT ITSELF, RIGHT?
EXACTLY.
CASE CLOSED, COURT DISMISSED!!
B-BUT!

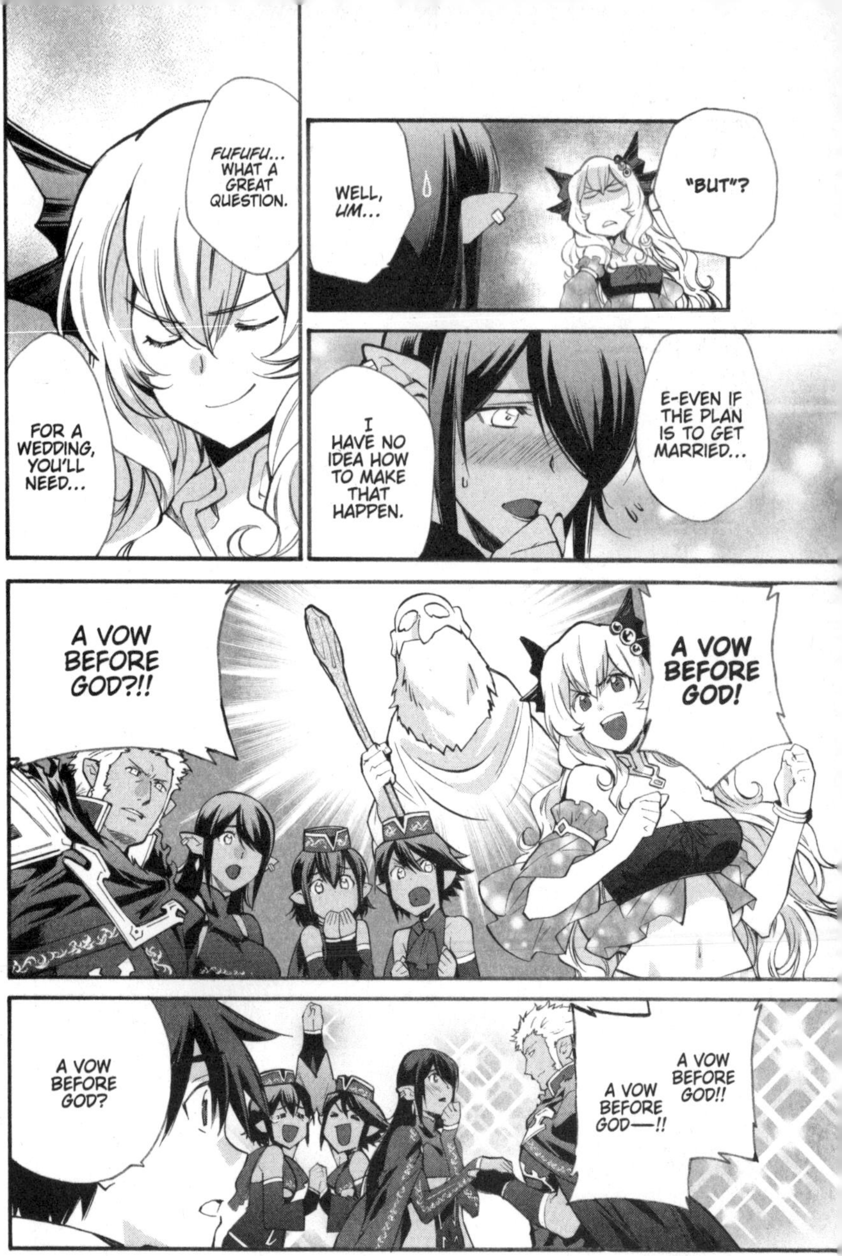
"BUT"?
WELL, UM...
E-EVEN IF THE PLAN IS TO GET MARRIED...
I HAVE NO IDEA HOW TO MAKE THAT HAPPEN.
FUFUFU... WHAT A GREAT QUESTION.
FOR A WEDDING, YOU'LL NEED...
A VOW BEFORE GOD!
A VOW BEFORE GOD?!!
A VOW BEFORE GOD!!
A VOW BEFORE GOD—!!
A VOW BEFORE GOD?

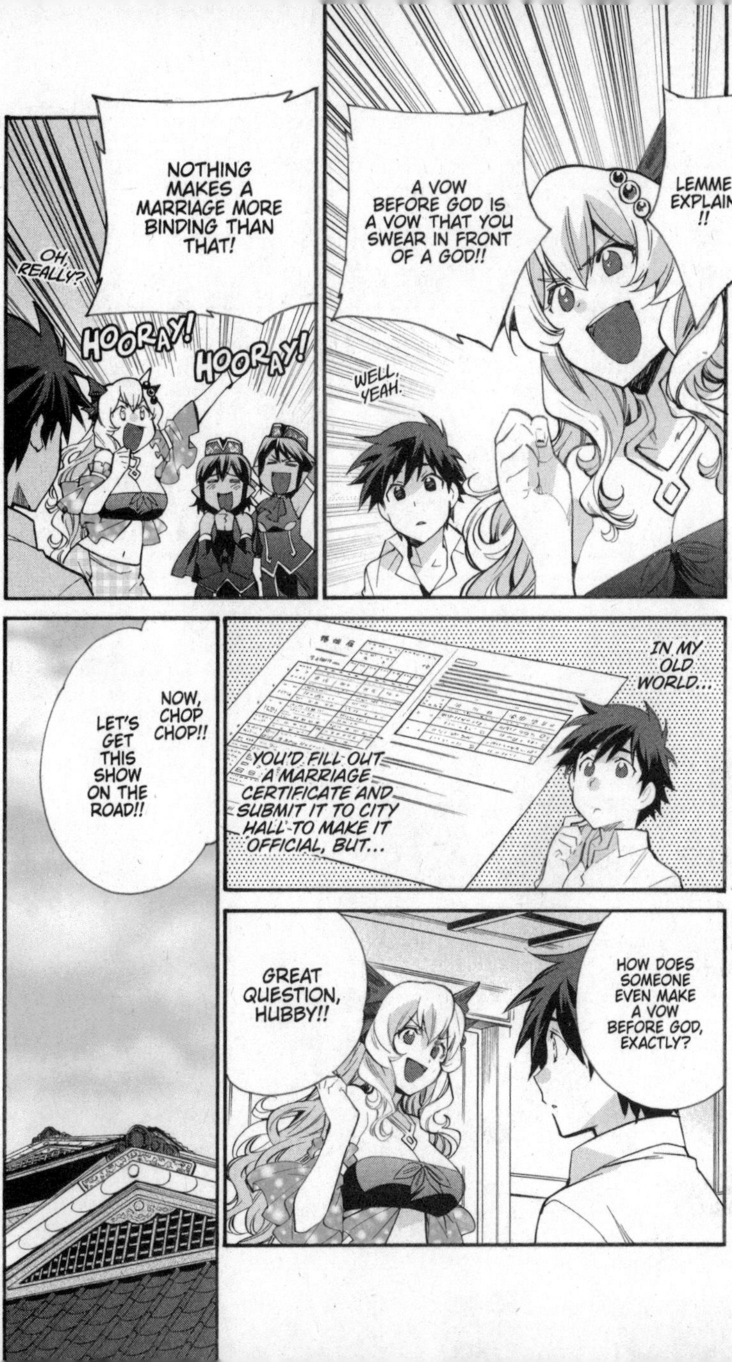
LEMME EXPLAIN!!
A VOW BEFORE GOD IS A VOW THAT YOU SWEAR IN FRONT OF A GOD!!
WELL, YEAH.
NOTHING MAKES A MARRIAGE MORE BINDING THAN THAT!
OH, REALLY?
HOORAY!
HOORAY!
IN MY OLD WORLD...
YOU'D FILL OUT A MARRIAGE CERTIFICATE AND SUBMIT IT TO CITY HALL TO MAKE IT OFFICIAL, BUT...
HOW DOES SOMEONE EVEN MAKE A VOW BEFORE GOD, EXACTLY?
GREAT QUESTION, HUBBY!!
NOW, CHOP CHOP!!
LET'S GET THIS SHOW ON THE ROAD!!

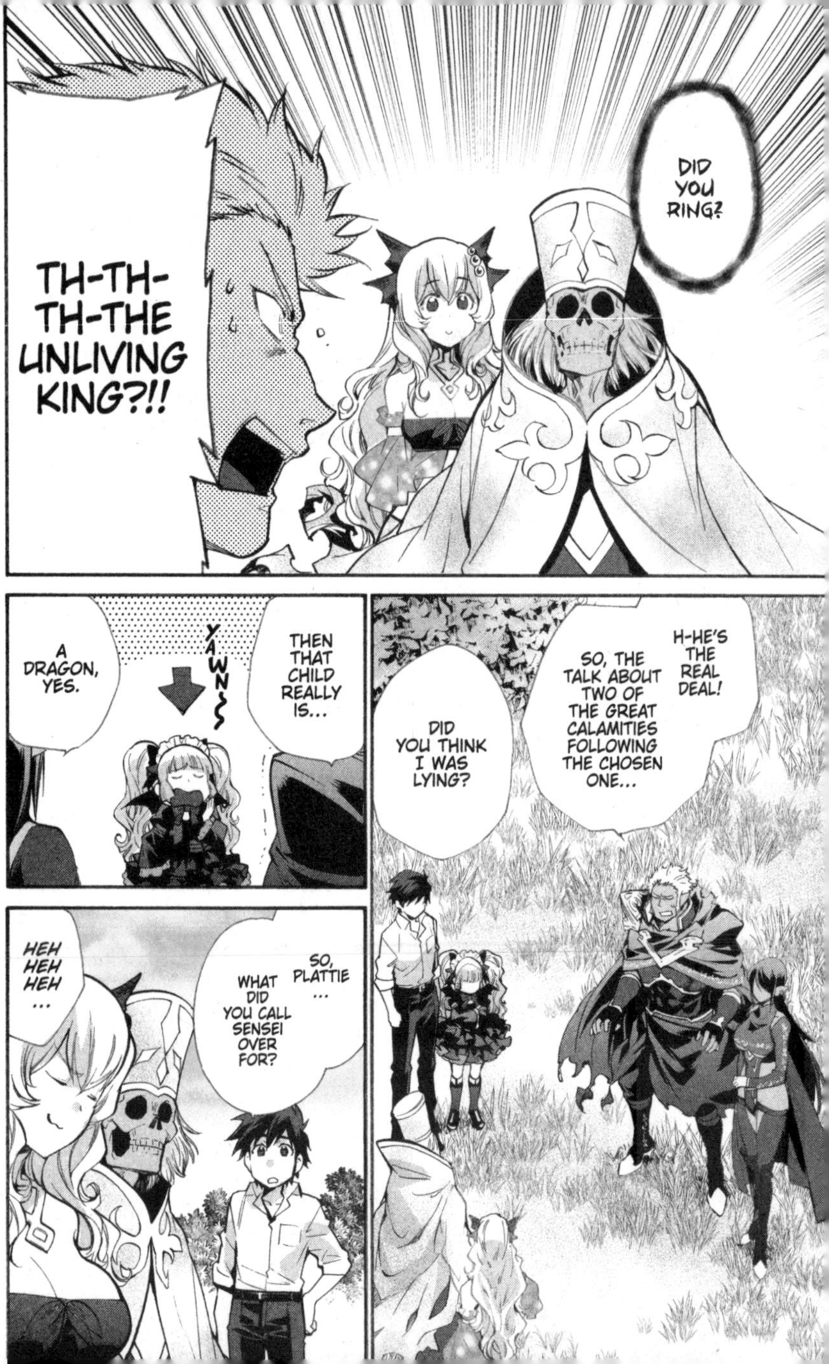
DID YOU RING?
TH-TH-TH-THE UNLIVING KING?!!
H-HE'S THE REAL DEAL!
SO, THE TALK ABOUT TWO OF THE GREAT CALAMITIES FOLLOWING THE CHOSEN ONE...
DID YOU THINK I WAS LYING?
THEN THAT CHILD REALLY IS...
YAWN~
A DRAGON, YES.
SO, PLATTIE...
WHAT DID YOU CALL SENSEI OVER FOR?
HEH HEH HEH...

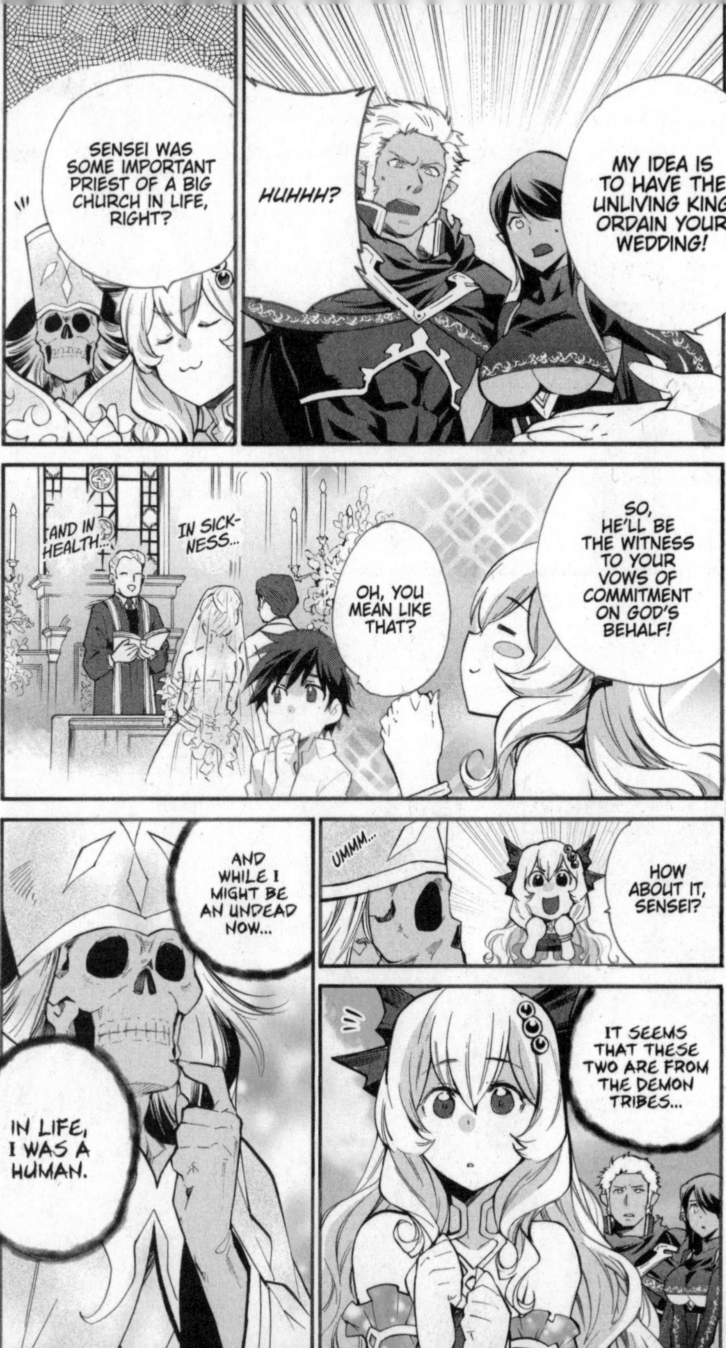
MY IDEA IS TO HAVE THE UNLIVING KING ORDAIN YOUR WEDDING!
HUHHH?
SENSEI WAS SOME IMPORTANT PRIEST OF A BIG CHURCH IN LIFE, RIGHT?
SO, HE'LL BE THE WITNESS TO YOUR VOWS OF COMMITMENT ON GOD'S BEHALF!
OH, YOU MEAN LIKE THAT?
IN SICKNESS...
AND IN HEALTH...
HOW ABOUT IT, SENSEI?
UMMM...
IT SEEMS THAT THESE TWO ARE FROM THE DEMON TRIBES...
AND WHILE I MIGHT BE AN UNDEAD NOW...
IN LIFE, I WAS A HUMAN.

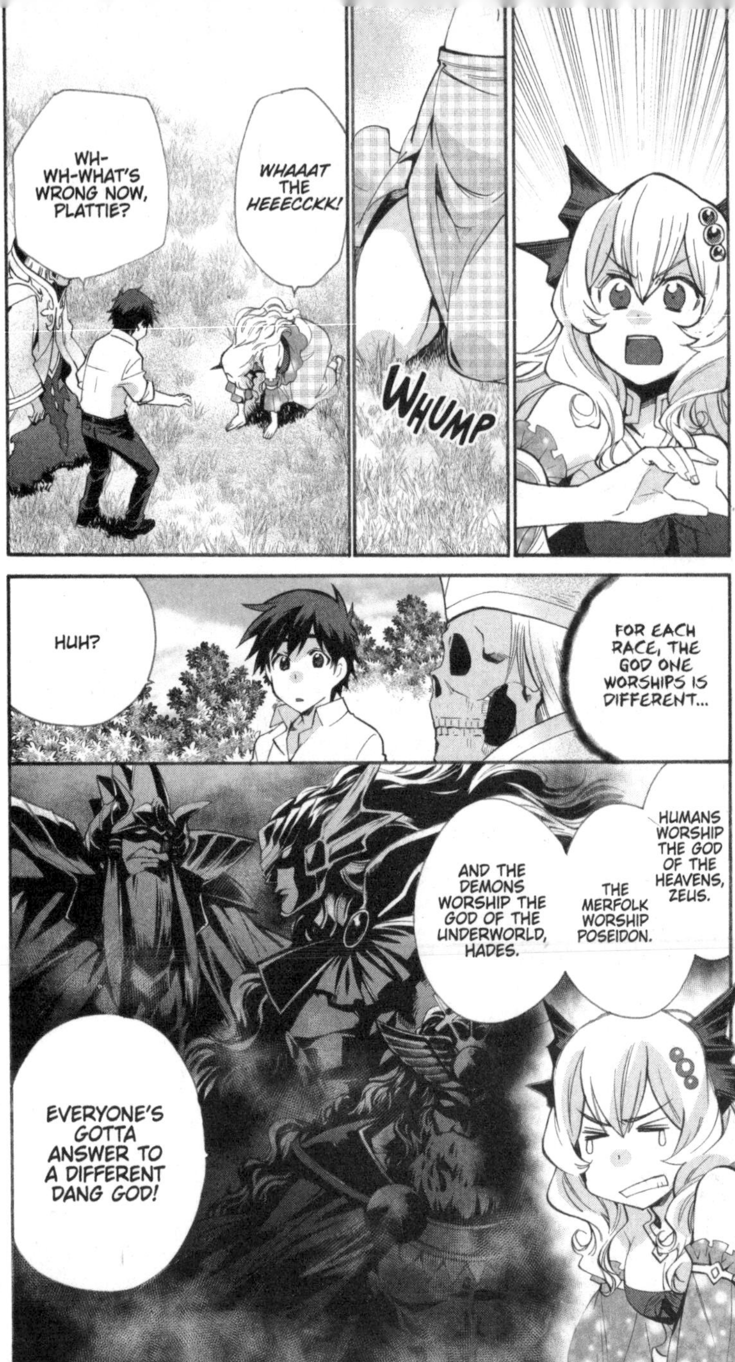
WHUMP
WHAAAT THE HEEECCKK!
WH- WH-WHAT'S WRONG NOW, PLATTIE?
FOR EACH RACE, THE GOD ONE WORSHIPS IS DIFFERENT...
HUH?
HUMANS WORSHIP THE GOD OF THE HEAVENS, ZEUS.
THE MERFOLK WORSHIP POSEIDON.
AND THE DEMONS WORSHIP THE GOD OF THE UNDERWORLD, HADES.
EVERYONE'S GOTTA ANSWER TO A DIFFERENT DANG GOD!

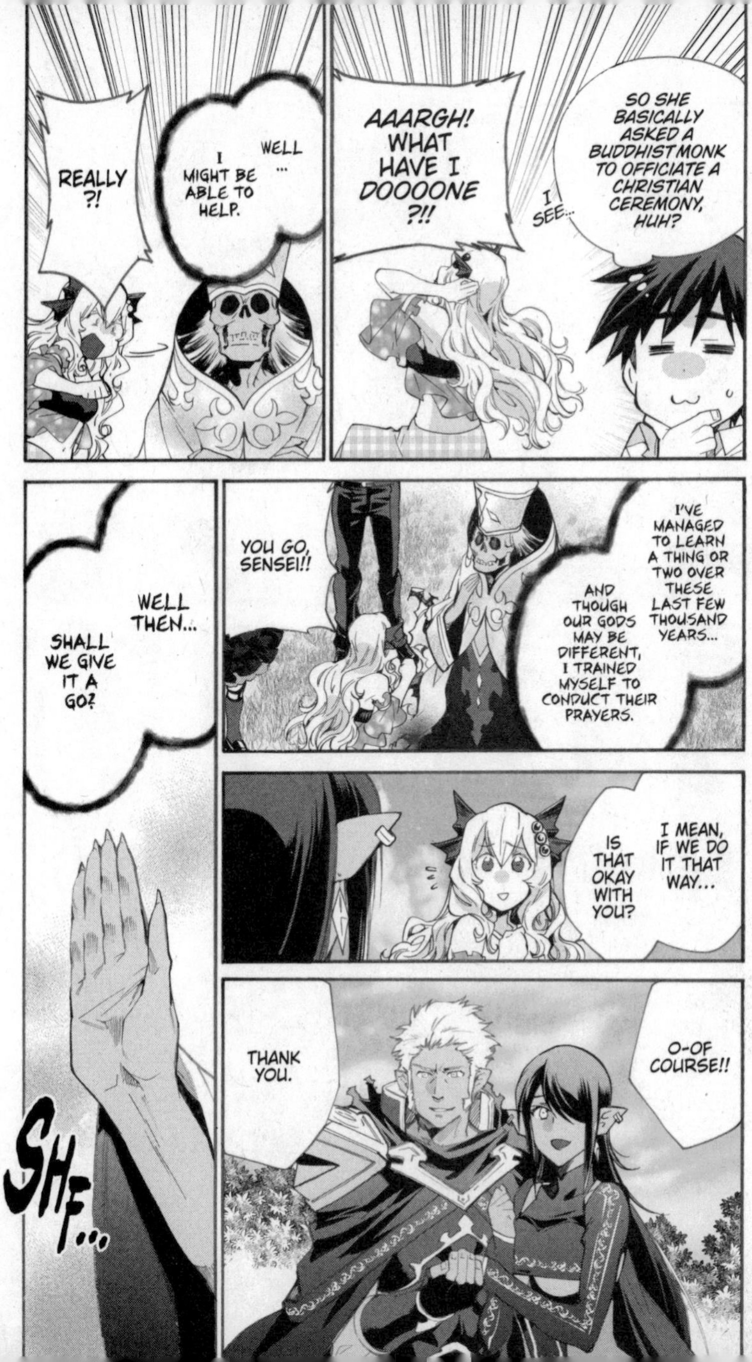
SO SHE BASICALLY ASKED A BUDDHIST MONK TO OFFICIATE A CHRISTIAN CEREMONY, HUH?
I SEE...
AAARGH! WHAT HAVE I DOOOONE ?!!
WELL ...
I MIGHT BE ABLE TO HELP.
REALLY ?!
I'VE MANAGED TO LEARN A THING OR TWO OVER THESE LAST FEW THOUSAND YEARS...
AND THOUGH OUR GODS MAY BE DIFFERENT, I TRAINED MYSELF TO CONDUCT THEIR PRAYERS.
YOU GO, SENSEI!!
I MEAN, IF WE DO IT THAT WAY...
IS THAT OKAY WITH YOU?
O-OF COURSE!!
THANK YOU.
WELL THEN...
SHALL WE GIVE IT A GO?
SHF...

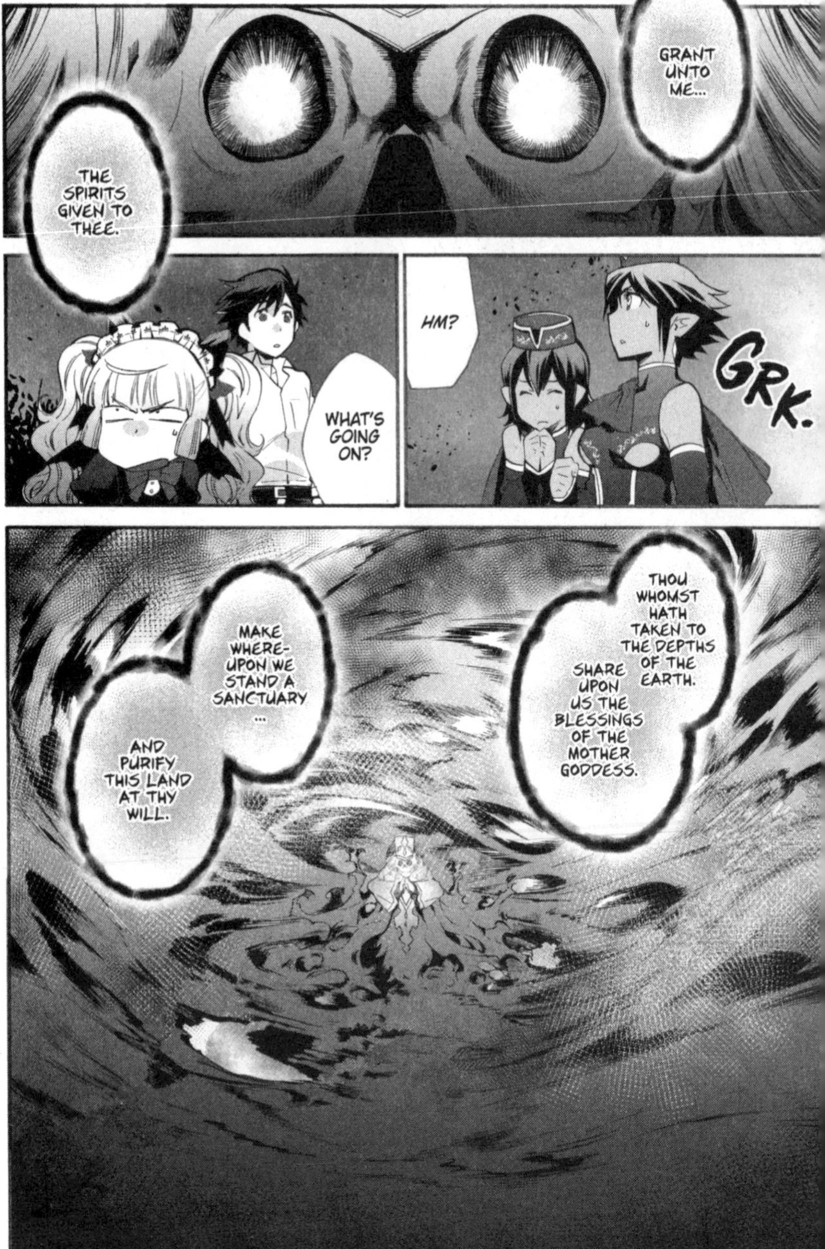
GRANT UNTO ME...
THE SPIRITS GIVEN TO THEE.
HM?
GRK.
WHAT'S GOING ON?
THOU WHOMST HATH TAKEN TO THE DEPTHS OF THE EARTH.
SHARE UPON US THE BLESSINGS OF THE MOTHER GODDESS.
MAKE WHERE-UPON WE STAND A SANCTUARY...
AND PURIFY THIS LAND AT THY WILL.

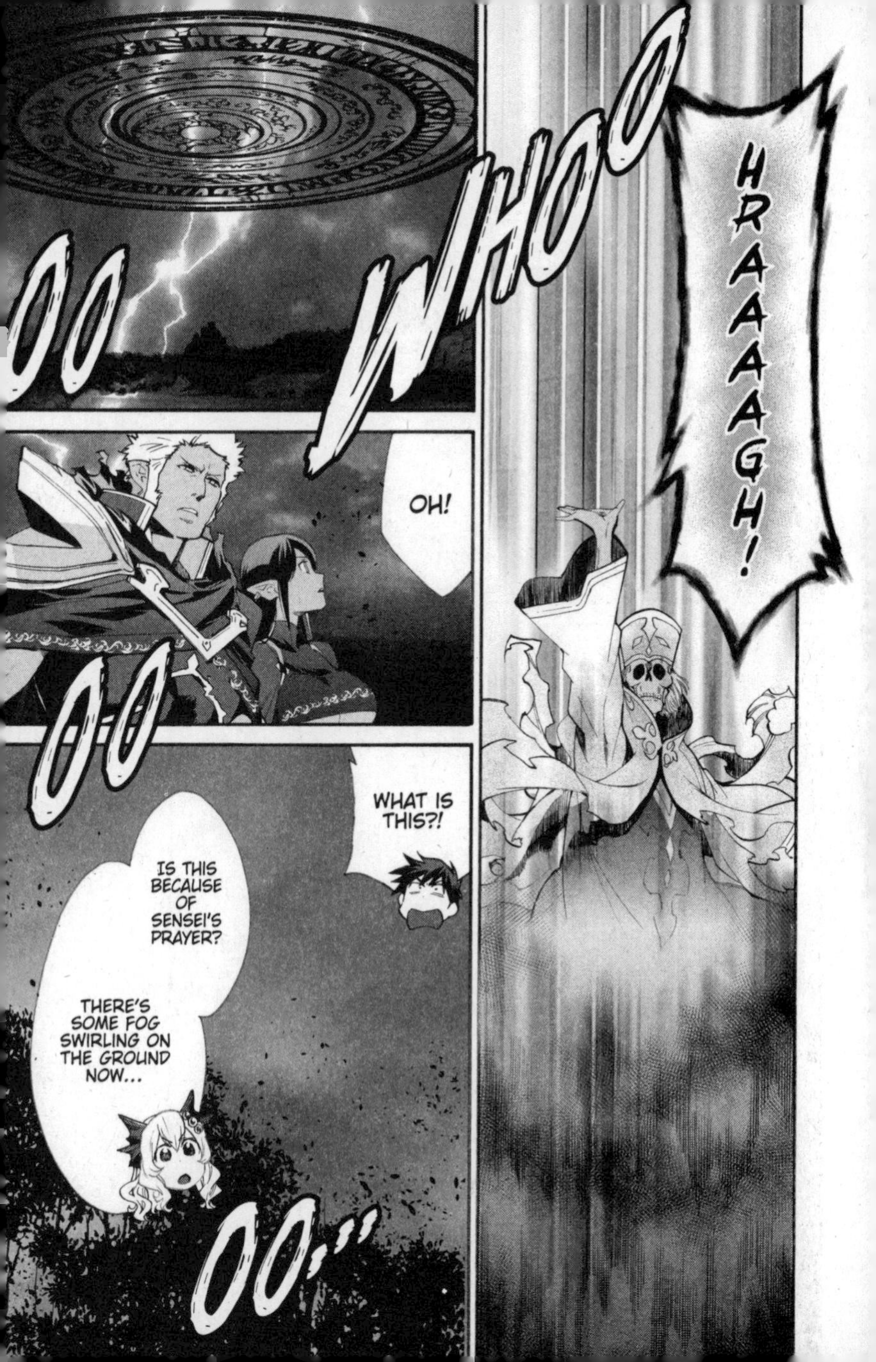
OOWHOO
HRAAAAGH!
OH!
O-O
WHAT IS THIS?!
IS THIS BECAUSE OF SENSEI'S PRAYER?
THERE'S SOME FOG SWIRLING ON THE GROUND NOW...
OO...

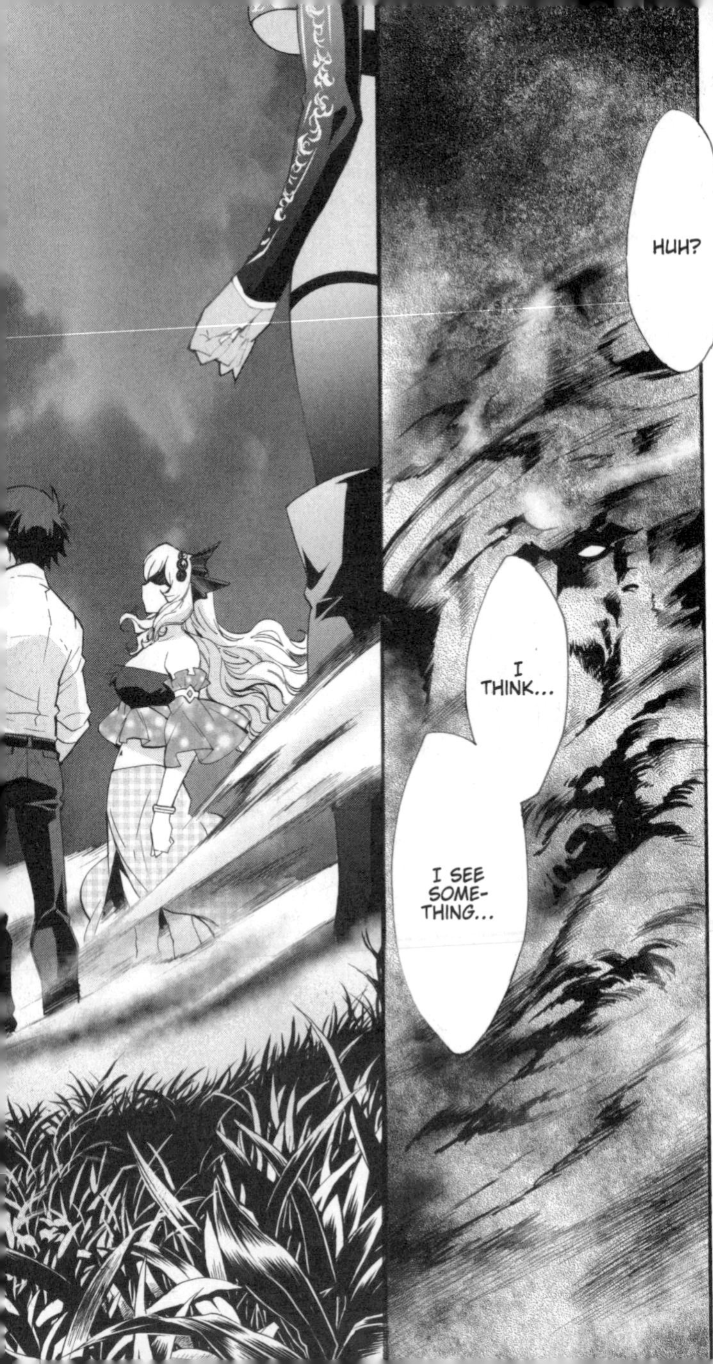
HUH?
I THINK...
I SEE SOME-THING...

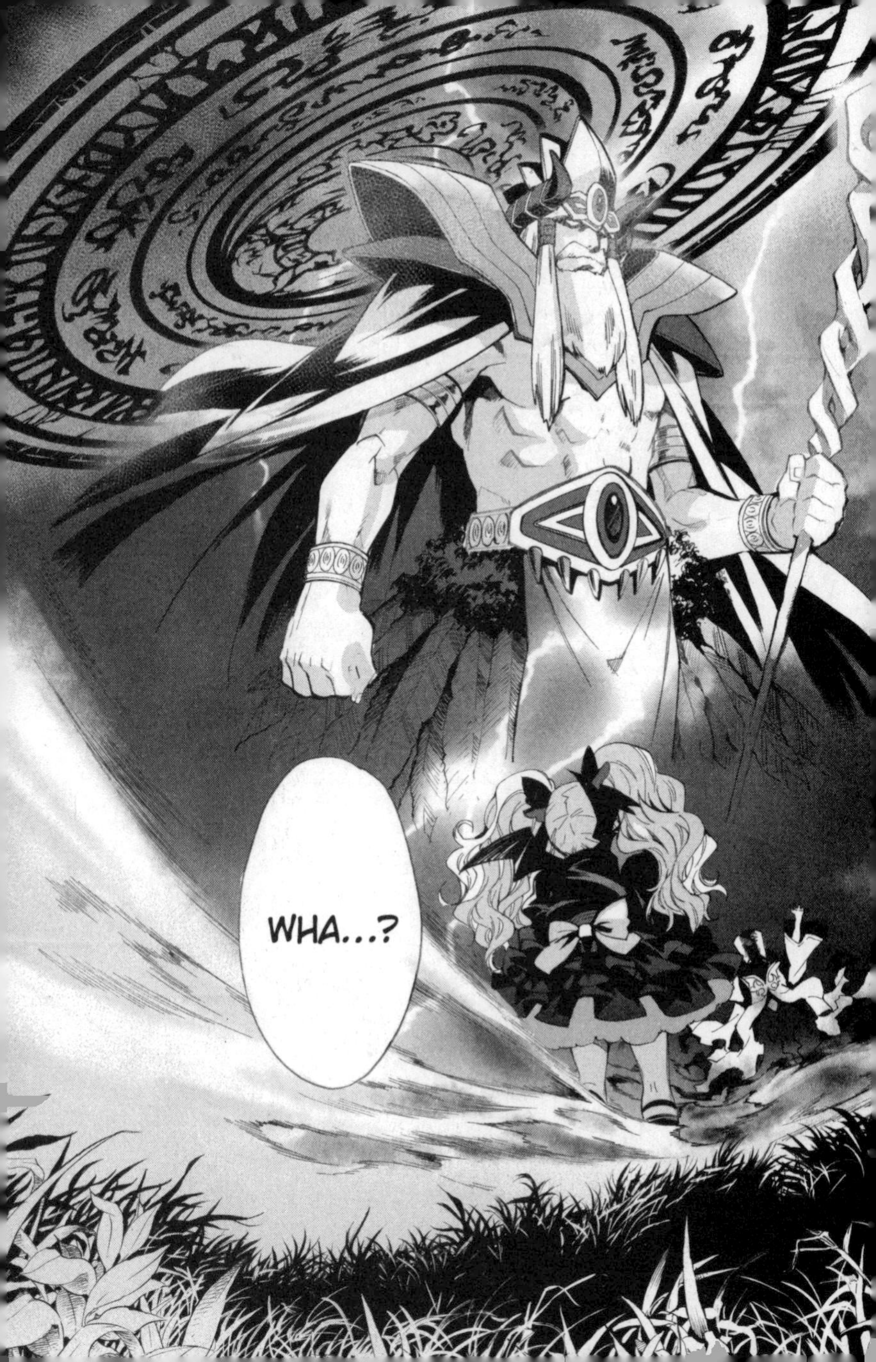
WHA...?

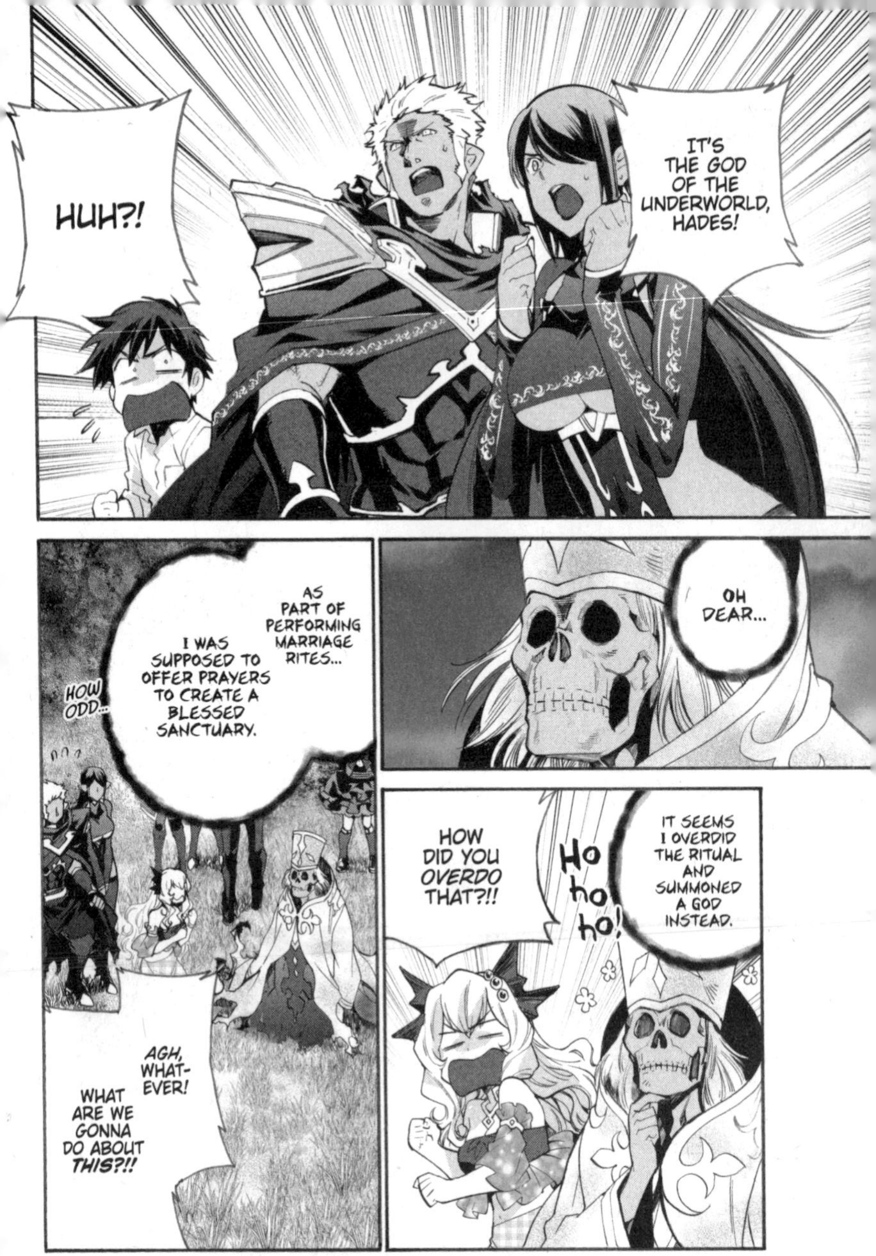
IT'S THE GOD OF THE UNDERWORLD, HADES!
HUH?!
OH DEAR...
IT SEEMS I OVERDID THE RITUAL AND SUMMONED A GOD INSTEAD.
Ho ho ho!
HOW DID YOU OVERDO THAT?!!
AS PART OF PERFORMING MARRIAGE RITES...
I WAS SUPPOSED TO OFFER PRAYERS TO CREATE A BLESSED SANCTUARY.
HOW ODD...
AGH, WHAT-EVER!
WHAT ARE WE GONNA DO ABOUT THIS?!!

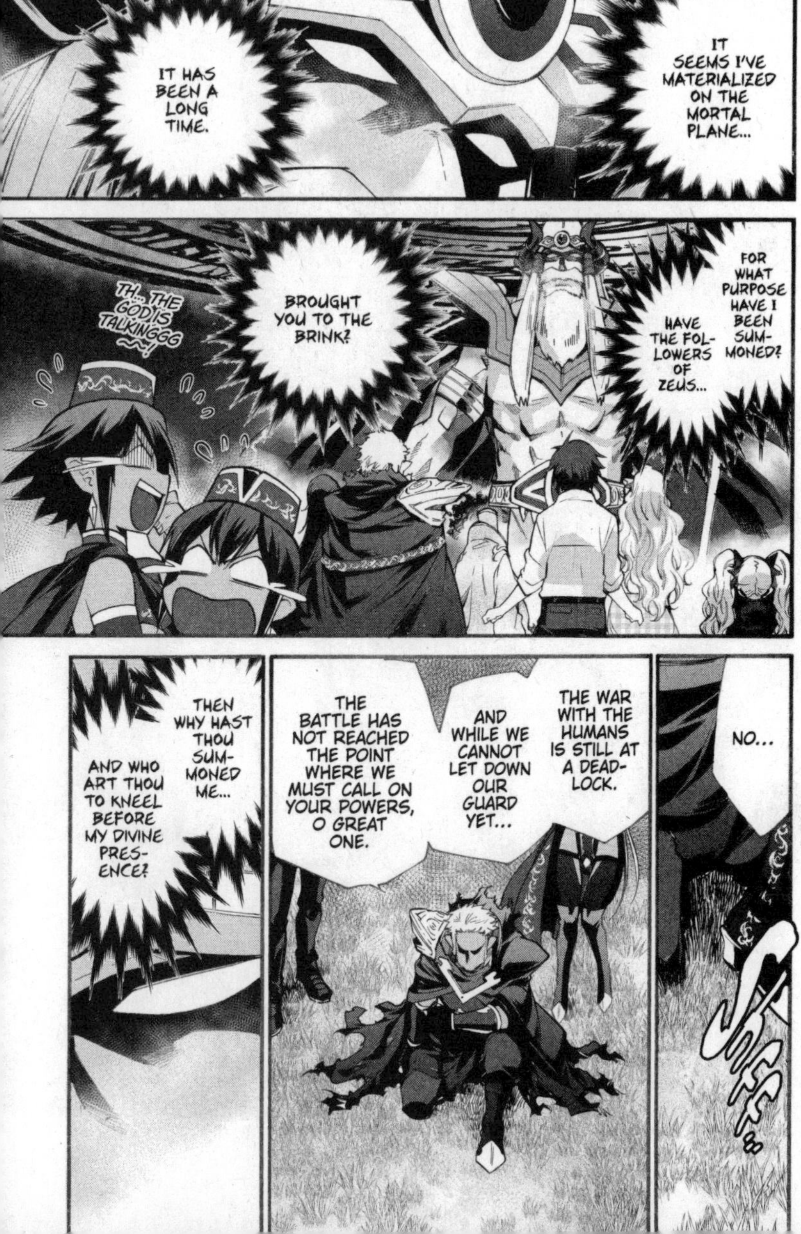
IT SEEMS I'VE MATERIALIZED ON THE MORTAL PLANE...
IT HAS BEEN A LONG TIME.
FOR WHAT PURPOSE HAVE I BEEN SUMMONED?
HAVE THE FOLLOWERS OF ZEUS...
BROUGHT YOU TO THE BRINK?
TH... THE GOD IS TALKINGGG~~!
NO...
THE WAR WITH THE HUMANS IS STILL AT A DEADLOCK.
AND WHILE WE CANNOT LET DOWN OUR GUARD YET...
THE BATTLE HAS NOT REACHED THE POINT WHERE WE MUST CALL ON YOUR POWERS, O GREAT ONE.
THEN WHY HAST THOU SUMMONED ME...
AND WHO ART THOU TO KNEEL BEFORE MY DIVINE PRESENCE?

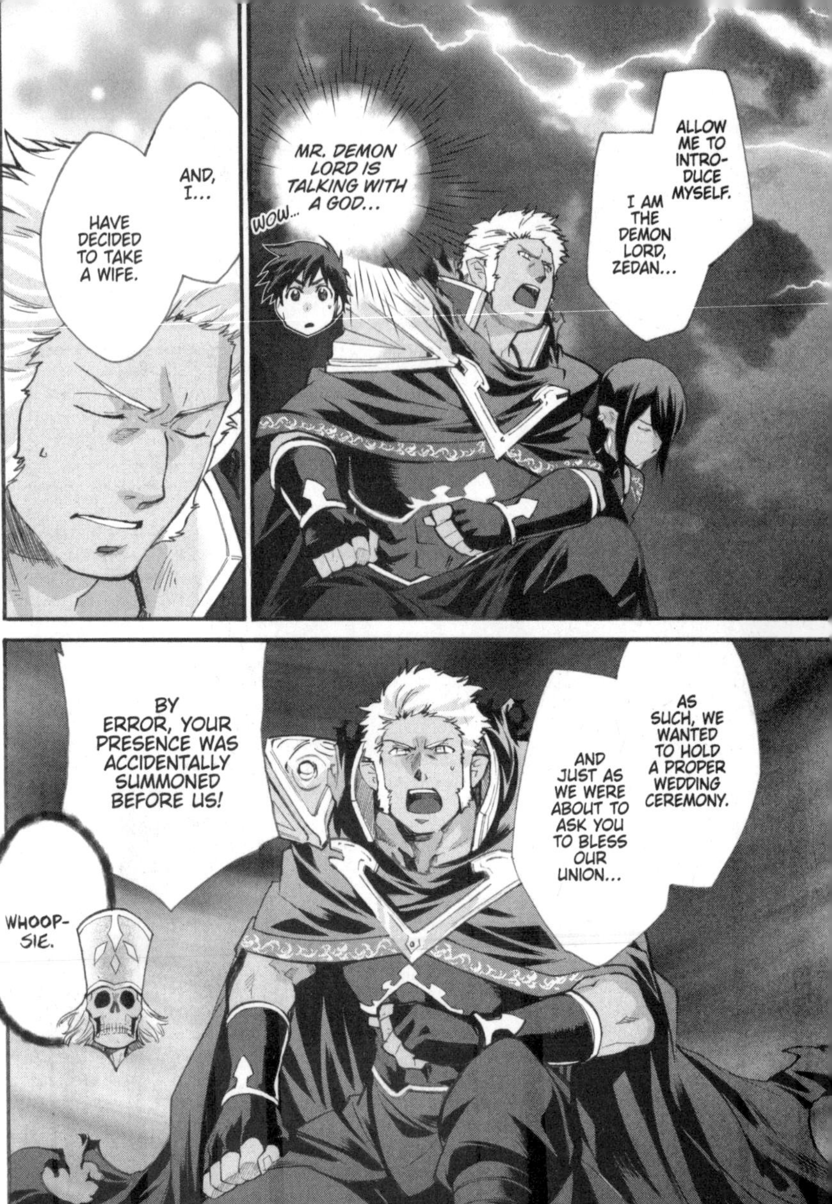
ALLOW ME TO INTRO-DUCE MYSELF.
I AM THE DEMON LORD, ZEDAN…
MR. DEMON LORD IS TALKING WITH A GOD…
WOW…
AND, I…
HAVE DECIDED TO TAKE A WIFE.
AS SUCH, WE WANTED TO HOLD A PROPER WEDDING CEREMONY.
AND JUST AS WE WERE ABOUT TO ASK YOU TO BLESS OUR UNION…
BY ERROR, YOUR PRESENCE WAS ACCIDENTALLY SUMMONED BEFORE US!
WHOOP-SIE.

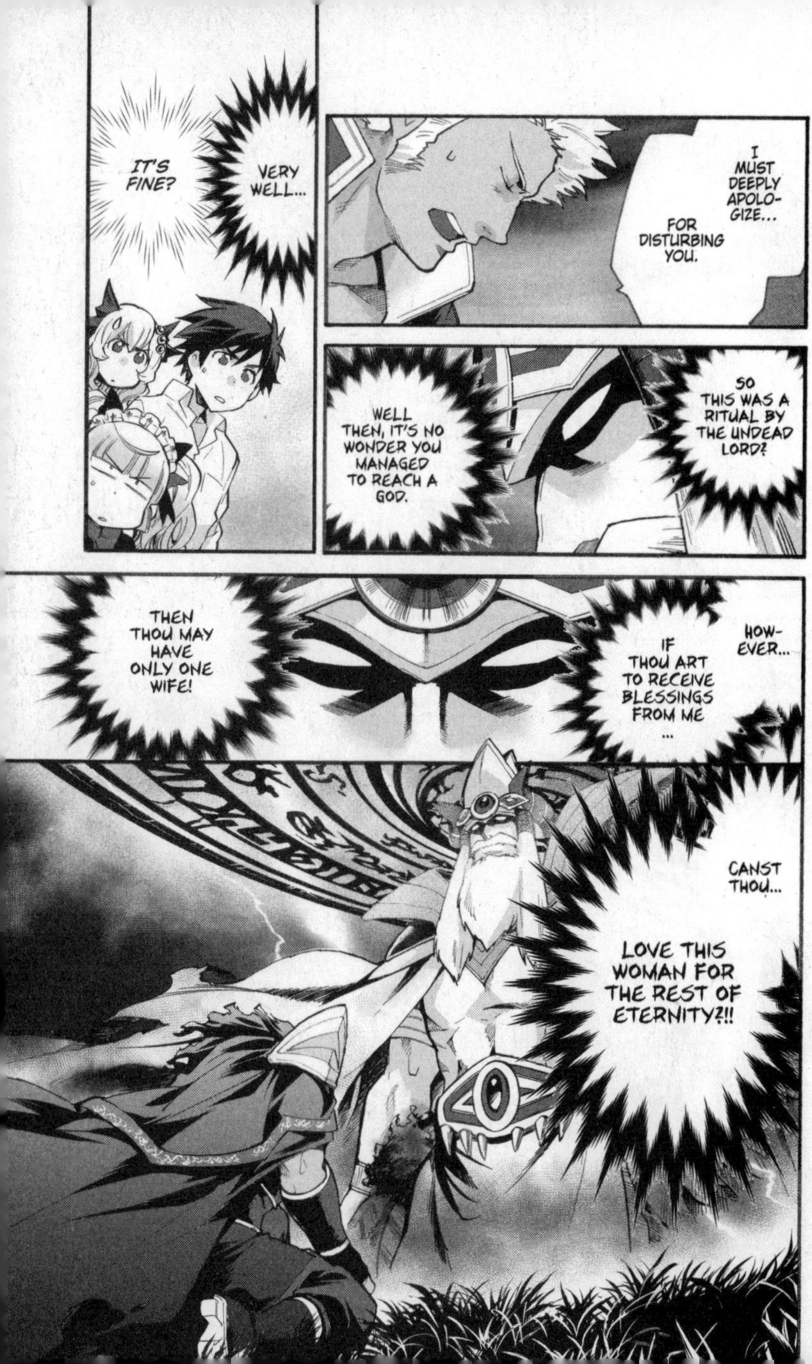
I MUST DEEPLY APOLOGIZE...
FOR DISTURBING YOU.
SO THIS WAS A RITUAL BY THE UNDEAD LORD?
WELL THEN, IT'S NO WONDER YOU MANAGED TO REACH A GOD.
VERY WELL...
IT'S FINE?
HOW-EVER...
IF THOU ART TO RECEIVE BLESSINGS FROM ME ...
THEN THOU MAY HAVE ONLY ONE WIFE!
CANST THOU...
LOVE THIS WOMAN FOR THE REST OF ETERNITY?!!

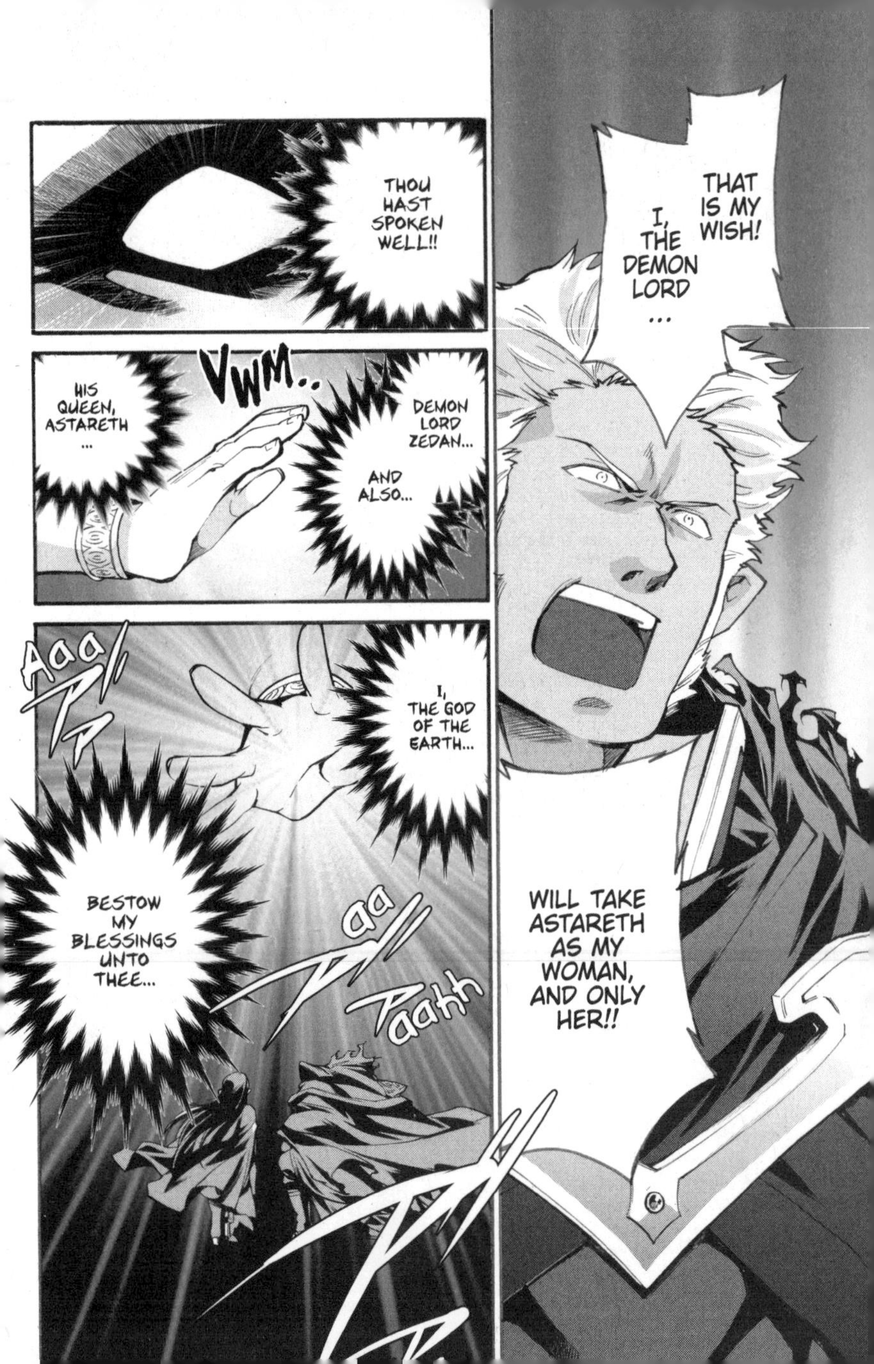
THAT IS MY WISH!
I, THE DEMON LORD ...
WILL TAKE ASTARETH AS MY WOMAN, AND ONLY HER!!
THOU HAST SPOKEN WELL!!
VWM..
DEMON LORD ZEDAN...
AND ALSO...
HIS QUEEN, ASTARETH ...
I, THE GOD OF THE EARTH...
Aaa
BESTOW MY BLESSINGS UNTO THEE...
aa
Paahh

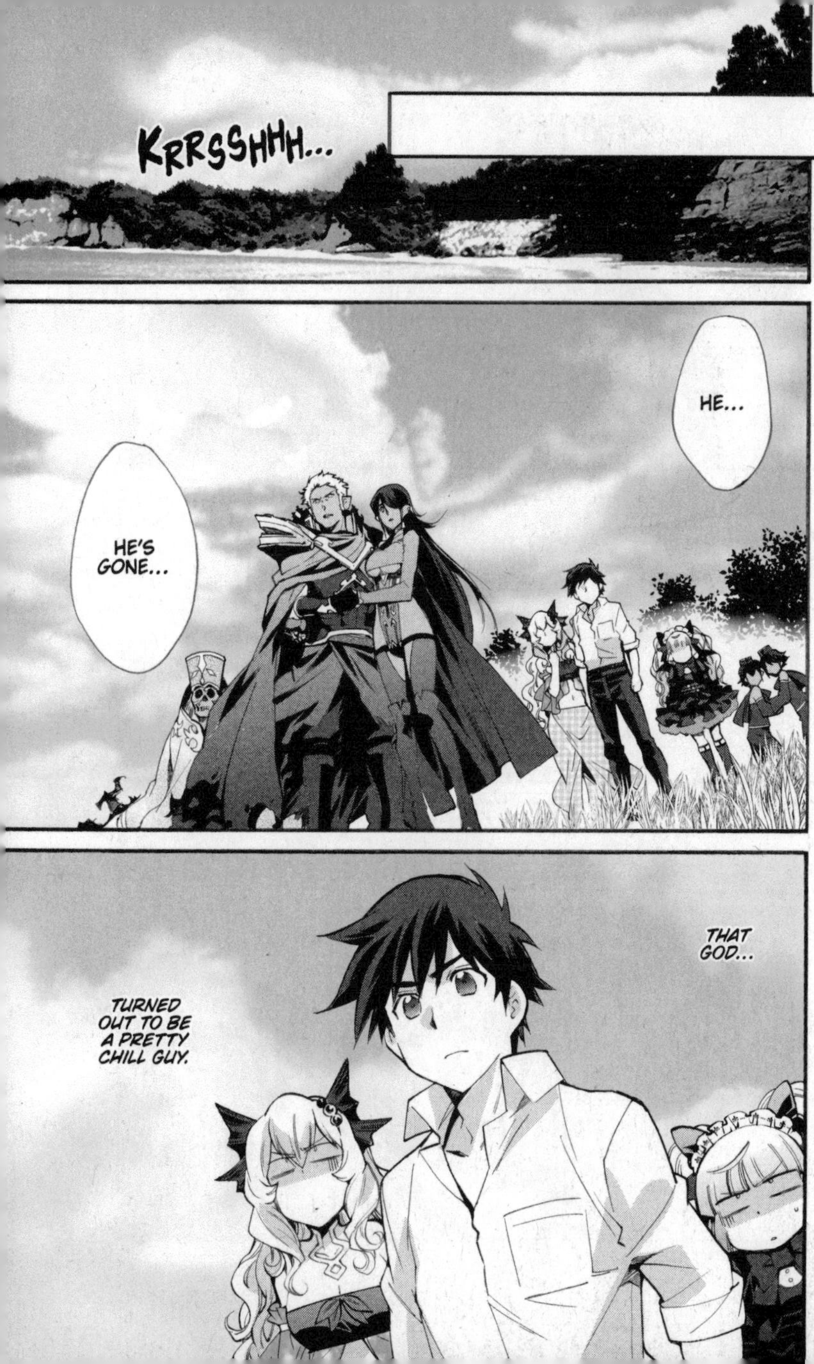
KRRSSHHH...
HE...
HE'S GONE...
THAT GOD...
TURNED OUT TO BE A PRETTY CHILL GUY.

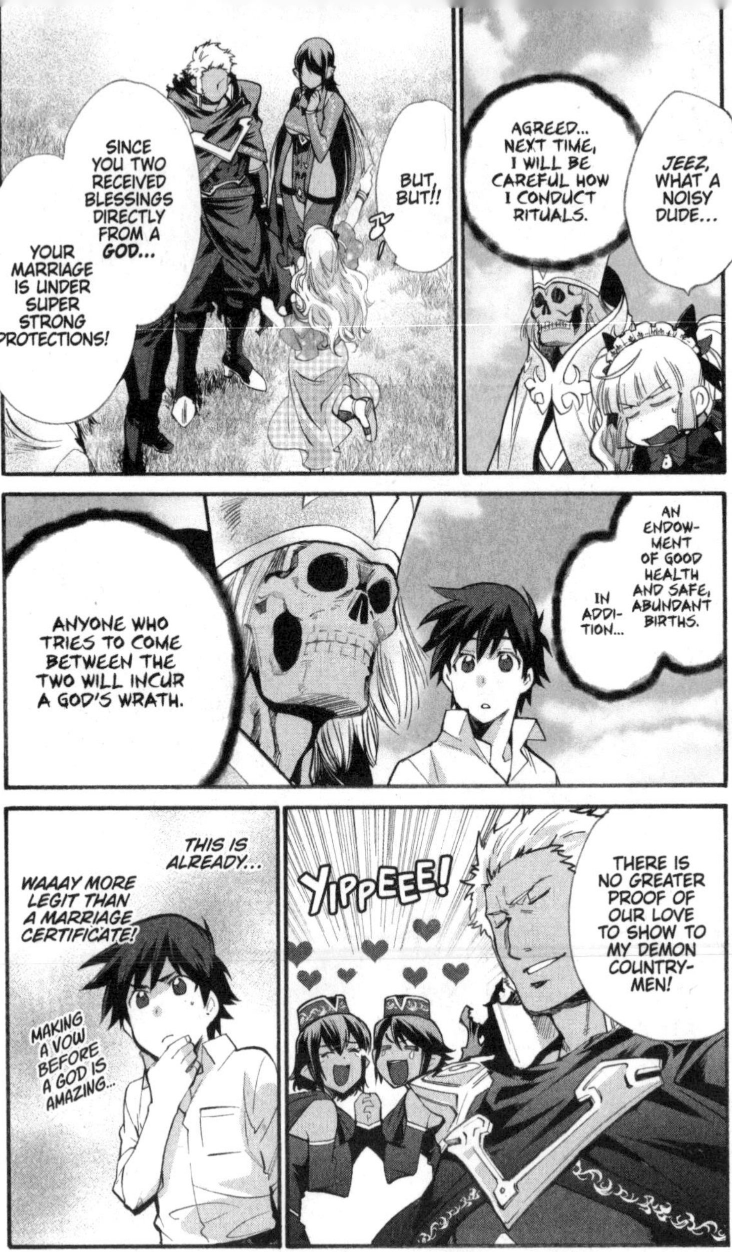
JEEZ, WHAT A NOISY DUDE...
AGREED... NEXT TIME, I WILL BE CAREFUL HOW I CONDUCT RITUALS.
BUT, BUT!!
SINCE YOU TWO RECEIVED BLESSINGS DIRECTLY FROM A GOD...
YOUR MARRIAGE IS UNDER SUPER STRONG PROTECTIONS!
AN ENDOWMENT OF GOOD HEALTH AND SAFE, ABUNDANT BIRTHS.
IN ADDITION...
ANYONE WHO TRIES TO COME BETWEEN THE TWO WILL INCUR A GOD'S WRATH.
THERE IS NO GREATER PROOF OF OUR LOVE TO SHOW TO MY DEMON COUNTRYMEN!
YIPPEEE!
THIS IS ALREADY...
WAAAY MORE LEGIT THAN A MARRIAGE CERTIFICATE!
MAKING A VOW BEFORE A GOD IS AMAZING...

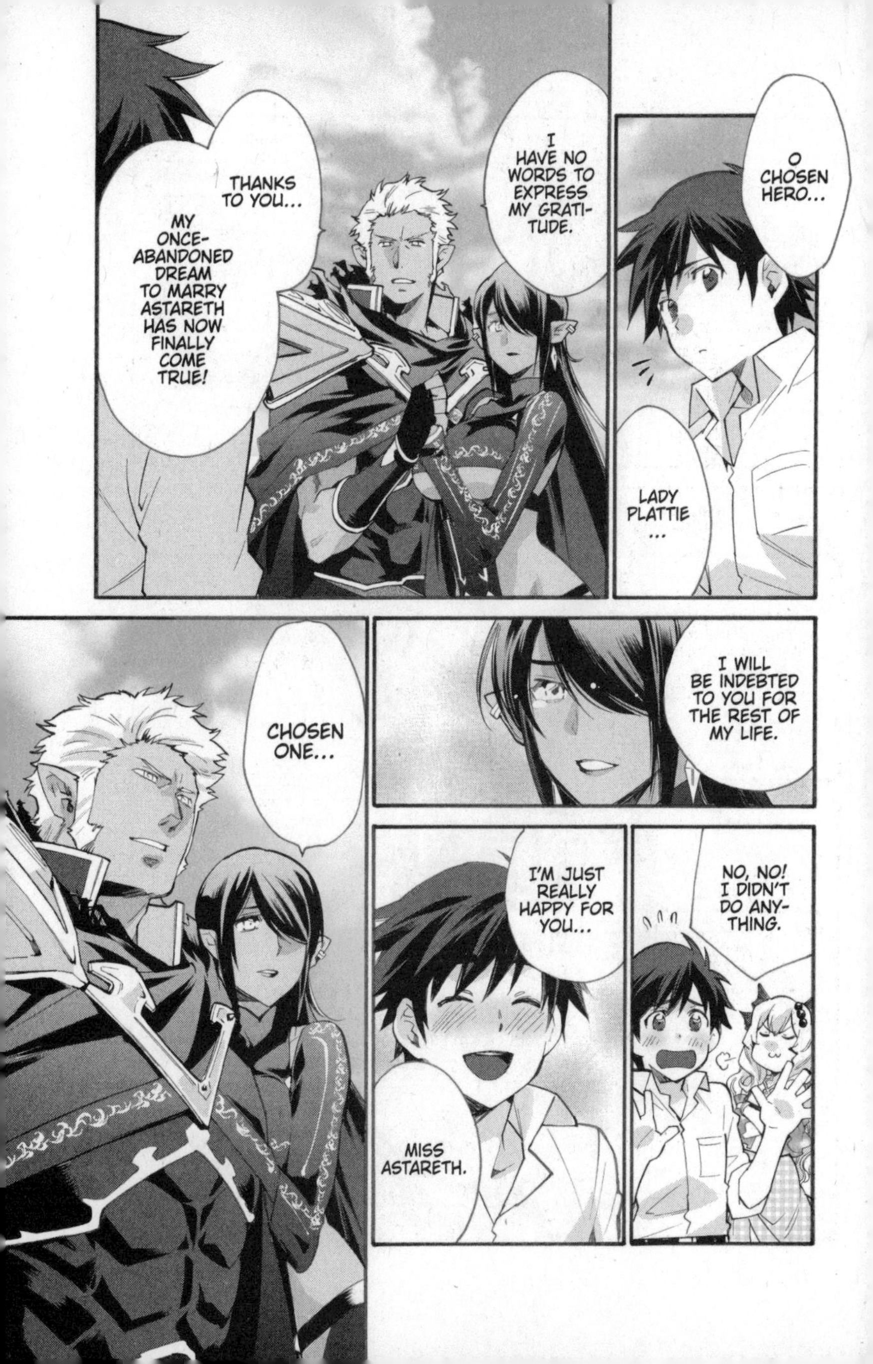
O CHOSEN HERO...
LADY PLATTIE ...
I HAVE NO WORDS TO EXPRESS MY GRATI-TUDE.
THANKS TO YOU...
MY ONCE-ABANDONED DREAM TO MARRY ASTARETH HAS NOW FINALLY COME TRUE!
I WILL BE INDEBTED TO YOU FOR THE REST OF MY LIFE.
NO, NO! I DIDN'T DO ANY-THING.
I'M JUST REALLY HAPPY FOR YOU...
MISS ASTARETH.
CHOSEN ONE...

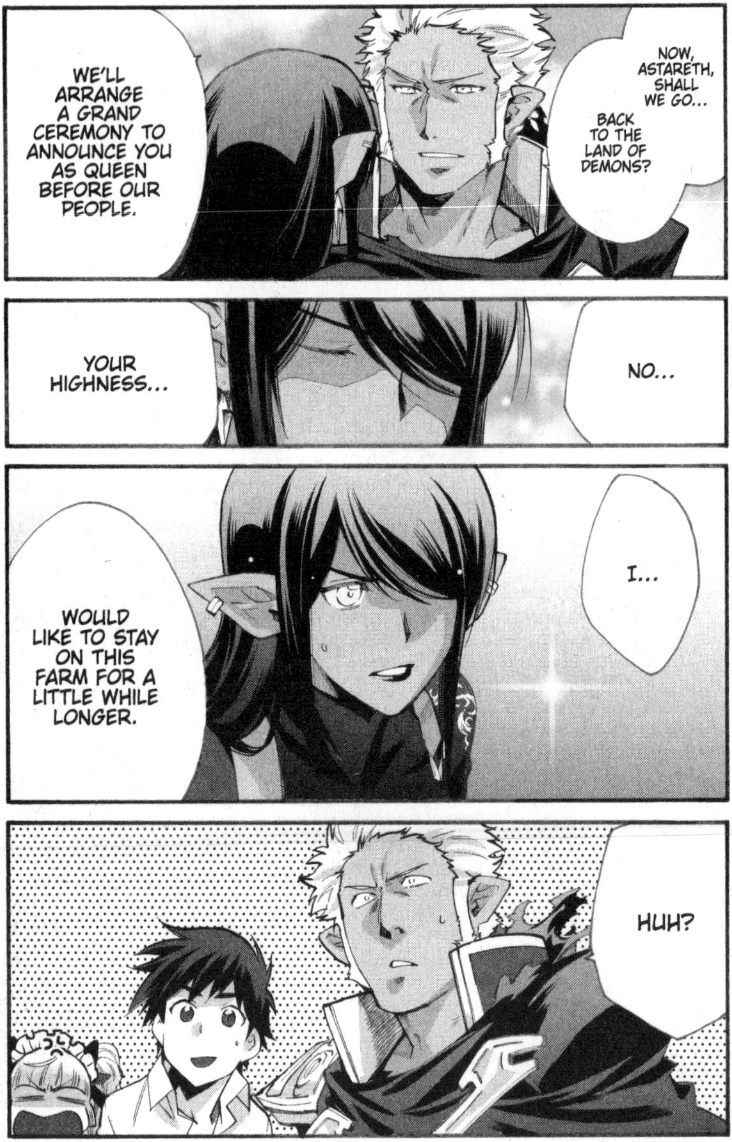
NOW, ASTARETH, SHALL WE GO...
BACK TO THE LAND OF DEMONS?
WE'LL ARRANGE A GRAND CEREMONY TO ANNOUNCE YOU AS QUEEN BEFORE OUR PEOPLE.
NO...
YOUR HIGHNESS...
I...
WOULD LIKE TO STAY ON THIS FARM FOR A LITTLE WHILE LONGER.
HUH?

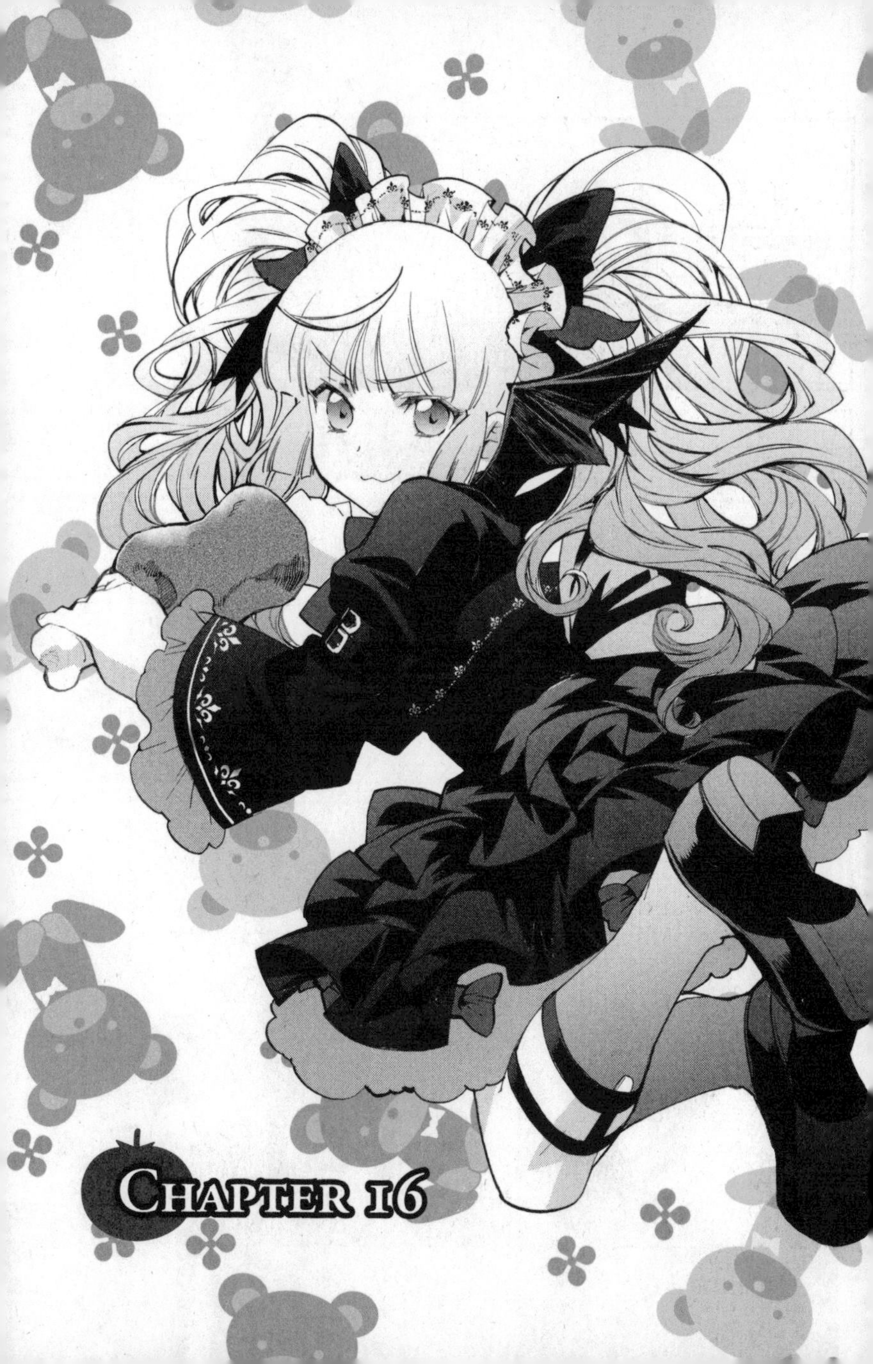
CHAPTER 16

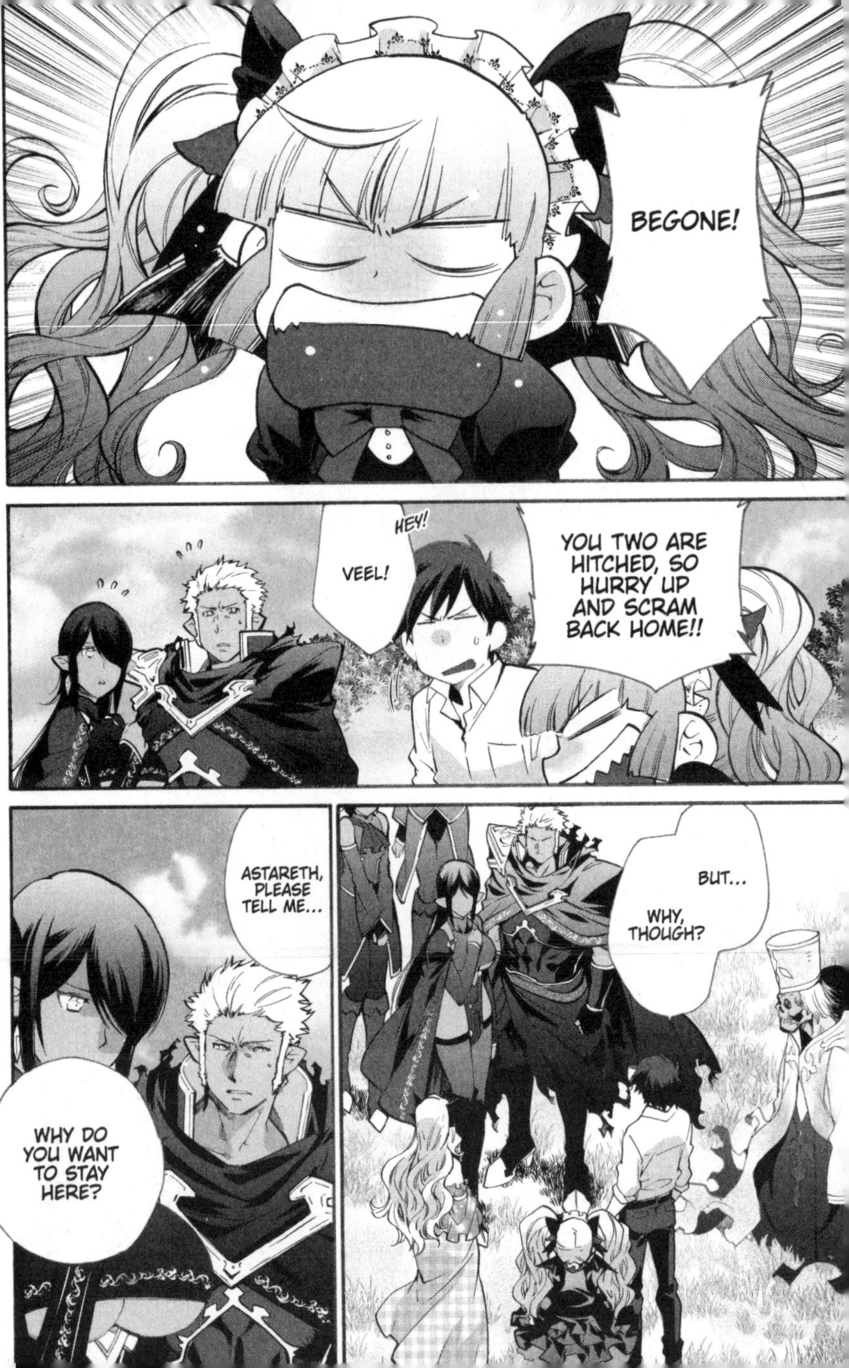
BEGONE!
YOU TWO ARE HITCHED, SO HURRY UP AND SCRAM BACK HOME!!
HEY!
VEEL!
BUT...
WHY, THOUGH?
ASTARETH, PLEASE TELL ME...
WHY DO YOU WANT TO STAY HERE?

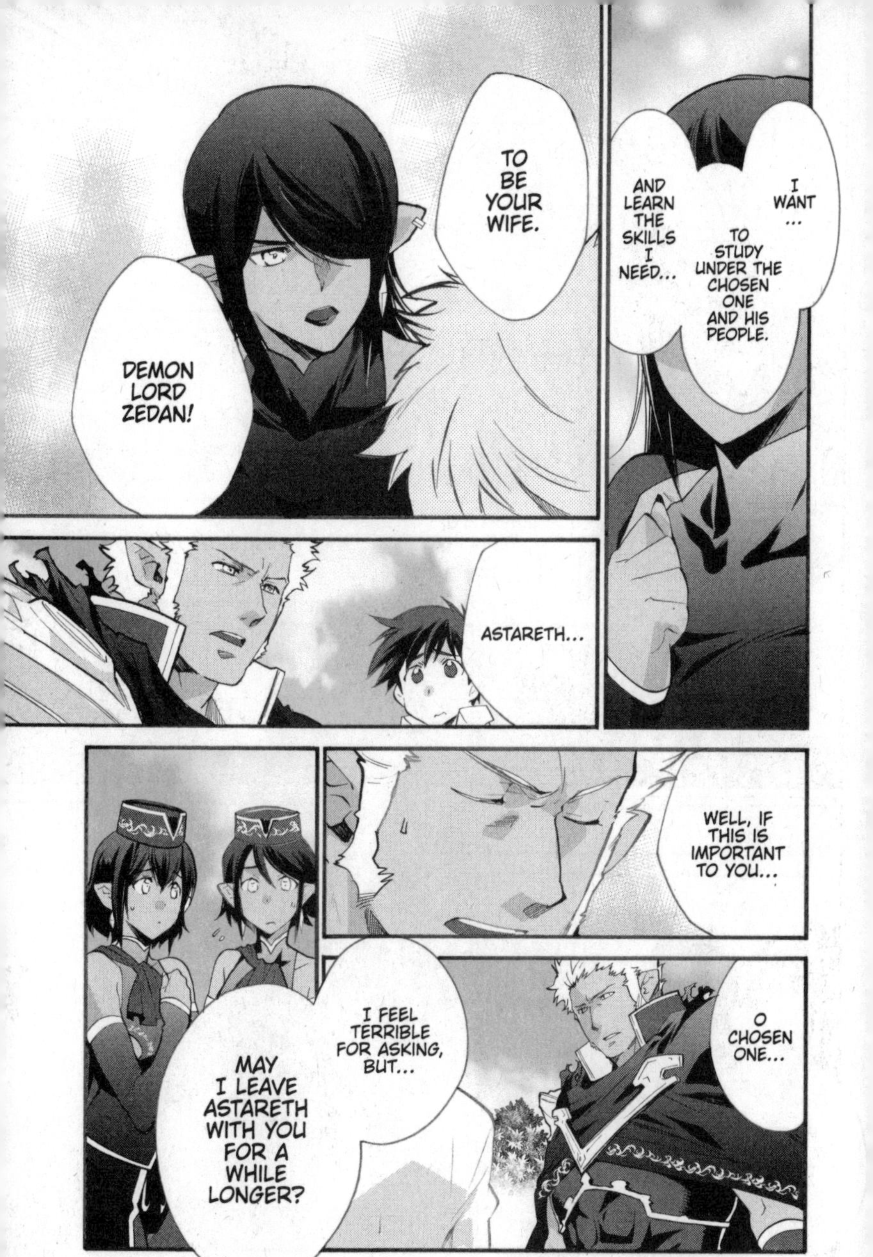
I WANT...
TO STUDY UNDER THE CHOSEN ONE AND HIS PEOPLE.
AND LEARN THE SKILLS I NEED...
TO BE YOUR WIFE.
DEMON LORD ZEDAN!
ASTARETH...
WELL, IF THIS IS IMPORTANT TO YOU...
O CHOSEN ONE...
I FEEL TERRIBLE FOR ASKING, BUT...
MAY I LEAVE ASTARETH WITH YOU FOR A WHILE LONGER?

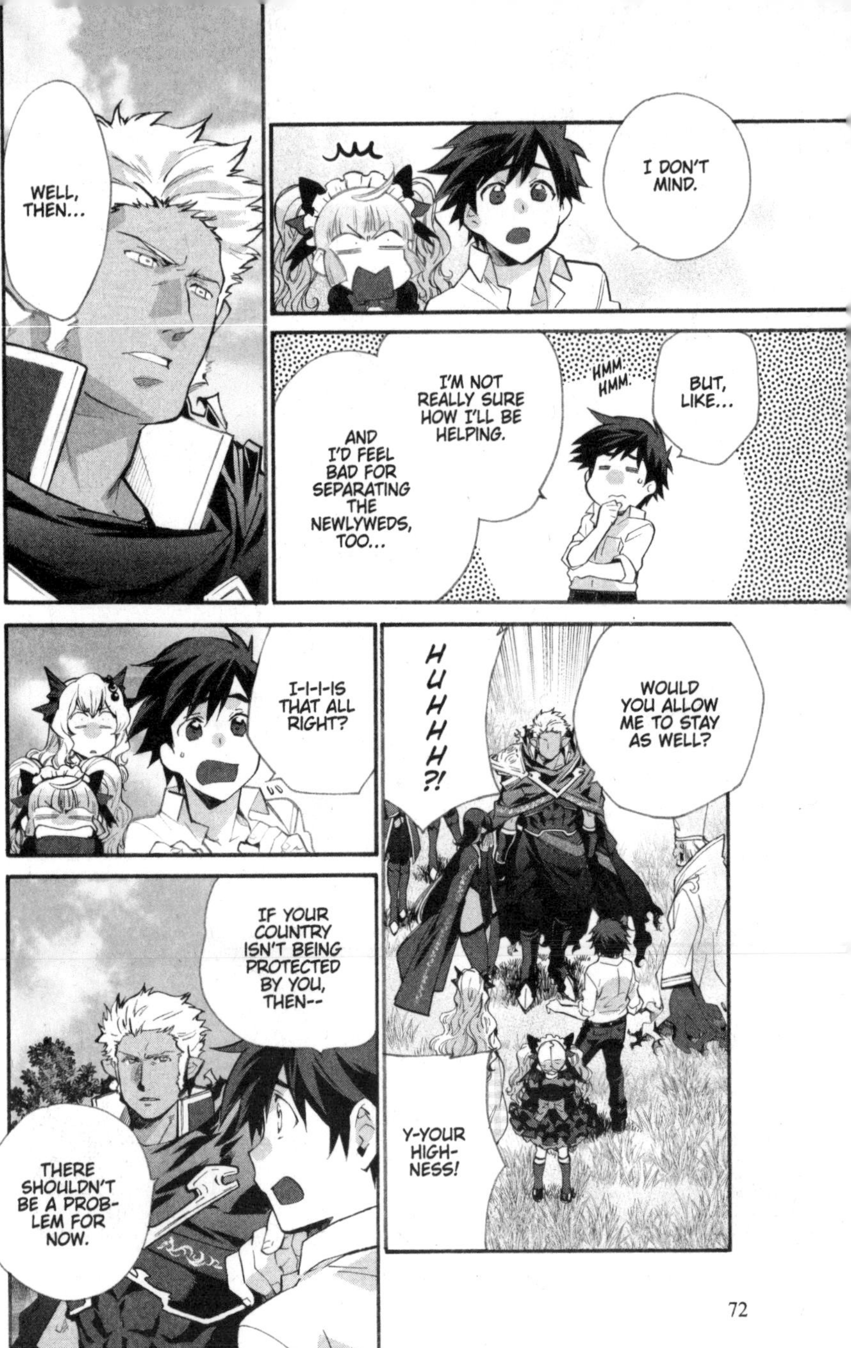
I DON'T MIND.
BUT, LIKE...
HMM HMM.
I'M NOT REALLY SURE HOW I'LL BE HELPING.
AND I'D FEEL BAD FOR SEPARATING THE NEWLYWEDS, TOO...
WELL, THEN...
WOULD YOU ALLOW ME TO STAY AS WELL?
HUHHHH?!
Y-YOUR HIGH-NESS!
I-I-I-IS THAT ALL RIGHT?
IF YOUR COUNTRY ISN'T BEING PROTECTED BY YOU, THEN--
THERE SHOULDN'T BE A PROB-LEM FOR NOW.

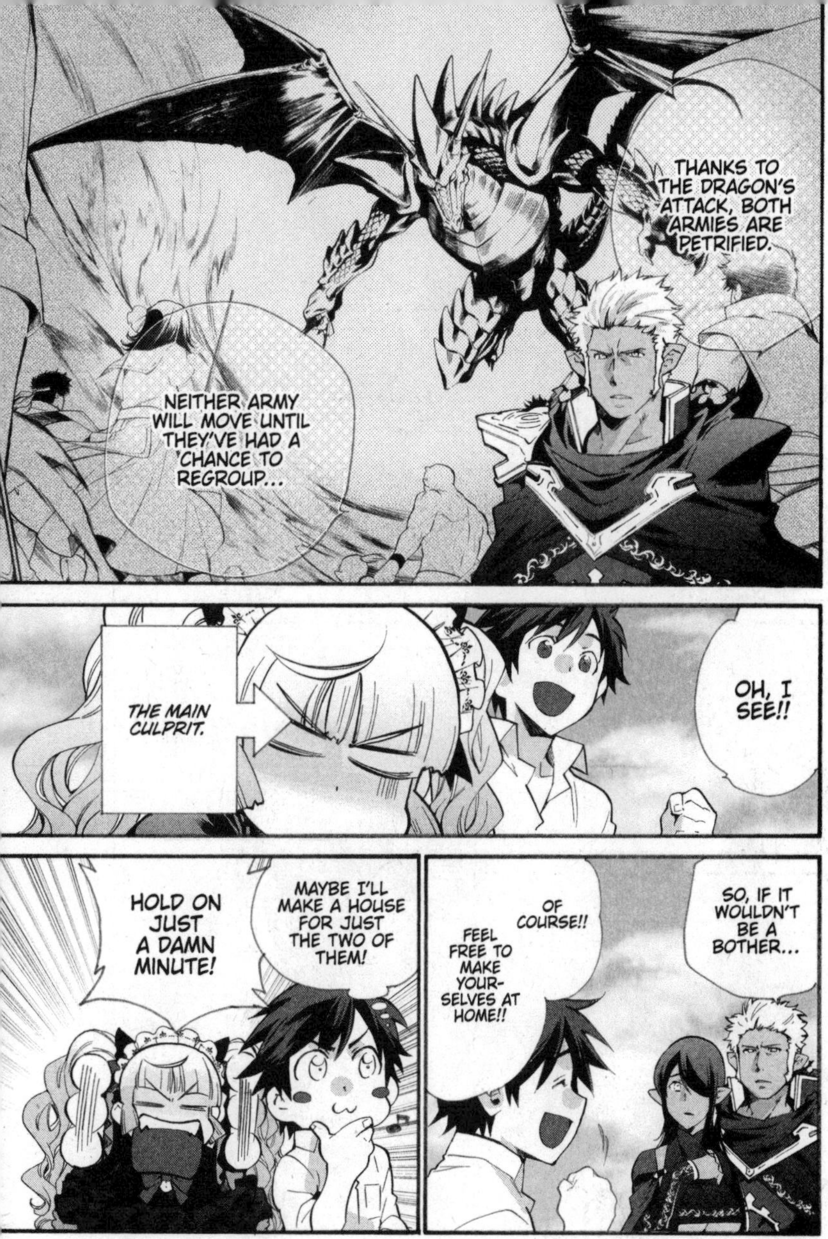
THANKS TO THE DRAGON'S ATTACK, BOTH ARMIES ARE PETRIFIED.
NEITHER ARMY WILL MOVE UNTIL THEY'VE HAD A CHANCE TO REGROUP...
OH, I SEE!!
THE MAIN CULPRIT.
SO, IF IT WOULDN'T BE A BOTHER...
OF COURSE!!
FEEL FREE TO MAKE YOUR-SELVES AT HOME!!
MAYBE I'LL MAKE A HOUSE FOR JUST THE TWO OF THEM!
HOLD ON JUST A DAMN MINUTE!

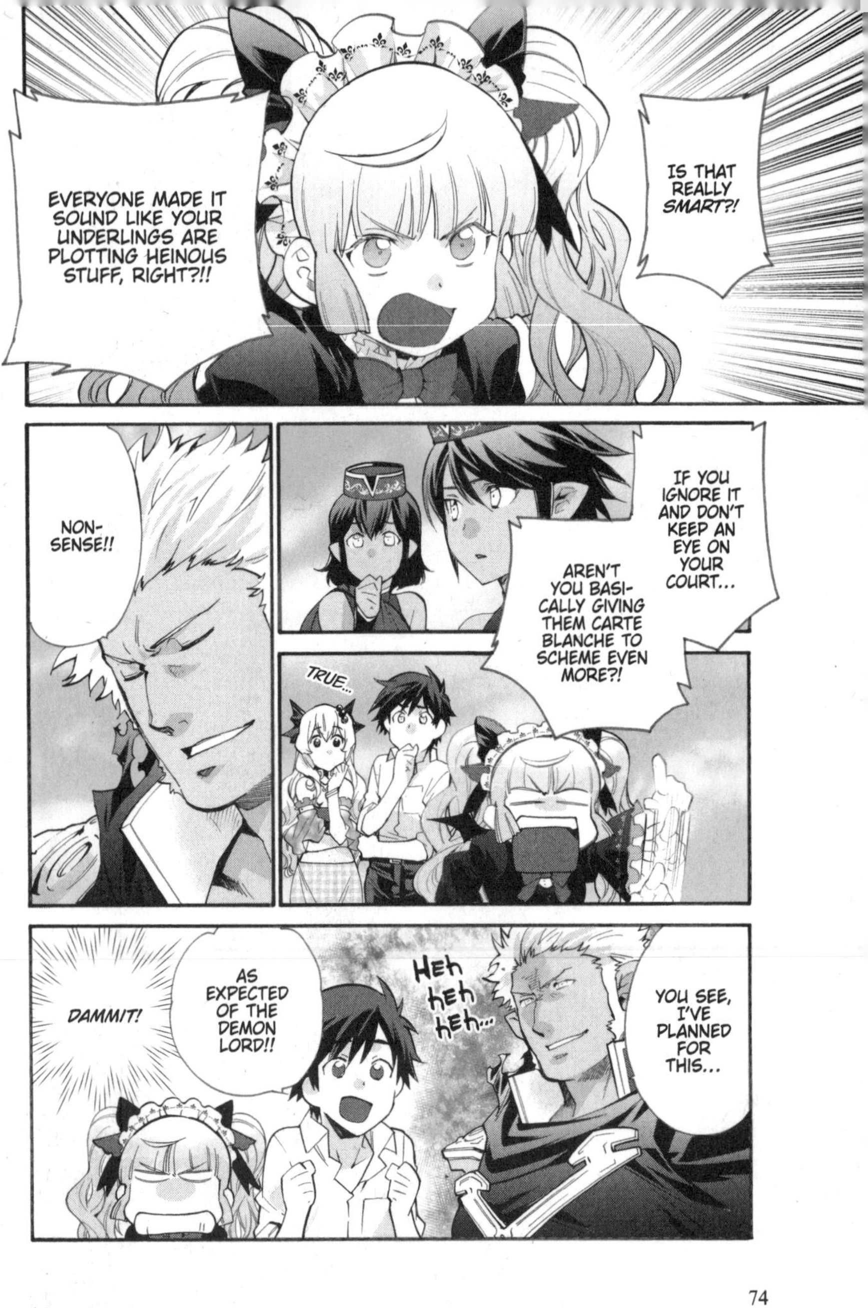
IS THAT REALLY SMART?!
EVERYONE MADE IT SOUND LIKE YOUR UNDERLINGS ARE PLOTTING HEINOUS STUFF, RIGHT?!!
IF YOU IGNORE IT AND DON'T KEEP AN EYE ON YOUR COURT...
AREN'T YOU BASICALLY GIVING THEM CARTE BLANCHE TO SCHEME EVEN MORE?!
TRUE...
NON-SENSE!!
YOU SEE, I'VE PLANNED FOR THIS...
Heh heh heh...
AS EXPECTED OF THE DEMON LORD!!
DAMMIT!

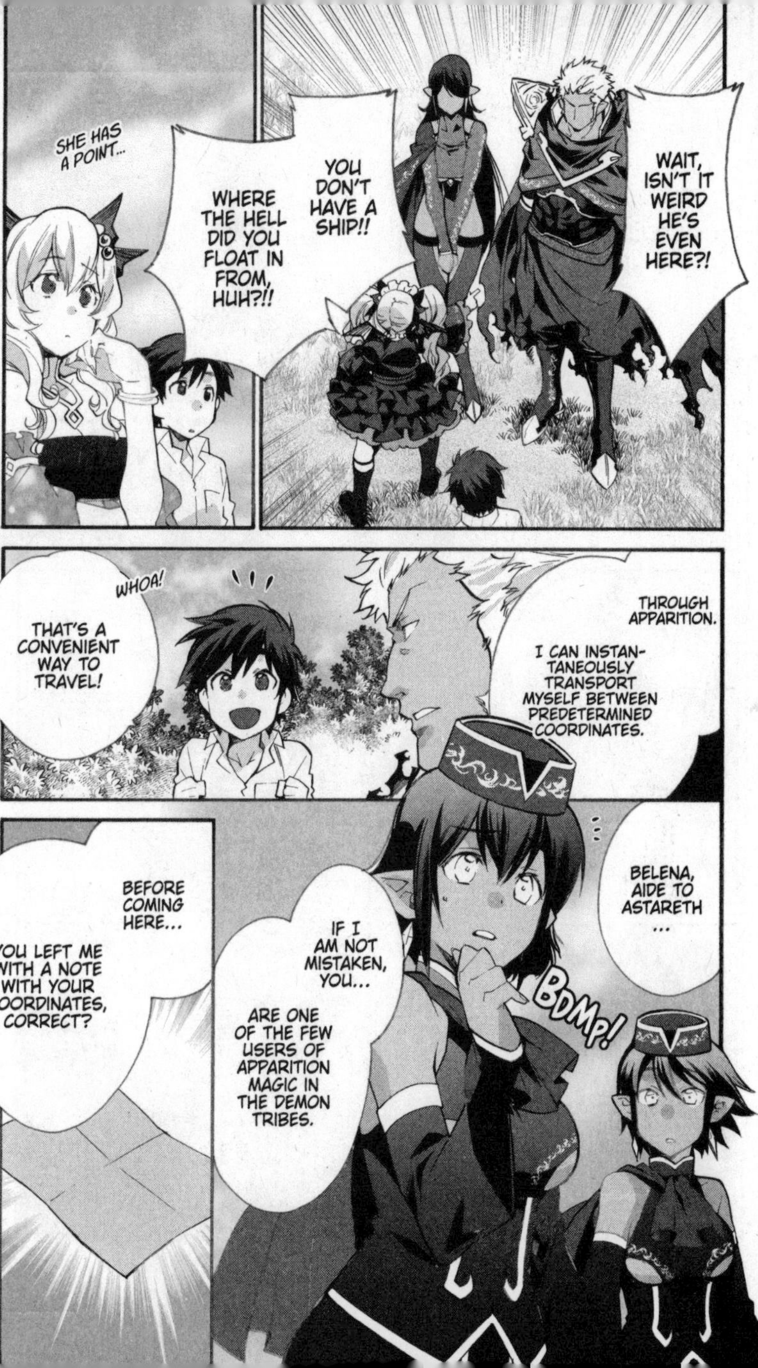
WAIT, ISN'T IT WEIRD HE'S EVEN HERE?!
YOU DON'T HAVE A SHIP!!
WHERE THE HELL DID YOU FLOAT IN FROM, HUH?!!
SHE HAS A POINT...
THROUGH APPARITION.
I CAN INSTANTANEOUSLY TRANSPORT MYSELF BETWEEN PREDETERMINED COORDINATES.
WHOA!
THAT'S A CONVENIENT WAY TO TRAVEL!
BELENA, AIDE TO ASTARETH...
BDMP!
IF I AM NOT MISTAKEN, YOU...
ARE ONE OF THE FEW USERS OF APPARITION MAGIC IN THE DEMON TRIBES.
BEFORE COMING HERE...
YOU LEFT ME WITH A NOTE WITH YOUR COORDINATES, CORRECT?

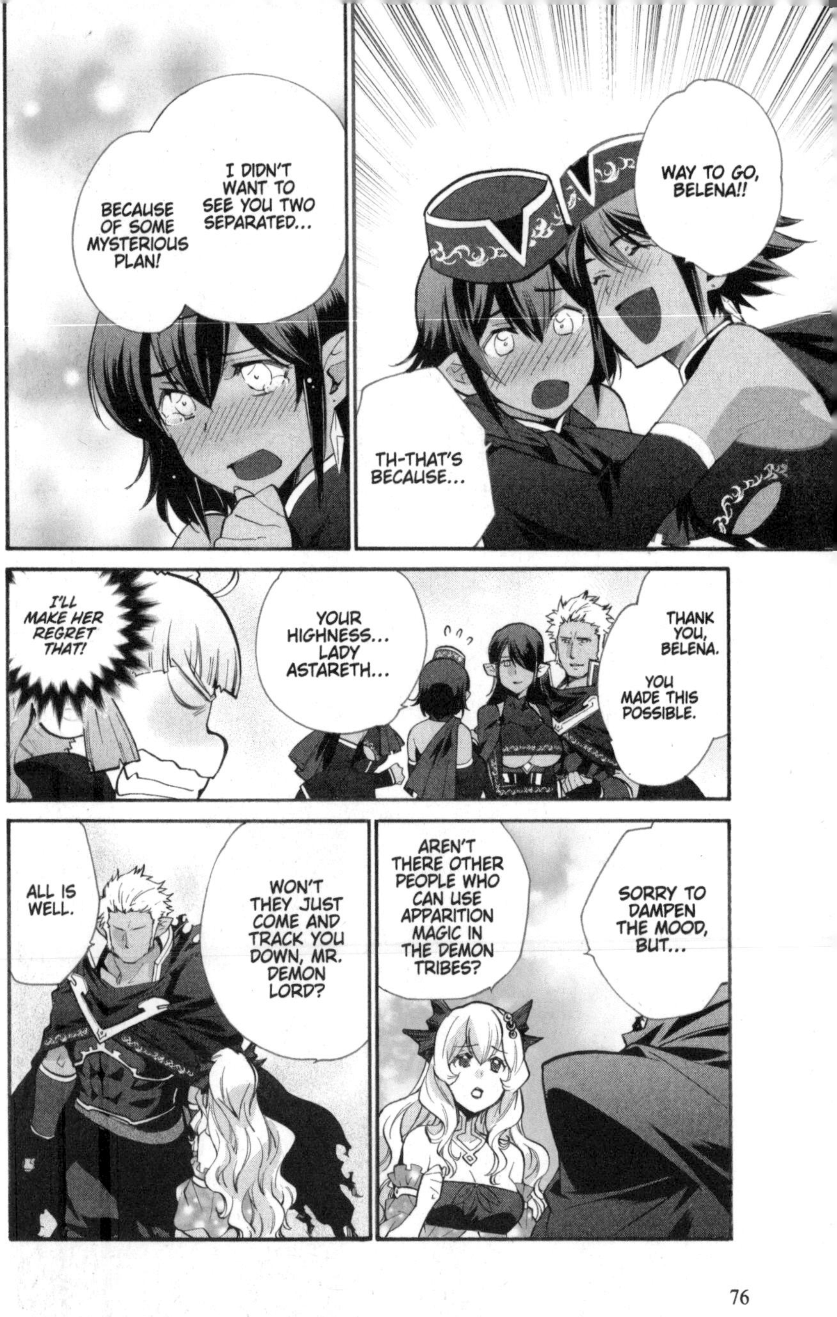
WAY TO GO, BELENA!!
TH-THAT'S BECAUSE...
I DIDN'T WANT TO SEE YOU TWO SEPARATED...
BECAUSE OF SOME MYSTERIOUS PLAN!
THANK YOU, BELENA.
YOU MADE THIS POSSIBLE.
YOUR HIGHNESS... LADY ASTARETH...
I'LL MAKE HER REGRET THAT!
SORRY TO DAMPEN THE MOOD, BUT...
AREN'T THERE OTHER PEOPLE WHO CAN USE APPARITION MAGIC IN THE DEMON TRIBES?
WON'T THEY JUST COME AND TRACK YOU DOWN, MR. DEMON LORD?
ALL IS WELL.

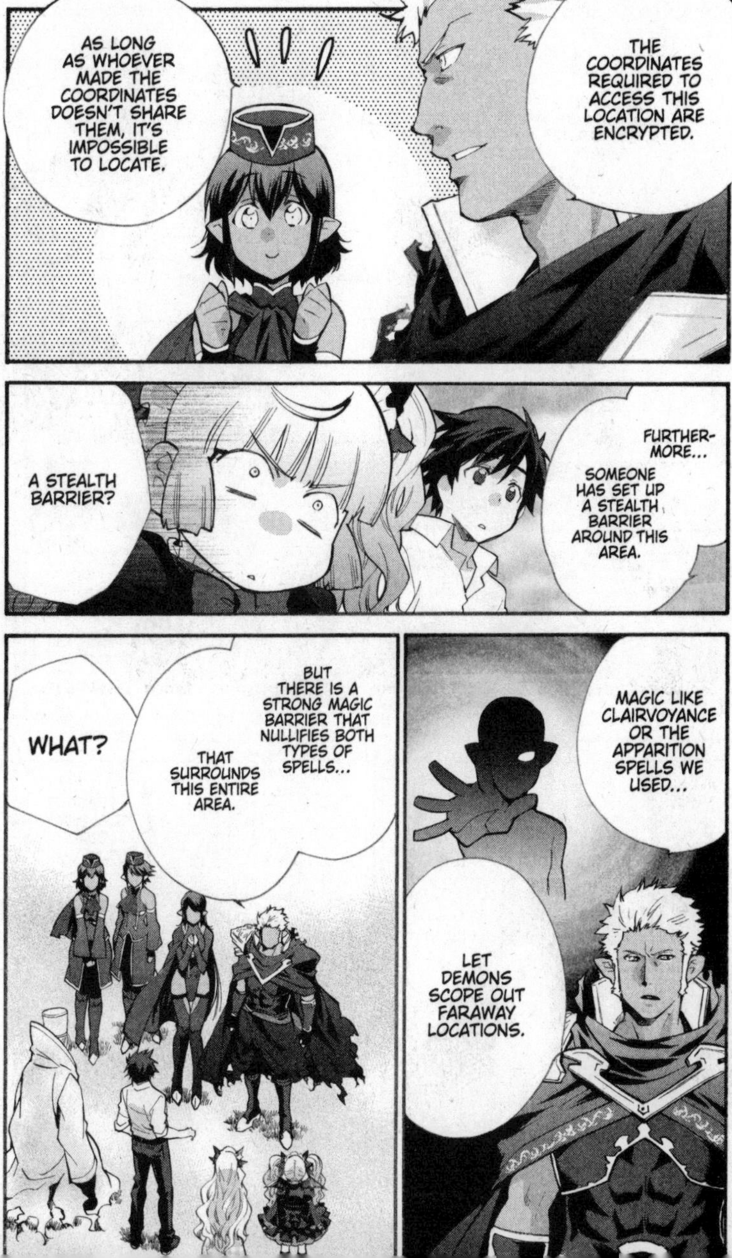
THE COORDINATES REQUIRED TO ACCESS THIS LOCATION ARE ENCRYPTED.
AS LONG AS WHOEVER MADE THE COORDINATES DOESN'T SHARE THEM, IT'S IMPOSSIBLE TO LOCATE.
FURTHER-MORE...
SOMEONE HAS SET UP A STEALTH BARRIER AROUND THIS AREA.
A STEALTH BARRIER?
MAGIC LIKE CLAIRVOYANCE OR THE APPARITION SPELLS WE USED...
LET DEMONS SCOPE OUT FARAWAY LOCATIONS.
BUT THERE IS A STRONG MAGIC BARRIER THAT NULLIFIES BOTH TYPES OF SPELLS...
THAT SURROUNDS THIS ENTIRE AREA.
WHAT?

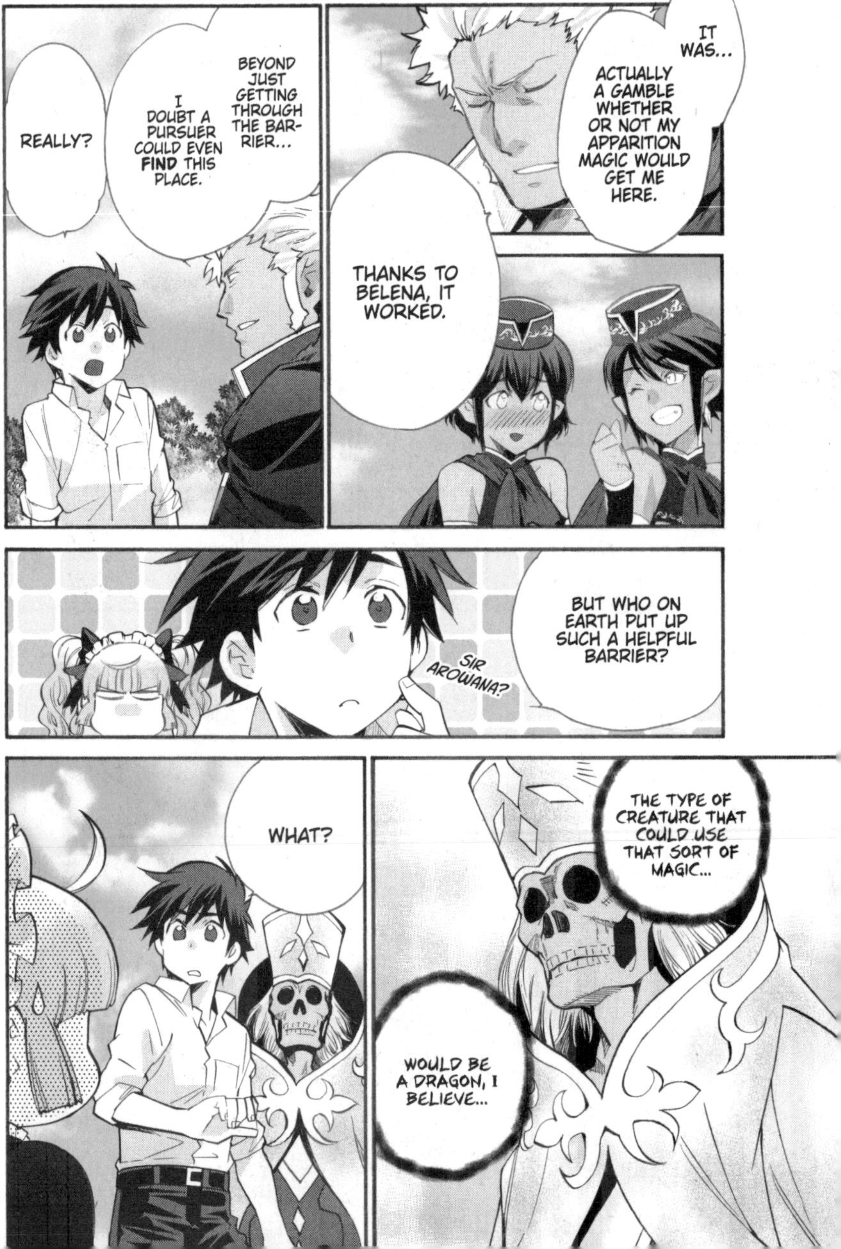
IT WAS...
ACTUALLY A GAMBLE WHETHER OR NOT MY APPARITION MAGIC WOULD GET ME HERE.
THANKS TO BELENA, IT WORKED.
BEYOND JUST GETTING THROUGH THE BARRIER...
I DOUBT A PURSUER COULD EVEN FIND THIS PLACE.
REALLY?
BUT WHO ON EARTH PUT UP SUCH A HELPFUL BARRIER?
SIR AROWANA?
THE TYPE OF CREATURE THAT COULD USE THAT SORT OF MAGIC...
WOULD BE A DRAGON, I BELIEVE...
WHAT?

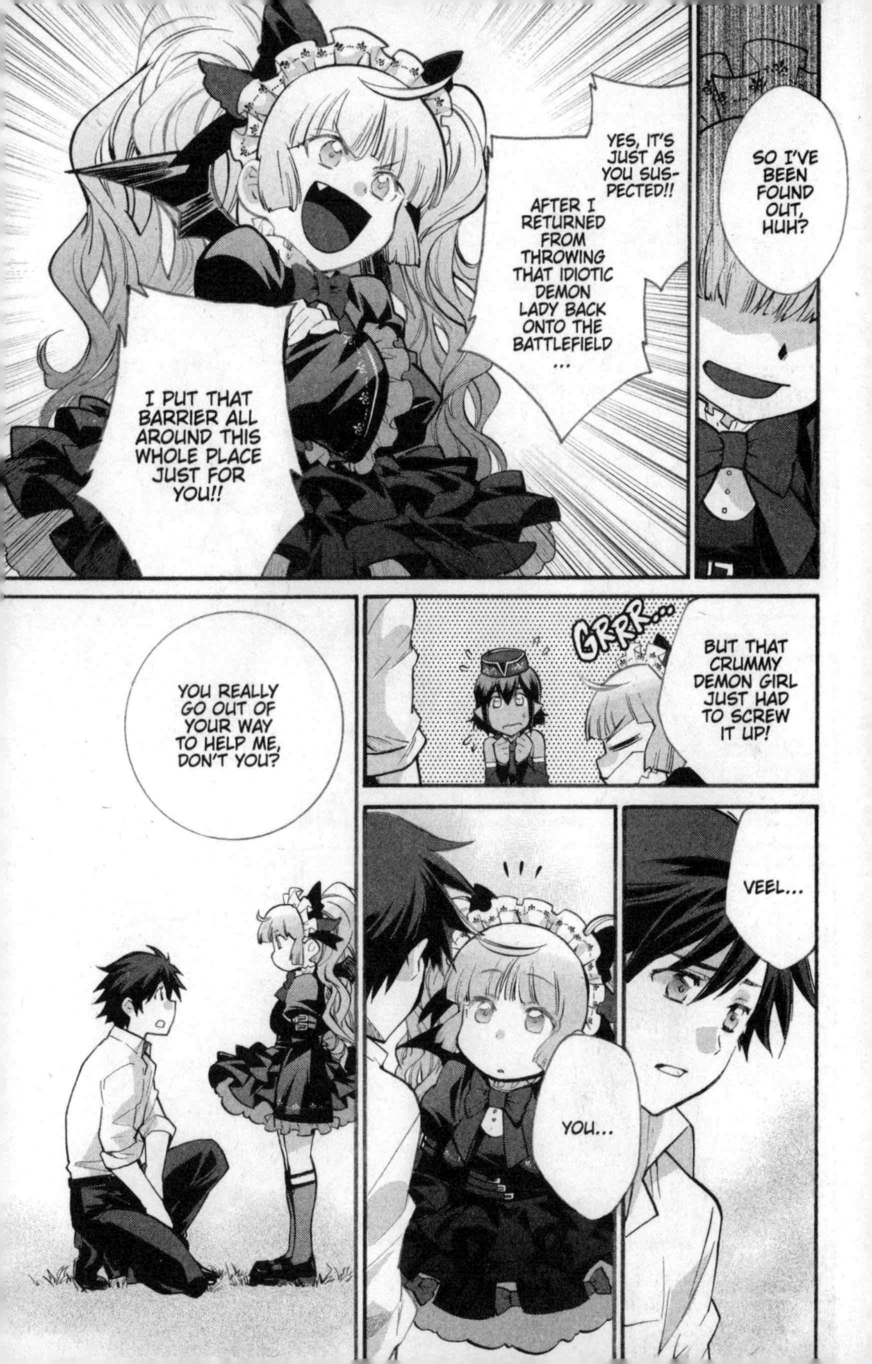
SO I'VE BEEN FOUND OUT, HUH?
YES, IT'S JUST AS YOU SUS-PECTED!!
AFTER I RETURNED FROM THROWING THAT IDIOTIC DEMON LADY BACK ONTO THE BATTLEFIELD ...
I PUT THAT BARRIER ALL AROUND THIS WHOLE PLACE JUST FOR YOU!!
BUT THAT CRUMMY DEMON GIRL JUST HAD TO SCREW IT UP!
GRRR...
VEEL...
YOU...
YOU REALLY GO OUT OF YOUR WAY TO HELP ME, DON'T YOU?

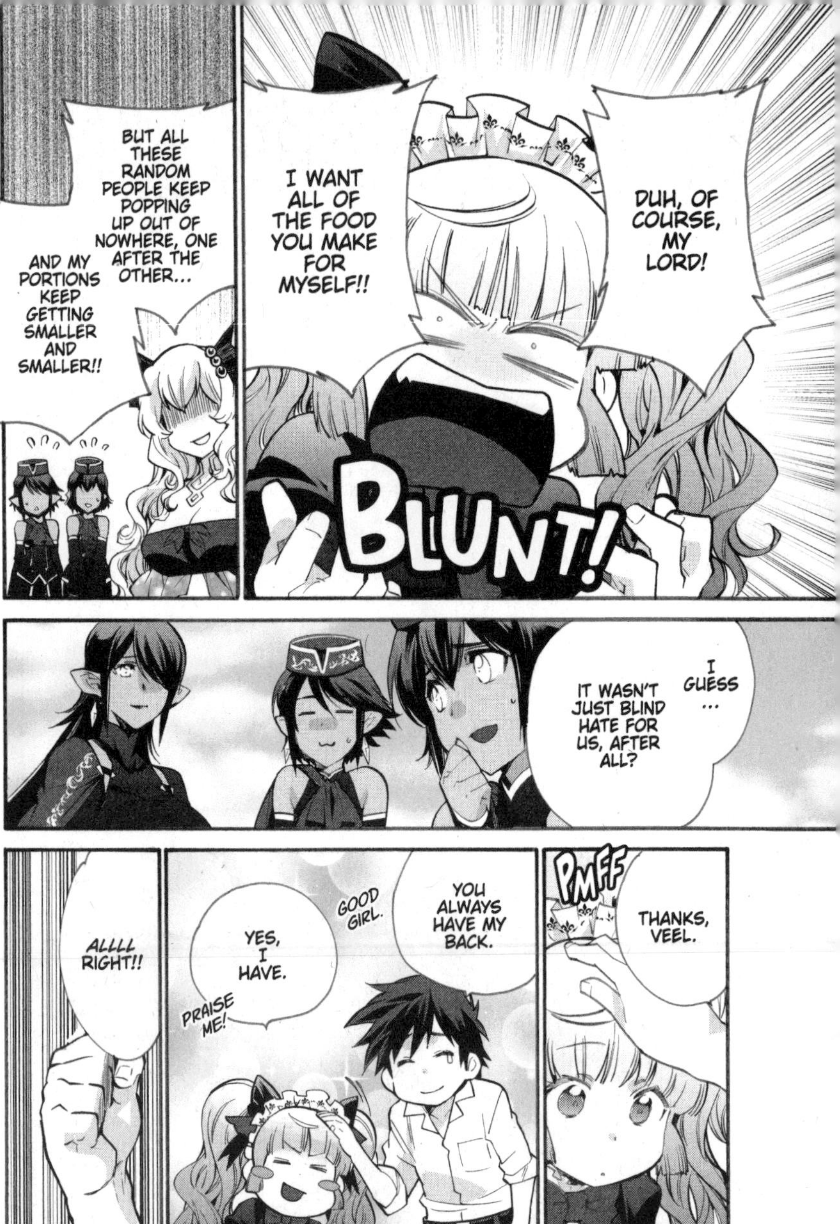
DUH, OF COURSE, MY LORD!
I WANT ALL OF THE FOOD YOU MAKE FOR MYSELF!!
BLUNT!
BUT ALL THESE RANDOM PEOPLE KEEP POPPING UP OUT OF NOWHERE, ONE AFTER THE OTHER...
AND MY PORTIONS KEEP GETTING SMALLER AND SMALLER!!
I GUESS...
IT WASN'T JUST BLIND HATE FOR US, AFTER ALL?
PMFF
THANKS, VEEL.
YOU ALWAYS HAVE MY BACK.
GOOD GIRL.
YES, I HAVE.
PRAISE ME!
ALLLL RIGHT!!

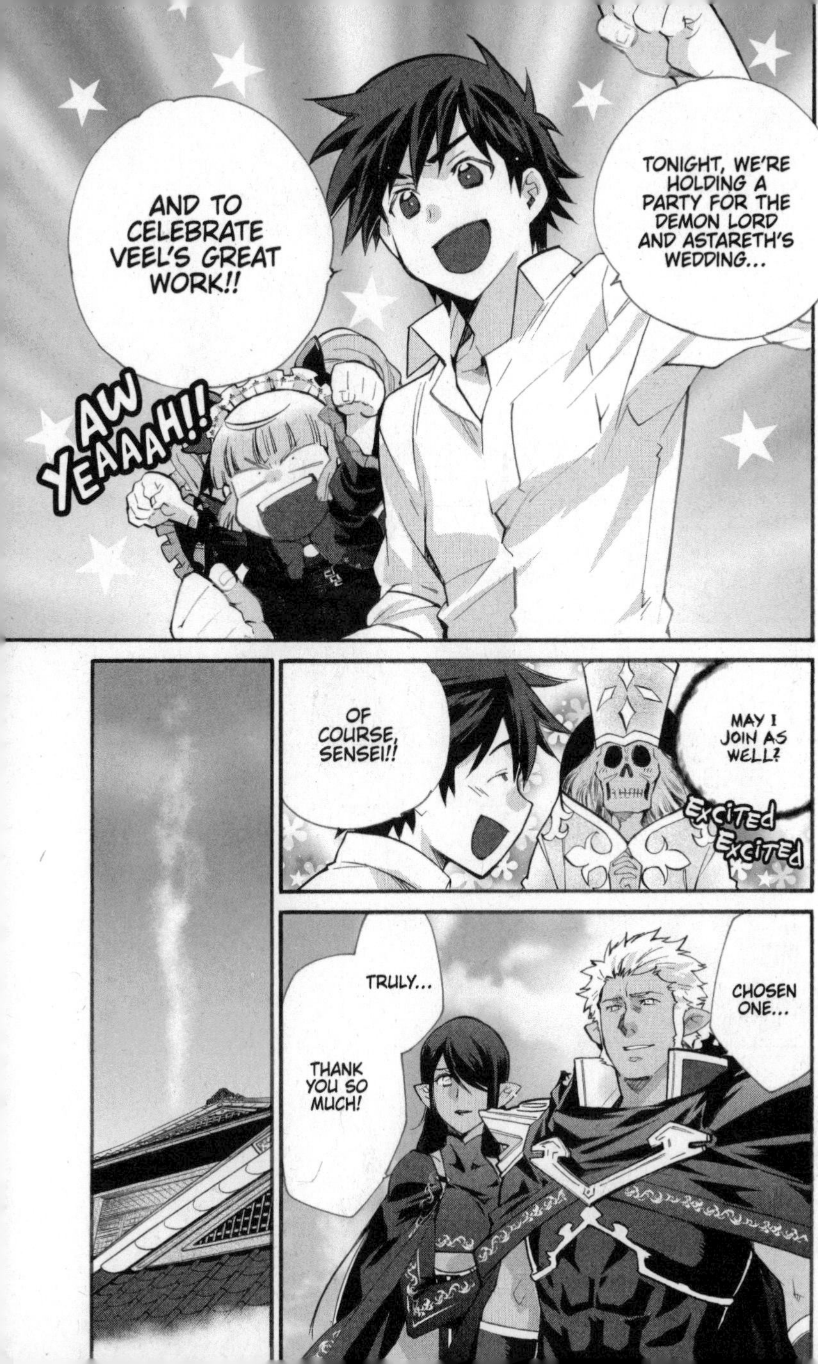
TONIGHT, WE'RE HOLDING A PARTY FOR THE DEMON LORD AND ASTARETH'S WEDDING...
AND TO CELEBRATE VEEL'S GREAT WORK!!
AW YEAAAH!!
MAY I JOIN AS WELL?
EXCITED EXCITED
OF COURSE, SENSEI!!
CHOSEN ONE...
TRULY...
THANK YOU SO MUCH!

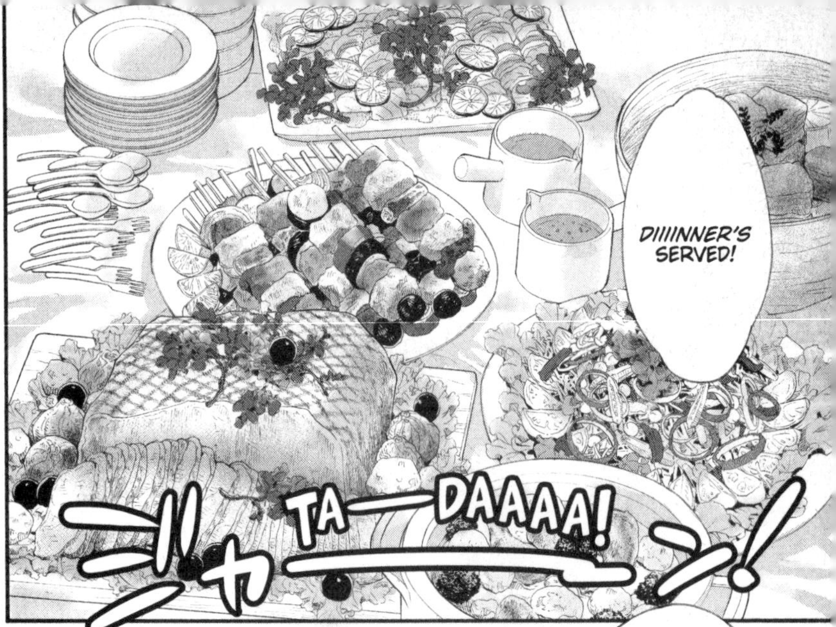
DIIIINNER'S SERVED!
TA—DAAAA!

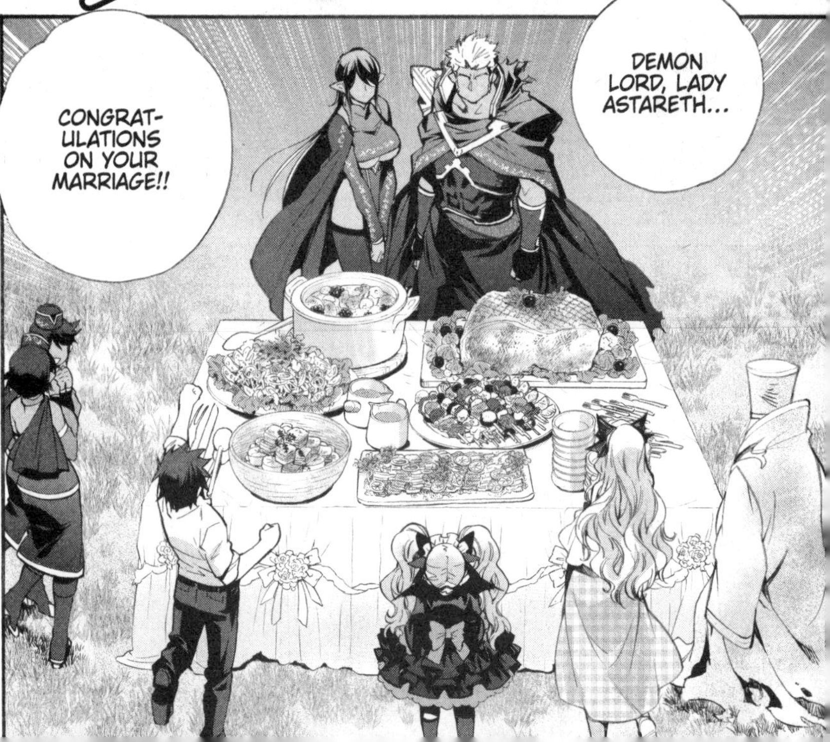
DEMON LORD, LADY ASTARETH…
CONGRAT-ULATIONS ON YOUR MARRIAGE!!

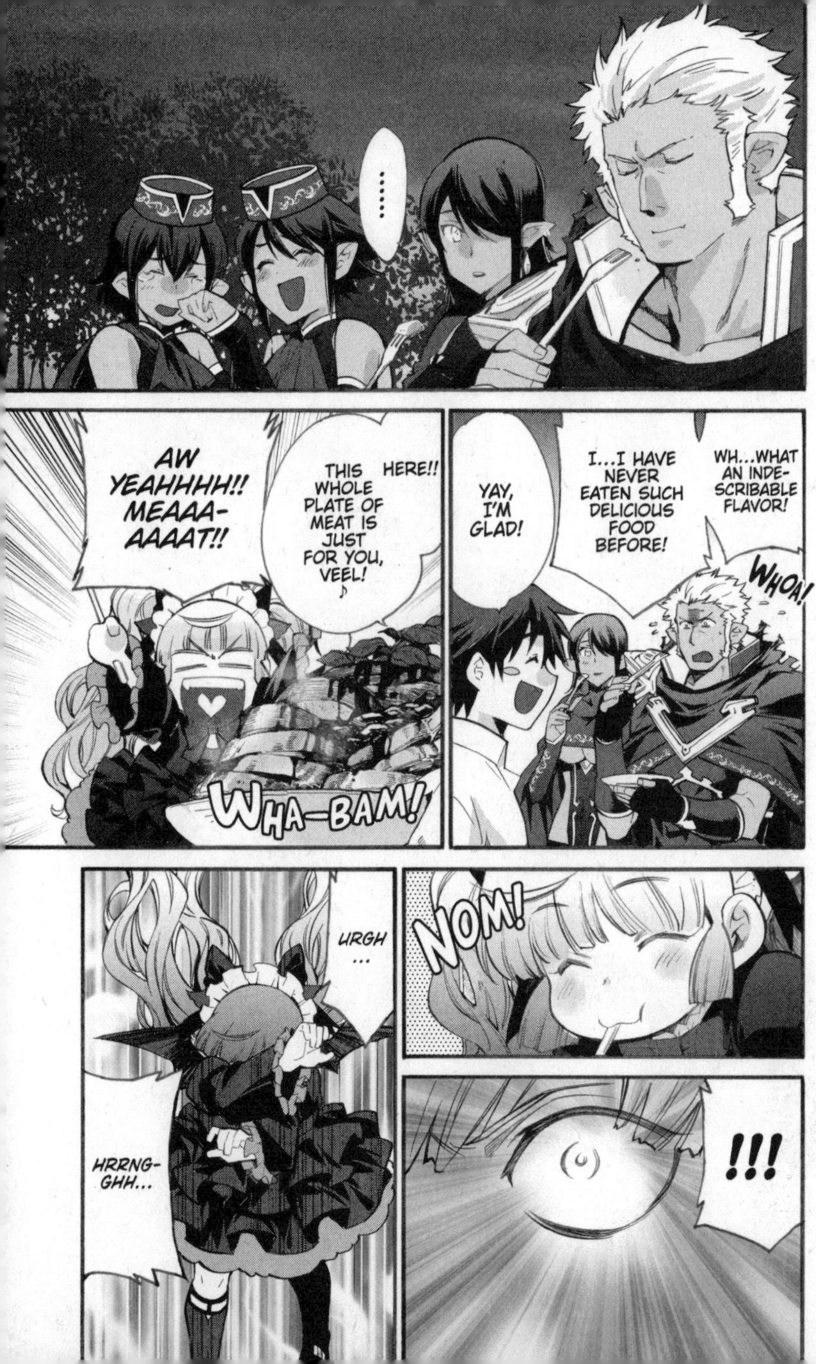
......
WH...WHAT AN INDE-SCRIBABLE FLAVOR!
I...I HAVE NEVER EATEN SUCH DELICIOUS FOOD BEFORE!
YAY, I'M GLAD!
WHOA!
HERE!!
THIS WHOLE PLATE OF MEAT IS JUST FOR YOU, VEEL! ♪
AW YEAHHHH!! MEAAA-AAAAT!!
WHA-BAM!
NOM!
!!!
URGH ...
HRRNG-GHH...

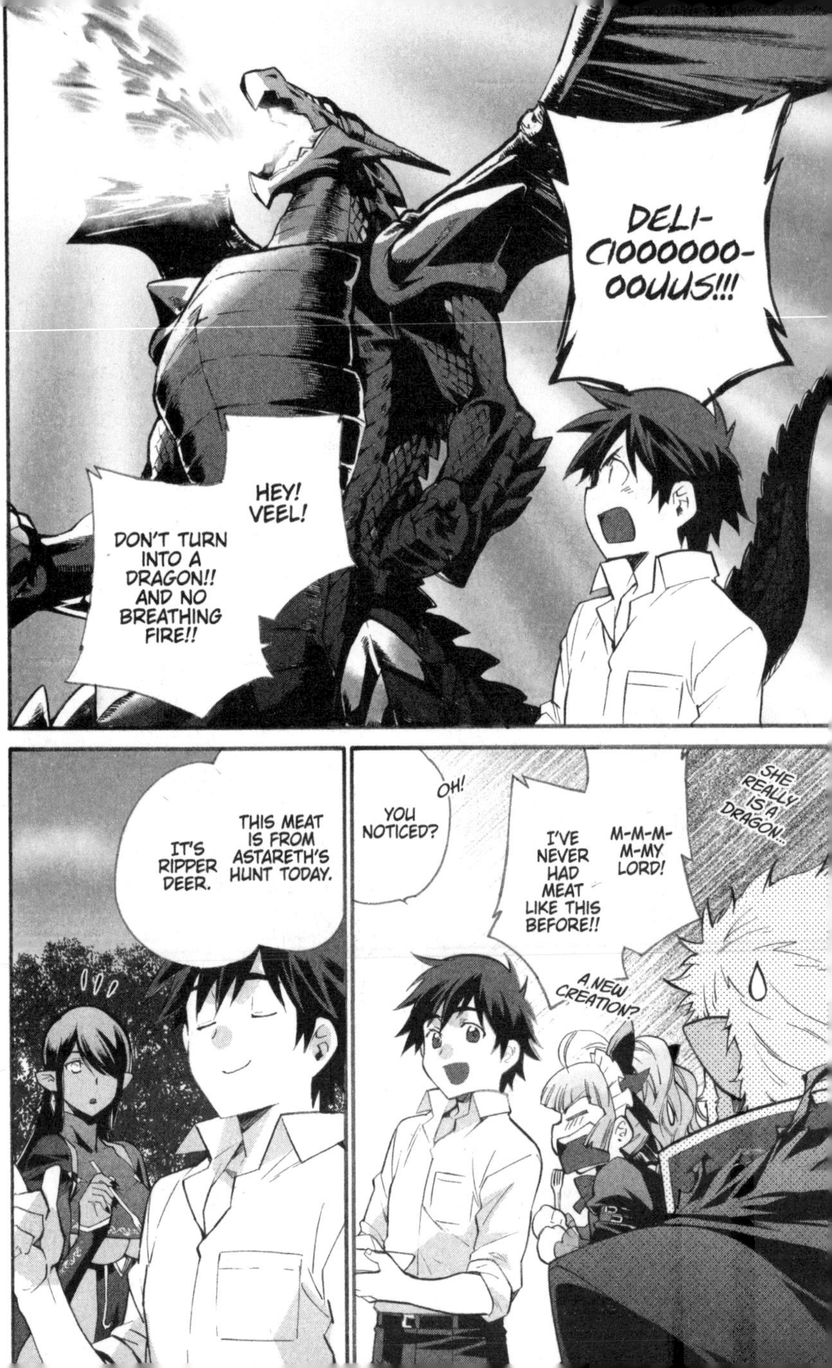
DELI-CIOOOOOO-OOUUS!!!
HEY! VEEL!
DON'T TURN INTO A DRAGON!! AND NO BREATHING FIRE!!
SHE REALLY IS A DRAGON...
M-M-M-M-MY LORD!
I'VE NEVER HAD MEAT LIKE THIS BEFORE!!
OH!
YOU NOTICED?
A NEW CREATION?
THIS MEAT IS FROM ASTARETH'S HUNT TODAY.
IT'S RIPPER DEER.

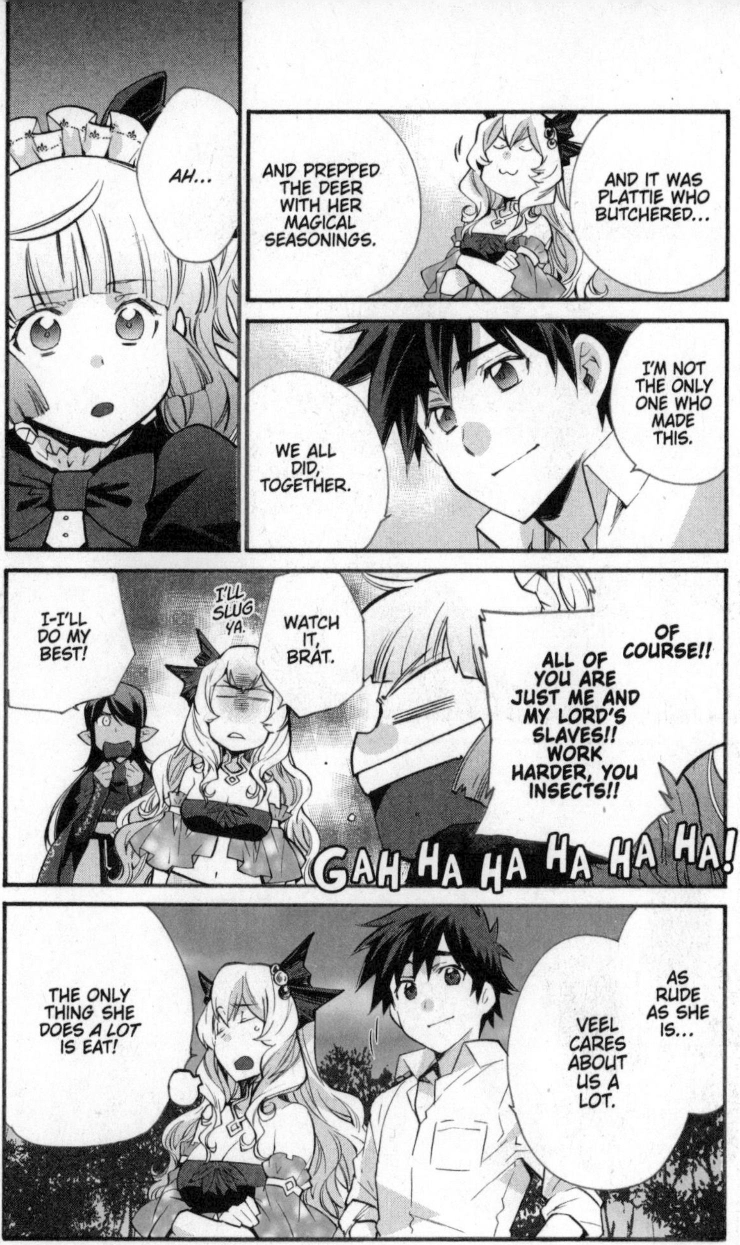
AND IT WAS PLATTIE WHO BUTCHERED...
AND PREPPED THE DEER WITH HER MAGICAL SEASONINGS.
I'M NOT THE ONLY ONE WHO MADE THIS.
WE ALL DID, TOGETHER.
AH...
OF COURSE!! ALL OF YOU ARE JUST ME AND MY LORD'S SLAVES!! WORK HARDER, YOU INSECTS!!
GAH HA HA HA HA HA HA!
WATCH IT, BRAT.
I'LL SLUG YA.
I-I'LL DO MY BEST!
AS RUDE AS SHE IS...
VEEL CARES ABOUT US A LOT.
THE ONLY THING SHE DOES A LOT IS EAT!

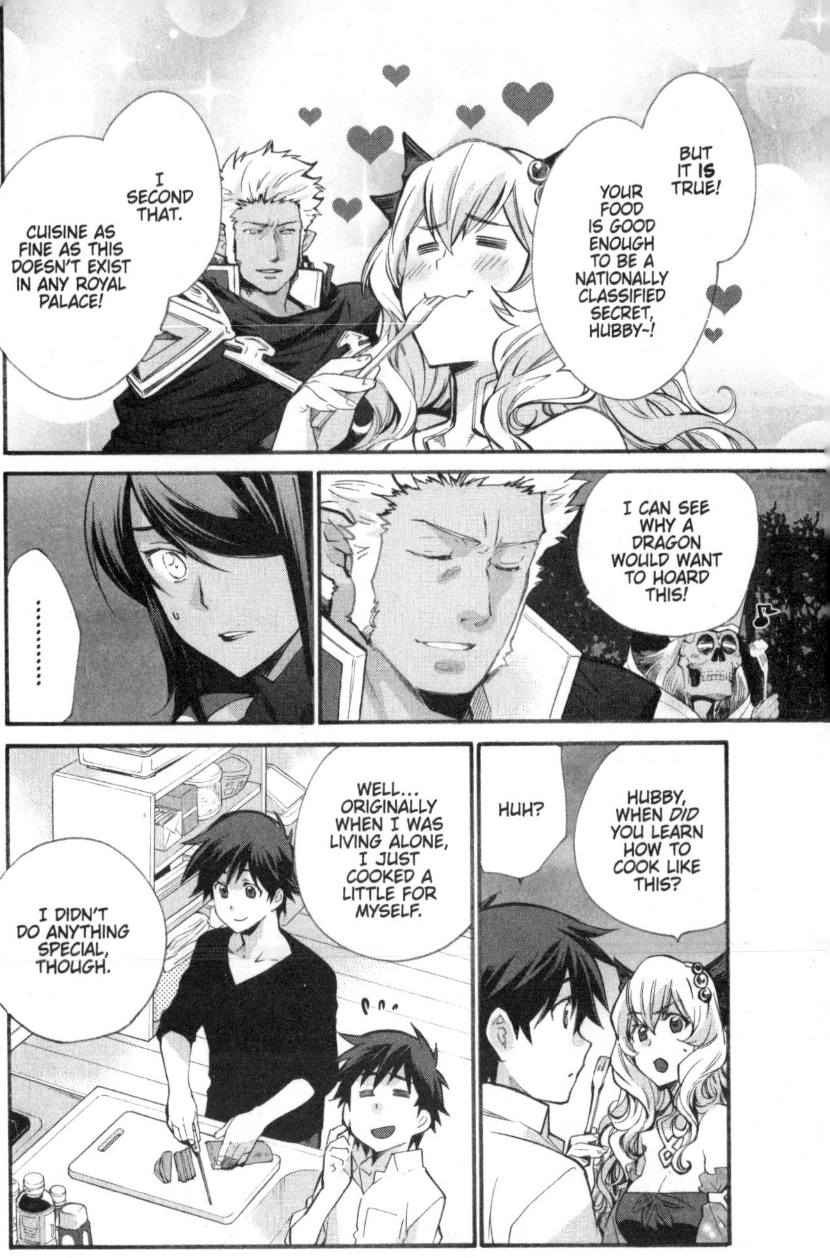
BUT IT **IS** TRUE!
YOUR FOOD IS GOOD ENOUGH TO BE A NATIONALLY CLASSIFIED SECRET, HUBBY~!
I SECOND THAT.
CUISINE AS FINE AS THIS DOESN'T EXIST IN ANY ROYAL PALACE!
I CAN SEE WHY A DRAGON WOULD WANT TO HOARD THIS!
....
HUBBY, WHEN *DID* YOU LEARN HOW TO COOK LIKE THIS?
HUH?
WELL... ORIGINALLY WHEN I WAS LIVING ALONE, I JUST COOKED A LITTLE FOR MYSELF.
I DIDN'T DO ANYTHING SPECIAL, THOUGH.

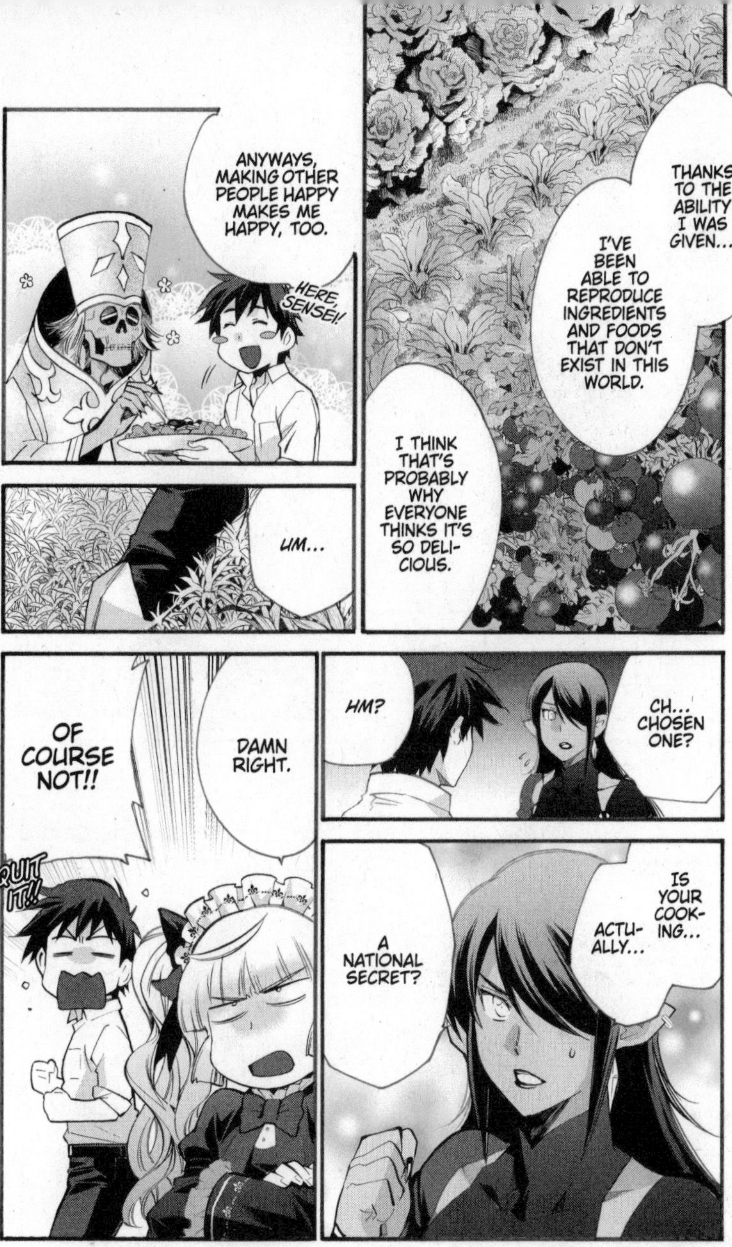
THANKS TO THE ABILITY I WAS GIVEN...
I'VE BEEN ABLE TO REPRODUCE INGREDIENTS AND FOODS THAT DON'T EXIST IN THIS WORLD.
I THINK THAT'S PROBABLY WHY EVERYONE THINKS IT'S SO DELICIOUS.
ANYWAYS, MAKING OTHER PEOPLE HAPPY MAKES ME HAPPY, TOO.
HERE, SENSEI!
UM...
CH... CHOSEN ONE?
HM?
IS YOUR COOKING...
ACTU-ALLY...
A NATIONAL SECRET?
DAMN RIGHT.
OF COURSE NOT!!
QUIT IT!!

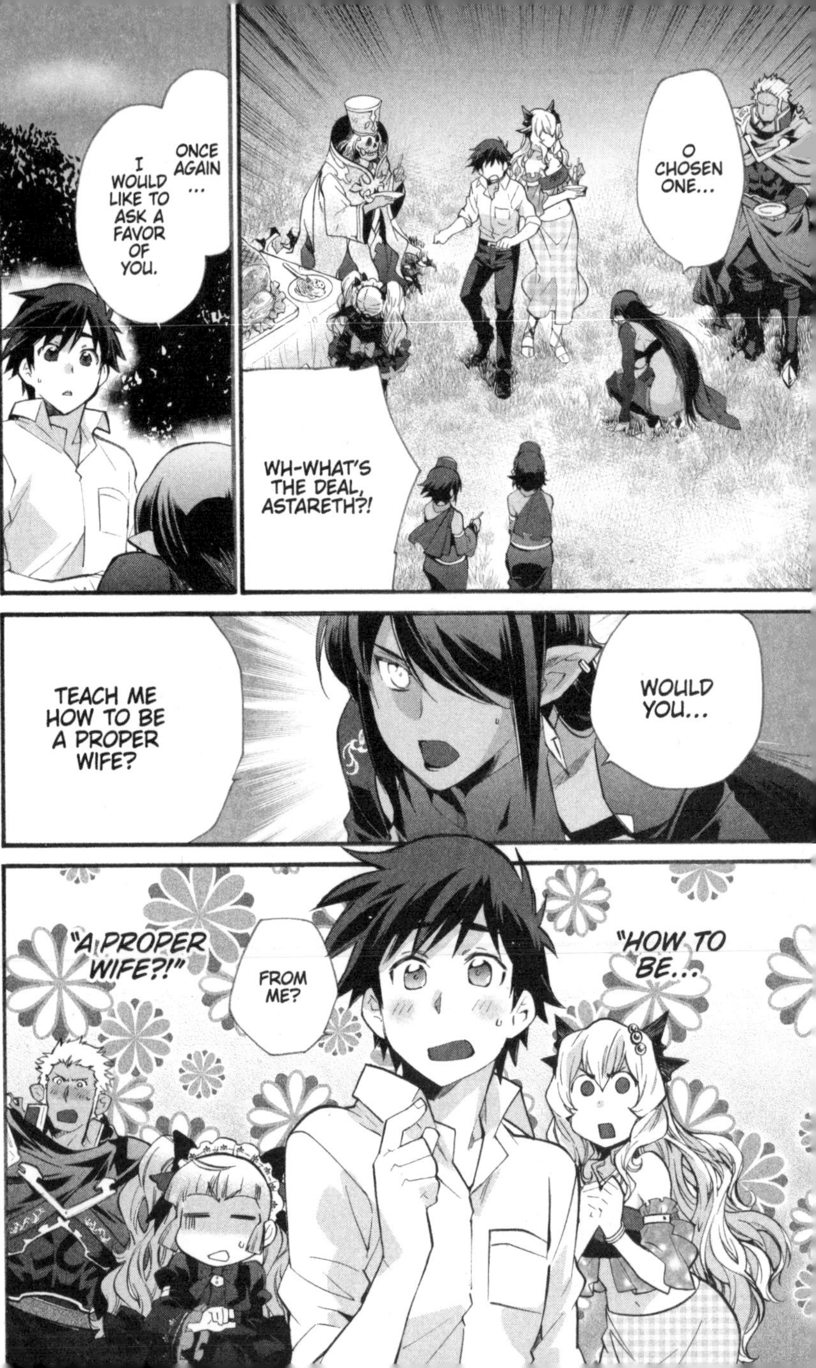
O CHOSEN ONE...
WH-WHAT'S THE DEAL, ASTARETH?!
ONCE AGAIN...
I WOULD LIKE TO ASK A FAVOR OF YOU.
WOULD YOU...
TEACH ME HOW TO BE A PROPER WIFE?
"HOW TO BE...
"A PROPER WIFE?!"
FROM ME?

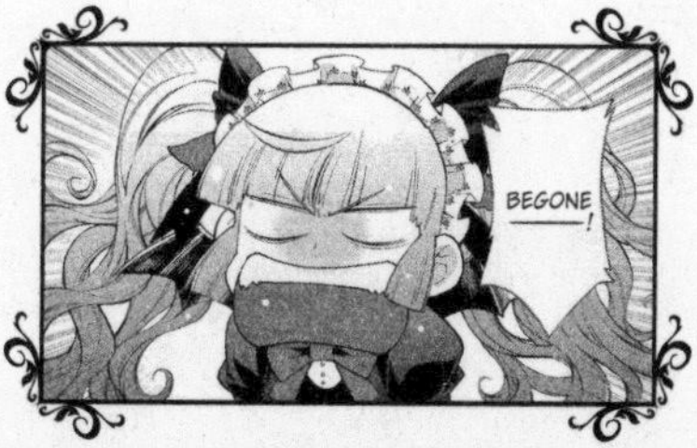
BEGONE—!

LET'S BUY THE LAND and CULTIVATE IT IN A DIFFERENT WORLD

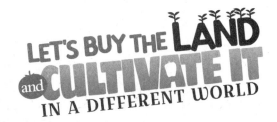

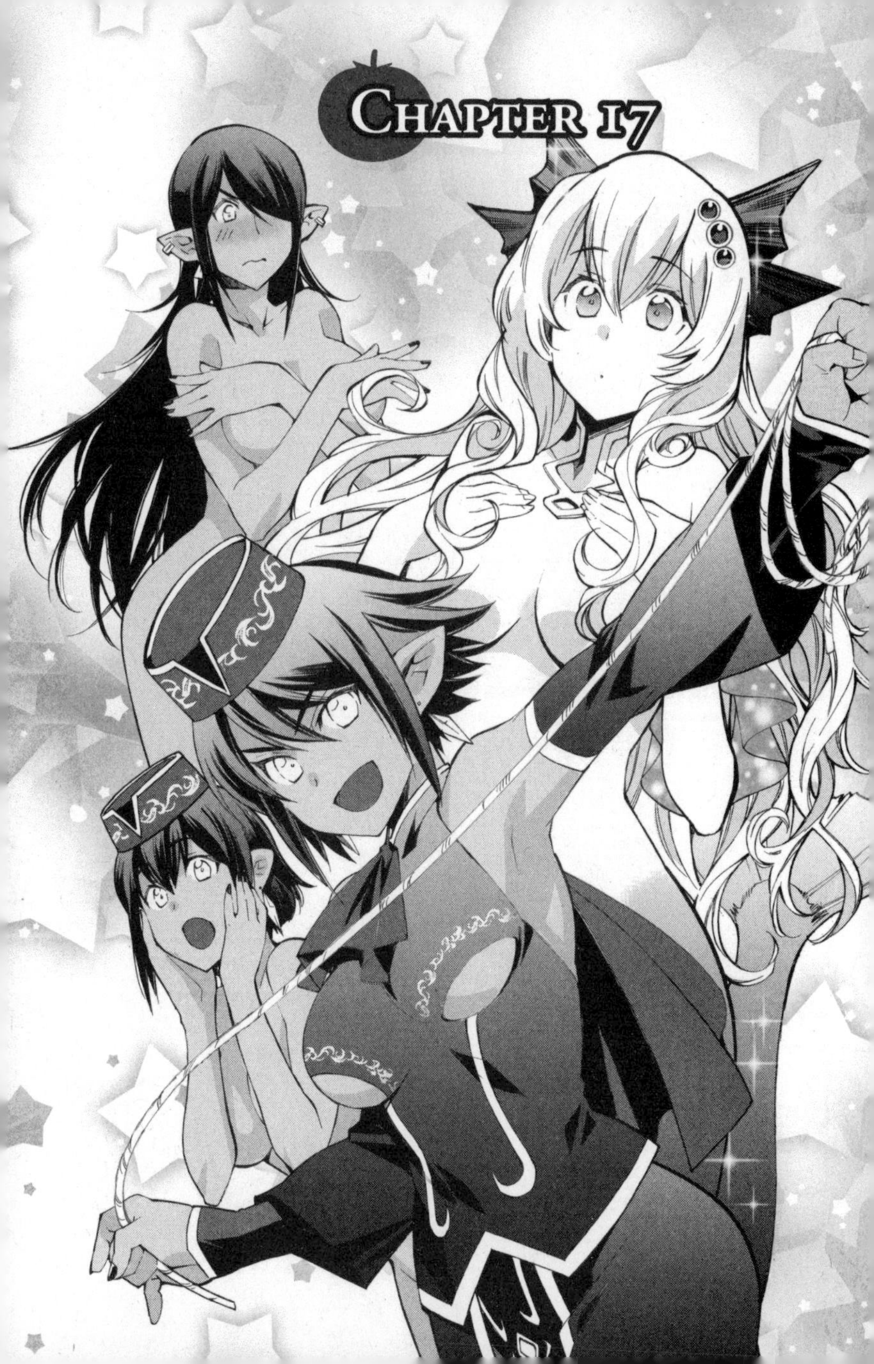
CHAPTER 17

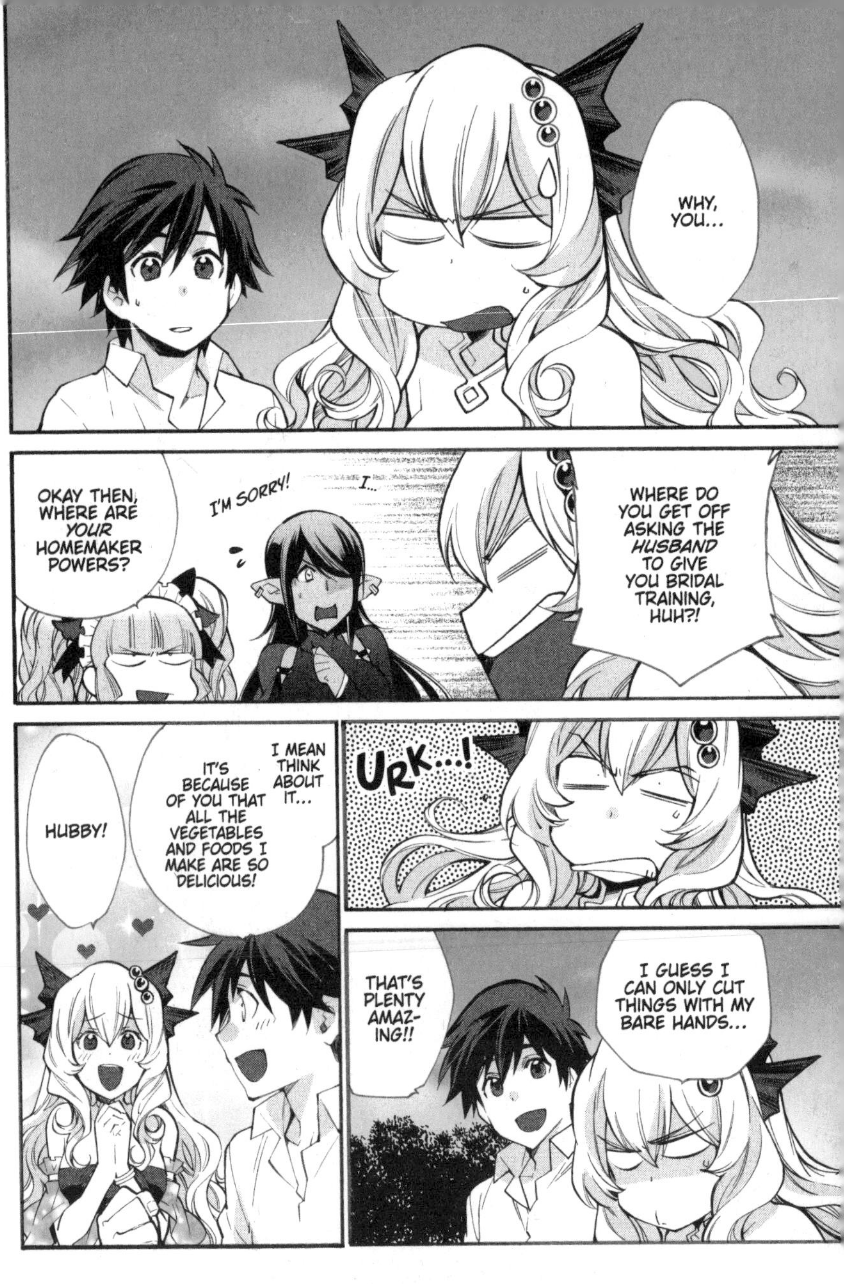
WHY, YOU...
WHERE DO YOU GET OFF ASKING THE *HUSBAND* TO GIVE YOU BRIDAL TRAINING, HUH?!
I...
I'M SORRY!
OKAY THEN, WHERE ARE *YOUR* HOMEMAKER POWERS?
URK...!
I GUESS I CAN ONLY CUT THINGS WITH MY BARE HANDS...
THAT'S PLENTY AMAZ-ING!!
I MEAN THINK ABOUT IT...
IT'S BECAUSE OF YOU THAT ALL THE VEGETABLES AND FOODS I MAKE ARE SO DELICIOUS!
HUBBY!

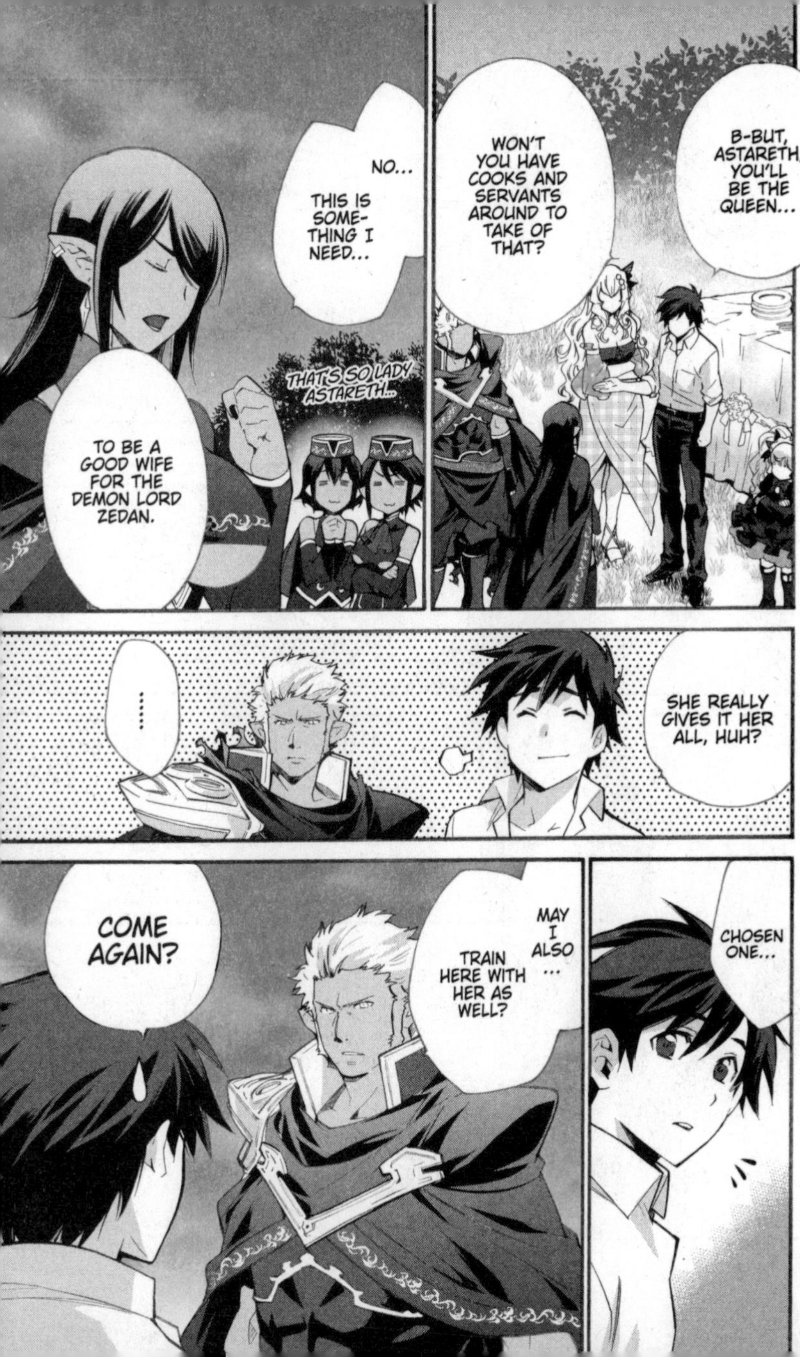
B-BUT, ASTARETH, YOU'LL BE THE QUEEN...
WON'T YOU HAVE COOKS AND SERVANTS AROUND TO TAKE OF THAT?
NO...
THIS IS SOME-THING I NEED...
THAT'S SO LADY ASTARETH...
TO BE A GOOD WIFE FOR THE DEMON LORD ZEDAN.
SHE REALLY GIVES IT HER ALL, HUH?
......
CHOSEN ONE...
MAY I ALSO...
TRAIN HERE WITH HER AS WELL?
COME AGAIN?

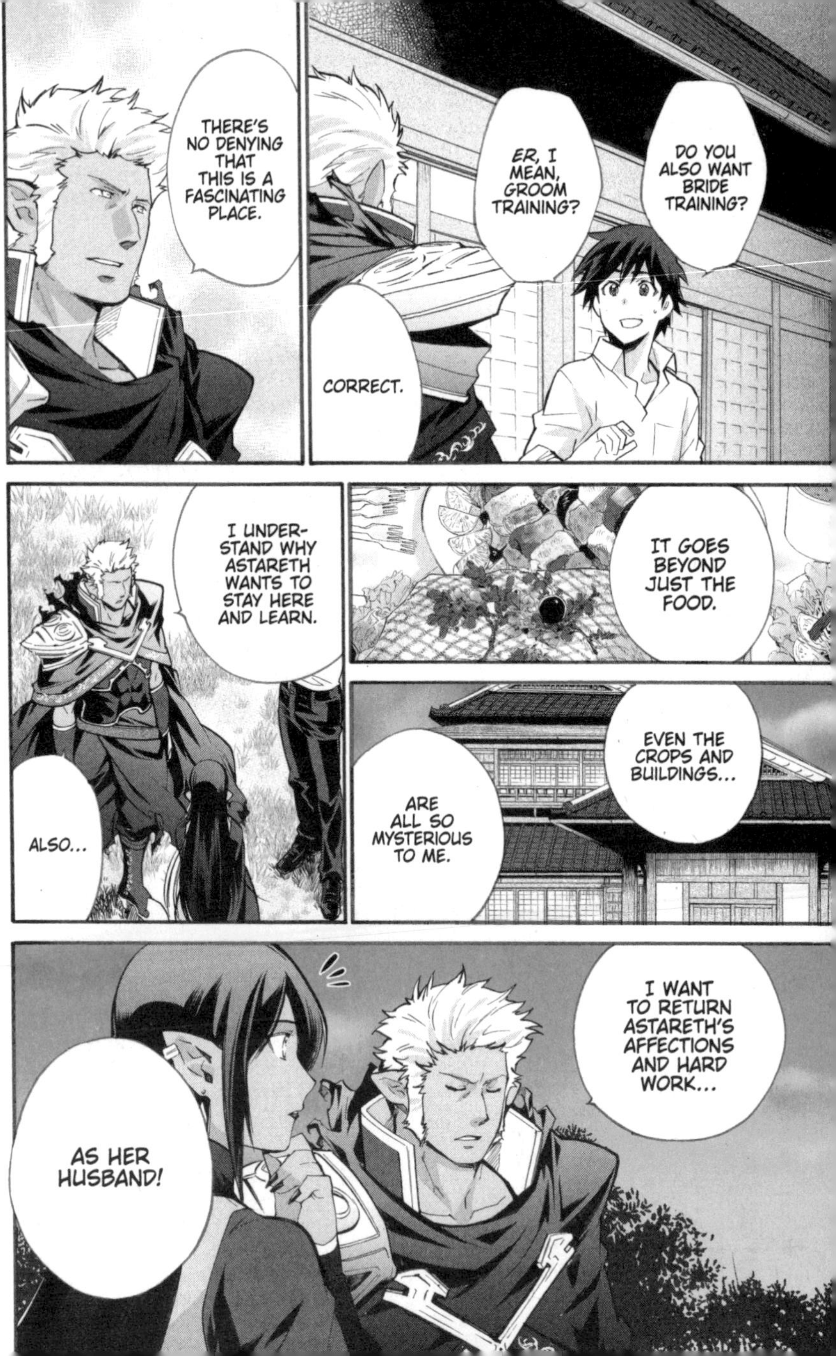
DO YOU ALSO WANT BRIDE TRAINING?
ER, I MEAN, GROOM TRAINING?
CORRECT.
THERE'S NO DENYING THAT THIS IS A FASCINATING PLACE.
IT GOES BEYOND JUST THE FOOD.
EVEN THE CROPS AND BUILDINGS...
ARE ALL SO MYSTERIOUS TO ME.
I UNDER-STAND WHY ASTARETH WANTS TO STAY HERE AND LEARN.
ALSO...
I WANT TO RETURN ASTARETH'S AFFECTIONS AND HARD WORK...
AS HER HUSBAND!

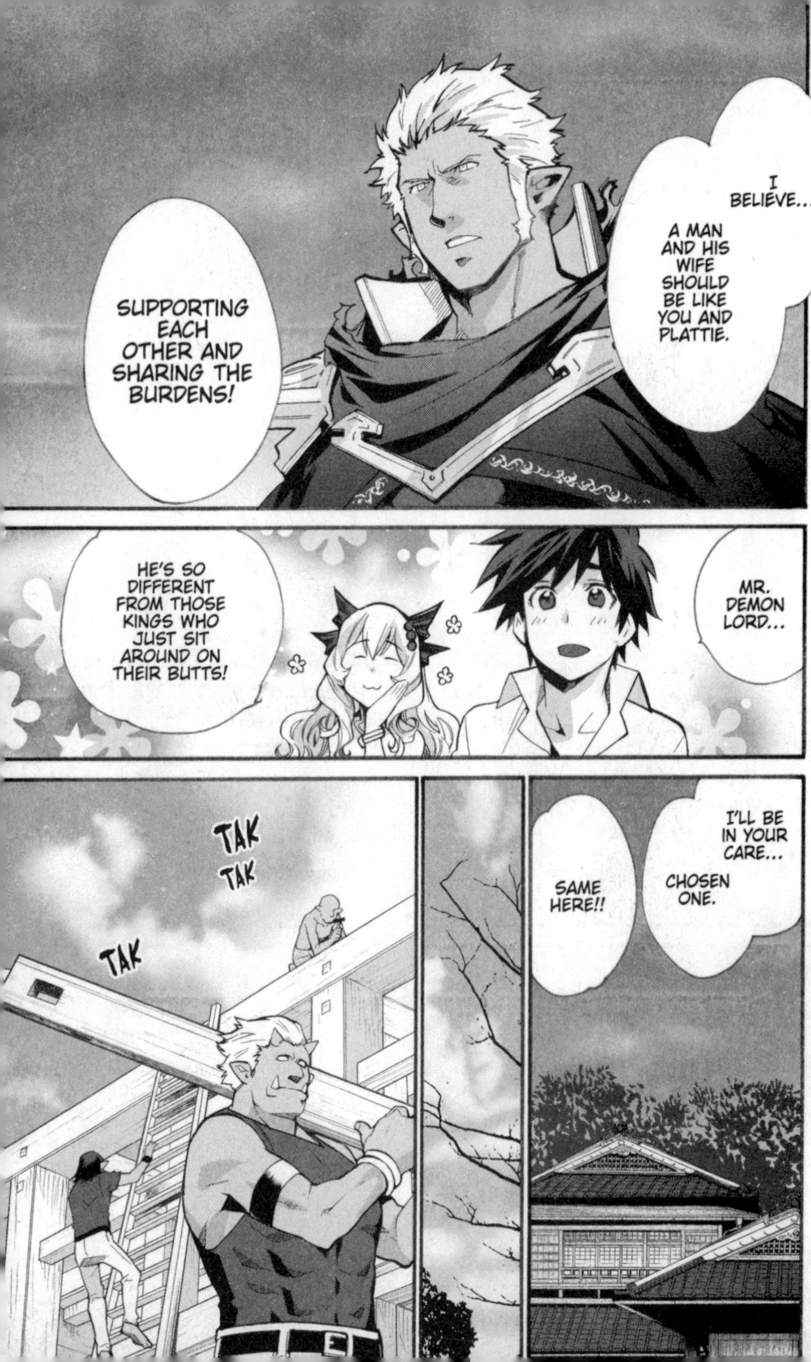
I BELIEVE...
A MAN AND HIS WIFE SHOULD BE LIKE YOU AND PLATTIE.
SUPPORTING EACH OTHER AND SHARING THE BURDENS!
MR. DEMON LORD...
HE'S SO DIFFERENT FROM THOSE KINGS WHO JUST SIT AROUND ON THEIR BUTTS!
I'LL BE IN YOUR CARE...
CHOSEN ONE.
SAME HERE!!
TAK
TAK
TAK

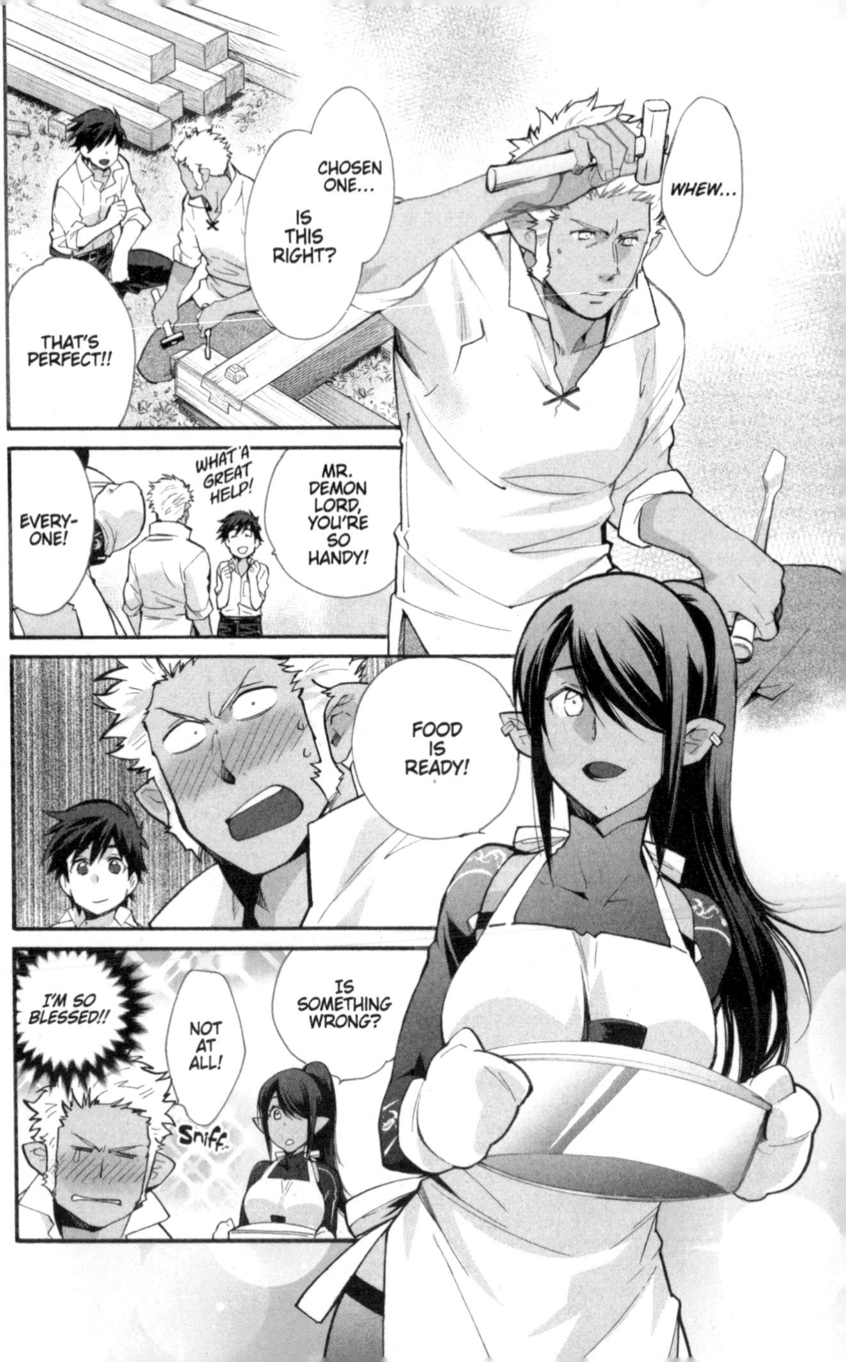
WHEW...
CHOSEN ONE...
IS THIS RIGHT?
THAT'S PERFECT!!
MR. DEMON LORD, YOU'RE SO HANDY!
WHAT A GREAT HELP!
EVERY-ONE!
FOOD IS READY!
IS SOMETHING WRONG?
NOT AT ALL!
Sniff...
I'M SO BLESSED!!

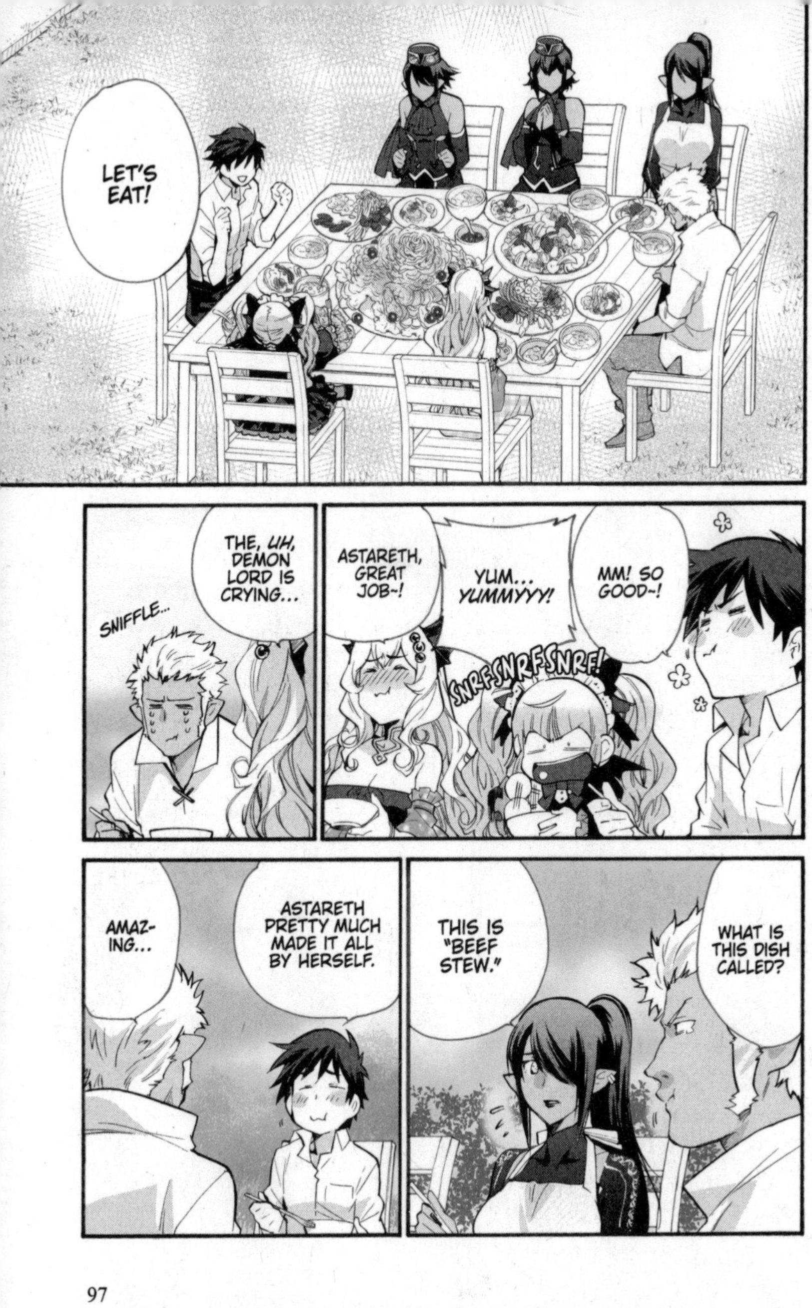
LET'S EAT!
MM! SO GOOD~!
YUM... YUMMYYY!
SNRFSNRFSNRF!
ASTARETH, GREAT JOB~!
THE, *UH,* DEMON LORD IS CRYING...
SNIFFLE...
WHAT IS THIS DISH CALLED?
THIS IS "BEEF STEW."
ASTARETH PRETTY MUCH MADE IT ALL BY HERSELF.
AMAZ-ING...

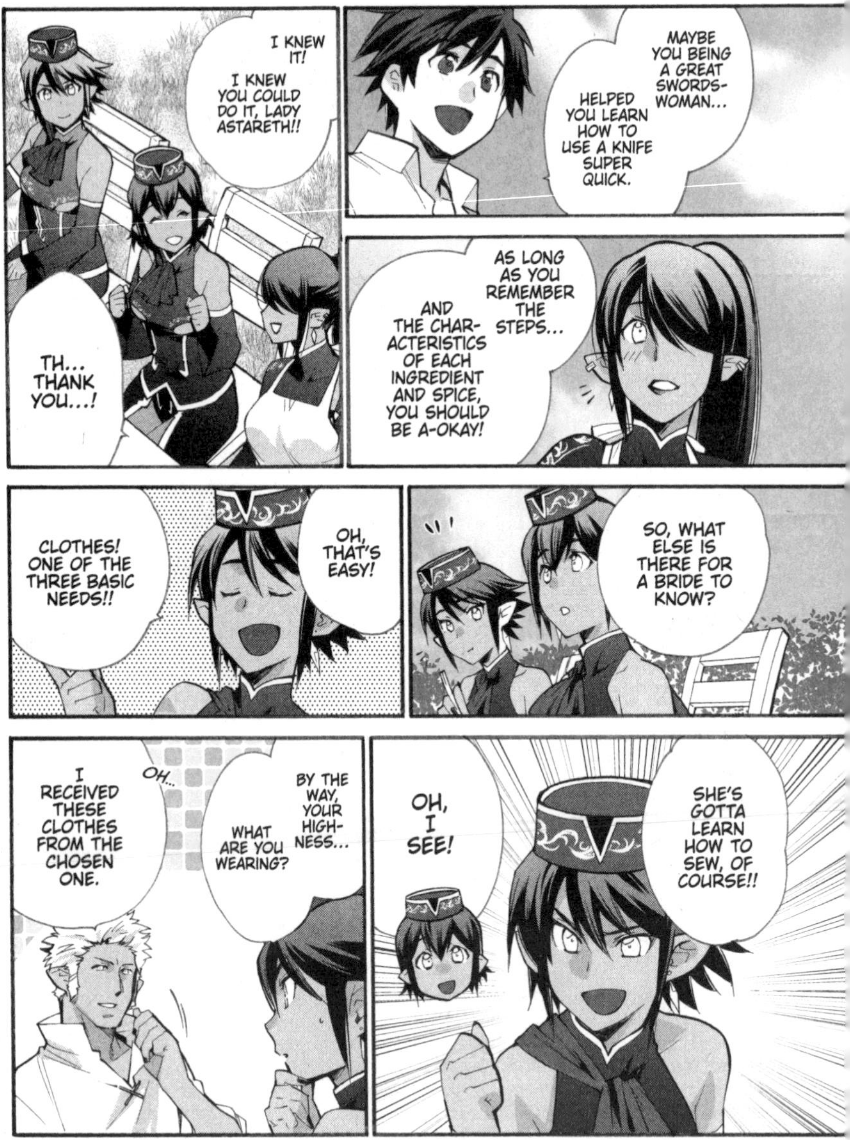
MAYBE YOU BEING A GREAT SWORDS-WOMAN...
HELPED YOU LEARN HOW TO USE A KNIFE SUPER QUICK.
AS LONG AS YOU REMEMBER THE STEPS...
AND THE CHAR-ACTERISTICS OF EACH INGREDIENT AND SPICE, YOU SHOULD BE A-OKAY!
I KNEW IT!
I KNEW YOU COULD DO IT, LADY ASTARETH!!
TH... THANK YOU...!
SO, WHAT ELSE IS THERE FOR A BRIDE TO KNOW?
OH, THAT'S EASY!
CLOTHES! ONE OF THE THREE BASIC NEEDS!!
SHE'S GOTTA LEARN HOW TO SEW, OF COURSE!!
OH, I SEE!
BY THE WAY, YOUR HIGH-NESS...
WHAT ARE YOU WEARING?
OH...
I RECEIVED THESE CLOTHES FROM THE CHOSEN ONE.

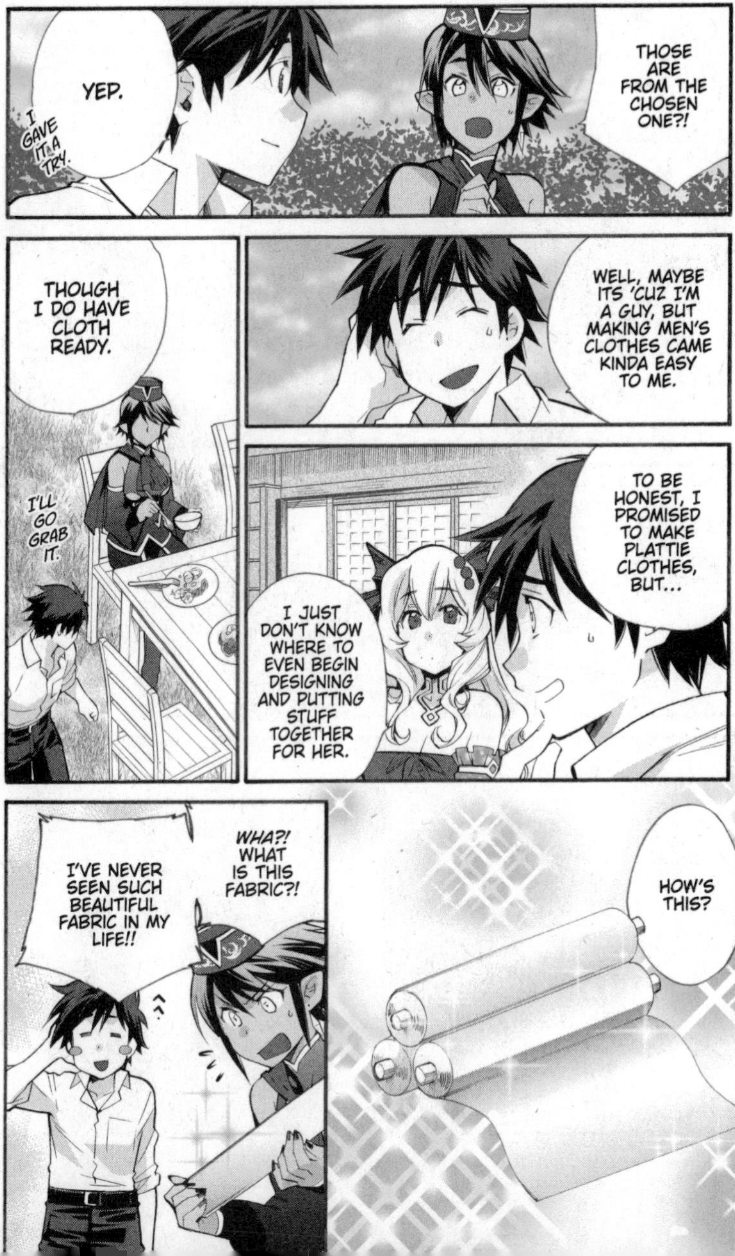
THOSE ARE FROM THE CHOSEN ONE?!
YEP.
I GAVE IT A TRY.
WELL, MAYBE ITS 'CUZ I'M A GUY, BUT MAKING MEN'S CLOTHES CAME KINDA EASY TO ME.
TO BE HONEST, I PROMISED TO MAKE PLATTIE CLOTHES, BUT...
I JUST DON'T KNOW WHERE TO EVEN BEGIN DESIGNING AND PUTTING STUFF TOGETHER FOR HER.
THOUGH I DO HAVE CLOTH READY.
I'LL GO GRAB IT.
HOW'S THIS?
WHA?! WHAT IS THIS FABRIC?!
I'VE NEVER SEEN SUCH BEAUTIFUL FABRIC IN MY LIFE!!

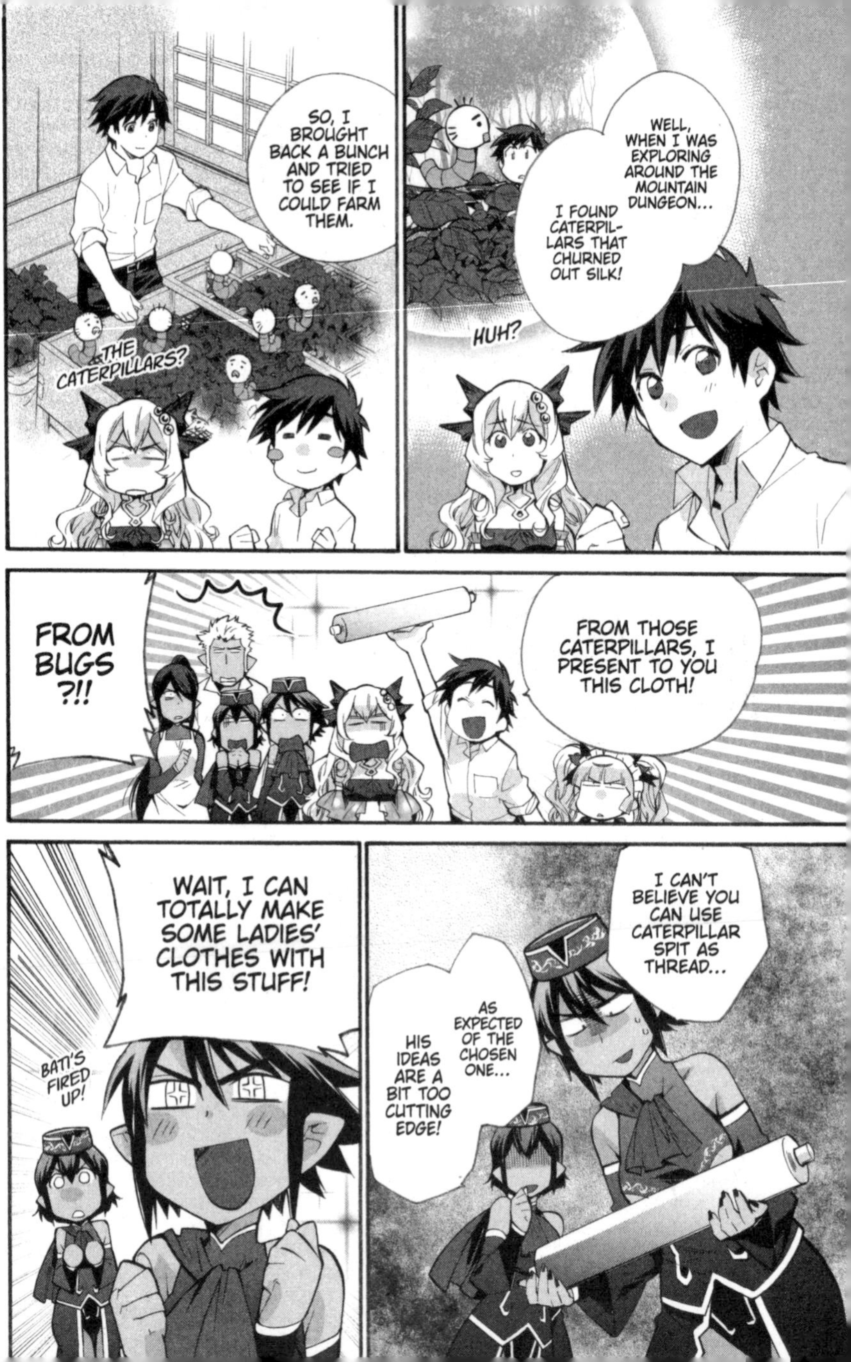
WELL, WHEN I WAS EXPLORING AROUND THE MOUNTAIN DUNGEON...
I FOUND CATERPIL-LARS THAT CHURNED OUT SILK!
HUH?
SO, I BROUGHT BACK A BUNCH AND TRIED TO SEE IF I COULD FARM THEM.
THE CATERPILLARS?
FROM THOSE CATERPILLARS, I PRESENT TO YOU THIS CLOTH!
FROM BUGS ?!!
I CAN'T BELIEVE YOU CAN USE CATERPILLAR SPIT AS THREAD...
AS EXPECTED OF THE CHOSEN ONE...
HIS IDEAS ARE A BIT TOO CUTTING EDGE!
WAIT, I CAN TOTALLY MAKE SOME LADIES' CLOTHES WITH THIS STUFF!
BATI'S FIRED UP!

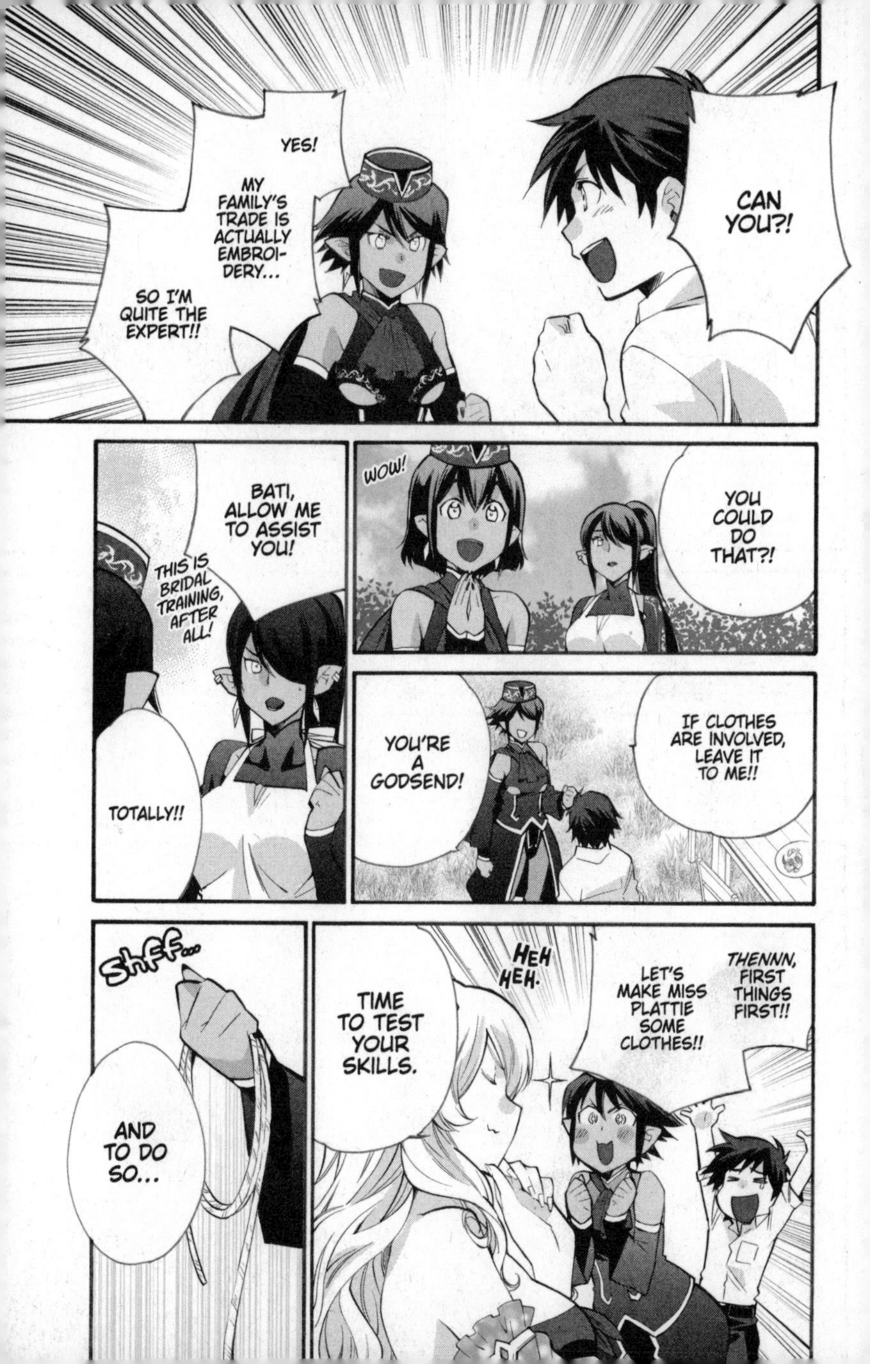
CAN YOU?!
YES!
MY FAMILY'S TRADE IS ACTUALLY EMBROIDERY...
SO I'M QUITE THE EXPERT!!
YOU COULD DO THAT?!
WOW!
IF CLOTHES ARE INVOLVED, LEAVE IT TO ME!!
YOU'RE A GODSEND!
BATI, ALLOW ME TO ASSIST YOU!
THIS IS BRIDAL TRAINING, AFTER ALL!
TOTALLY!!
THENNN, FIRST THINGS FIRST!!
LET'S MAKE MISS PLATTIE SOME CLOTHES!!
HEH HEH.
TIME TO TEST YOUR SKILLS.
Shff...
AND TO DO SO...

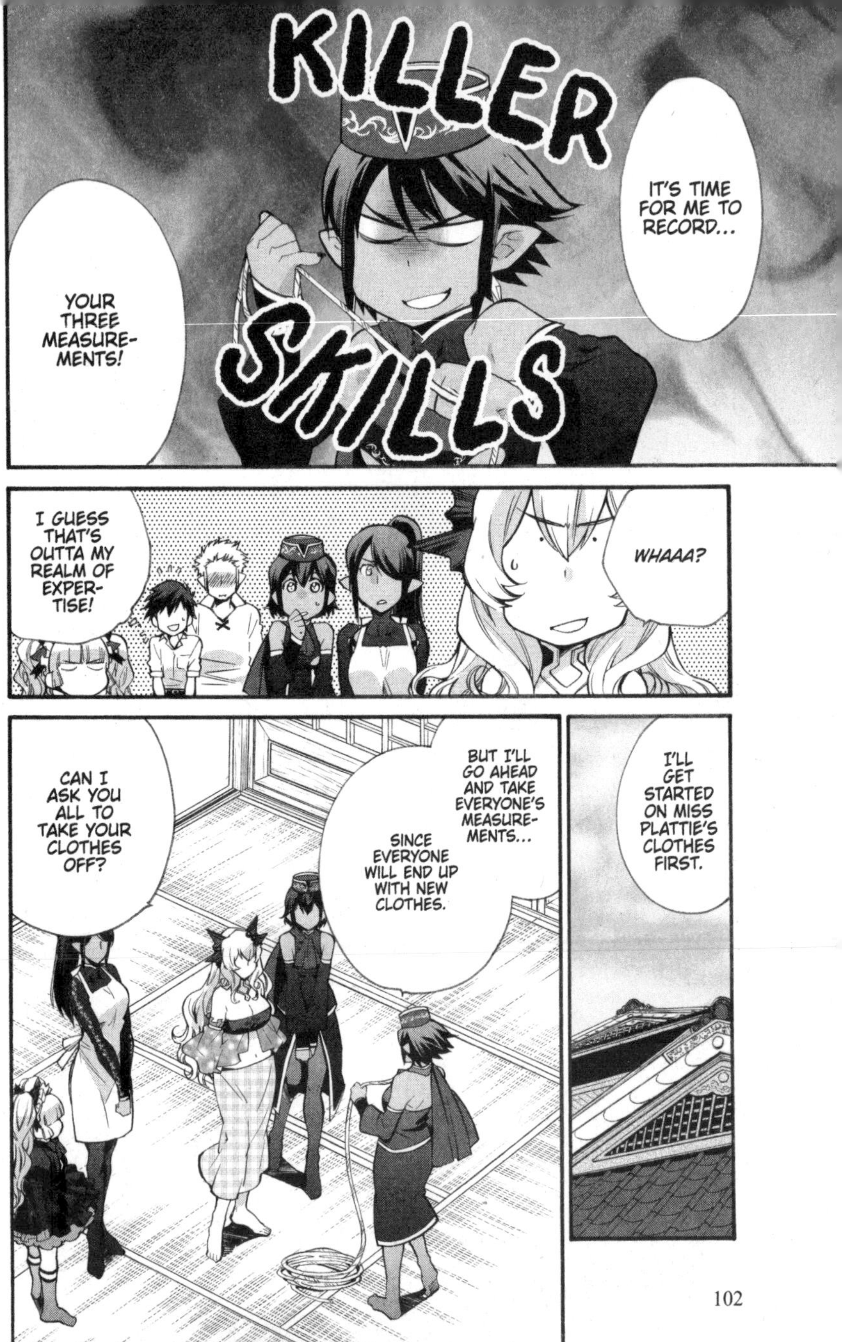
KILLER SKILLS
IT'S TIME FOR ME TO RECORD...
YOUR THREE MEASUREMENTS!
WHAAA?
I GUESS THAT'S OUTTA MY REALM OF EXPERTISE!
I'LL GET STARTED ON MISS PLATTIE'S CLOTHES FIRST.
BUT I'LL GO AHEAD AND TAKE EVERYONE'S MEASUREMENTS...
SINCE EVERYONE WILL END UP WITH NEW CLOTHES.
CAN I ASK YOU ALL TO TAKE YOUR CLOTHES OFF?

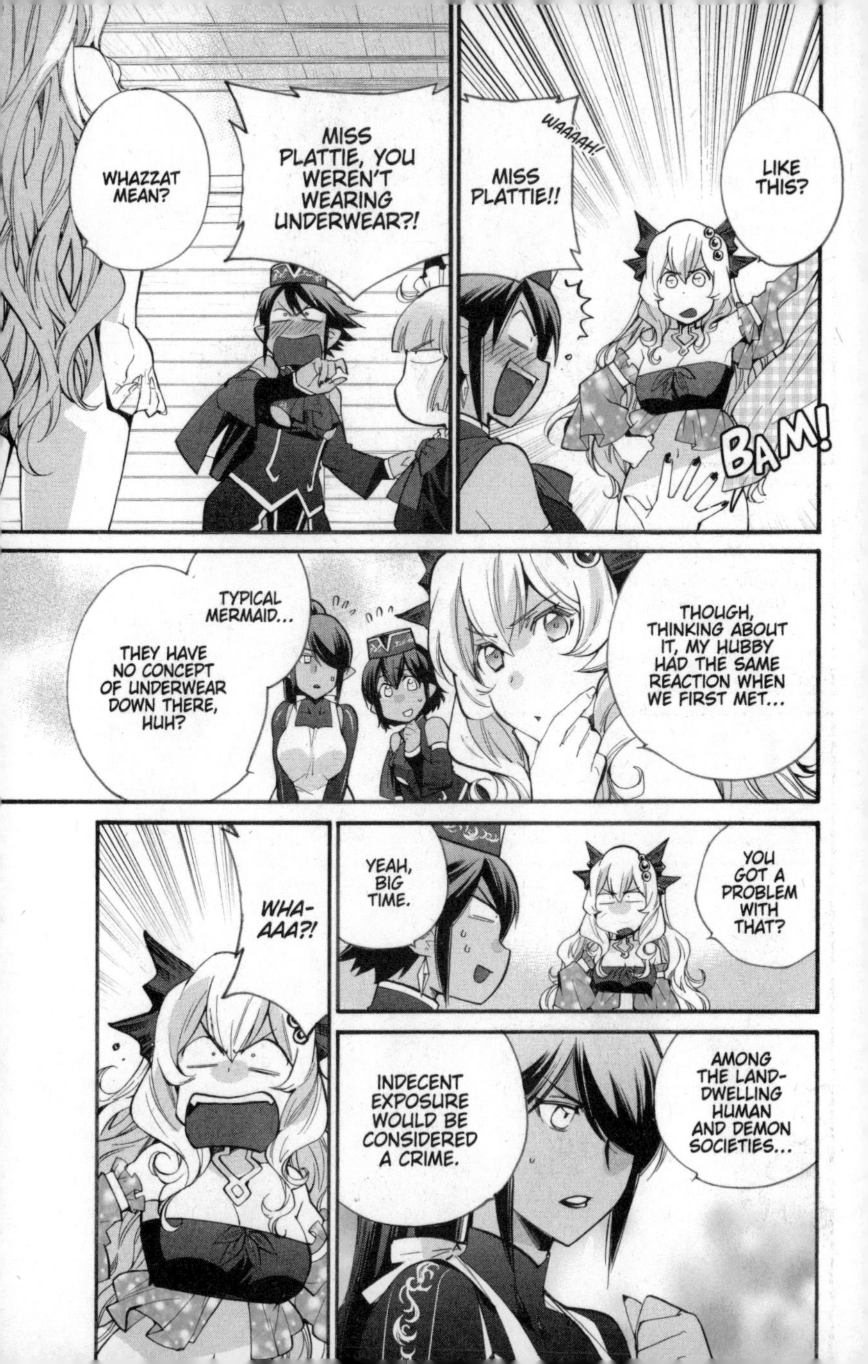
LIKE THIS?
WAAAAH!
MISS PLATTIE!!
BAM!
MISS PLATTIE, YOU WEREN'T WEARING UNDERWEAR?!
WHAZZAT MEAN?
THOUGH, THINKING ABOUT IT, MY HUBBY HAD THE SAME REACTION WHEN WE FIRST MET...
TYPICAL MERMAID...
THEY HAVE NO CONCEPT OF UNDERWEAR DOWN THERE, HUH?
YOU GOT A PROBLEM WITH THAT?
YEAH, BIG TIME.
AMONG THE LAND-DWELLING HUMAN AND DEMON SOCIETIES...
INDECENT EXPOSURE WOULD BE CONSIDERED A CRIME.
WHA-AAA?!

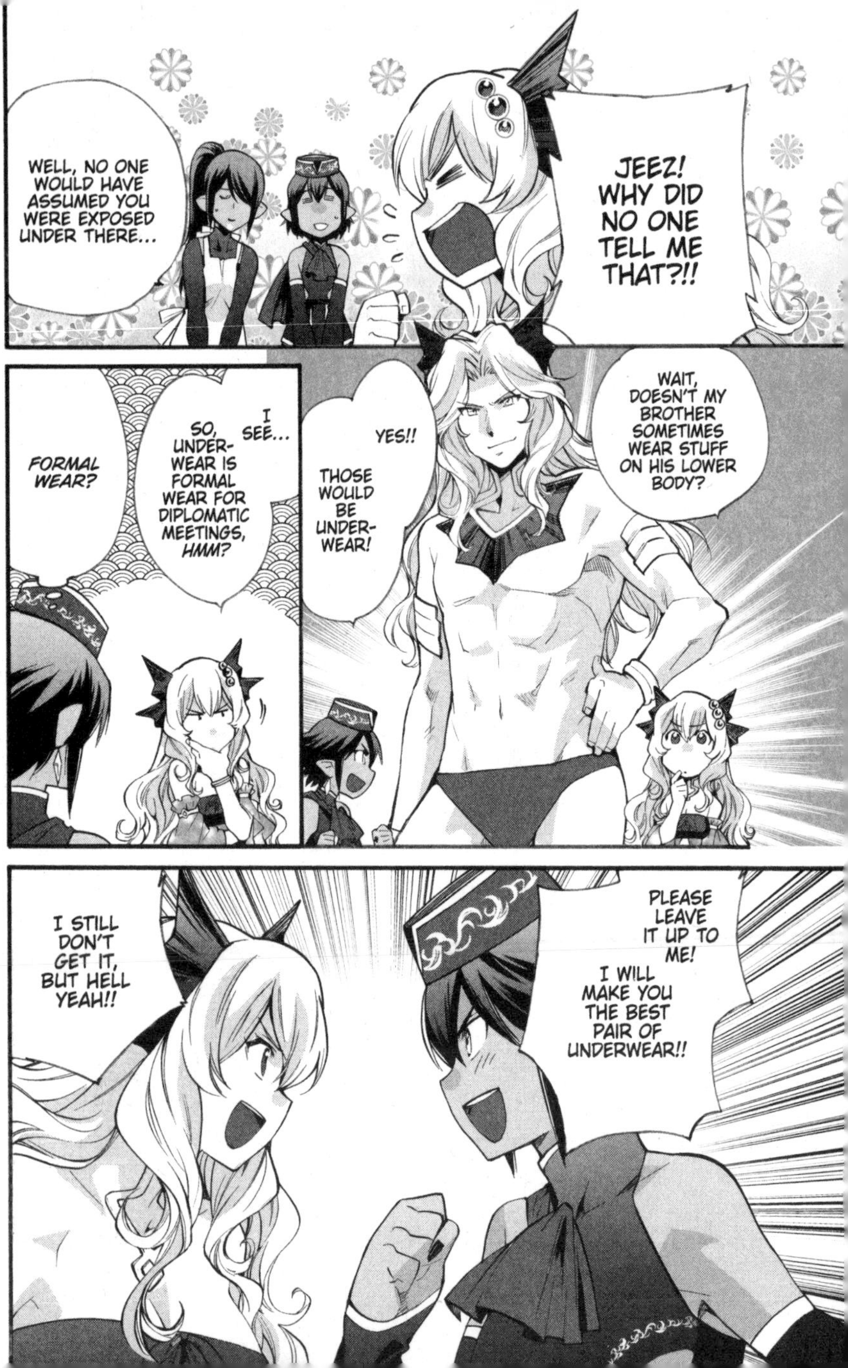
JEEZ! WHY DID NO ONE TELL ME THAT?!!
WELL, NO ONE WOULD HAVE ASSUMED YOU WERE EXPOSED UNDER THERE...
WAIT, DOESN'T MY BROTHER SOMETIMES WEAR STUFF ON HIS LOWER BODY?
YES!!
THOSE WOULD BE UNDER-WEAR!
I SEE...
SO, UNDER-WEAR IS FORMAL WEAR FOR DIPLOMATIC MEETINGS, *HMM?*
FORMAL WEAR?
PLEASE LEAVE IT UP TO ME!
I WILL MAKE YOU THE BEST PAIR OF UNDERWEAR!!
I STILL DON'T GET IT, BUT HELL YEAH!!

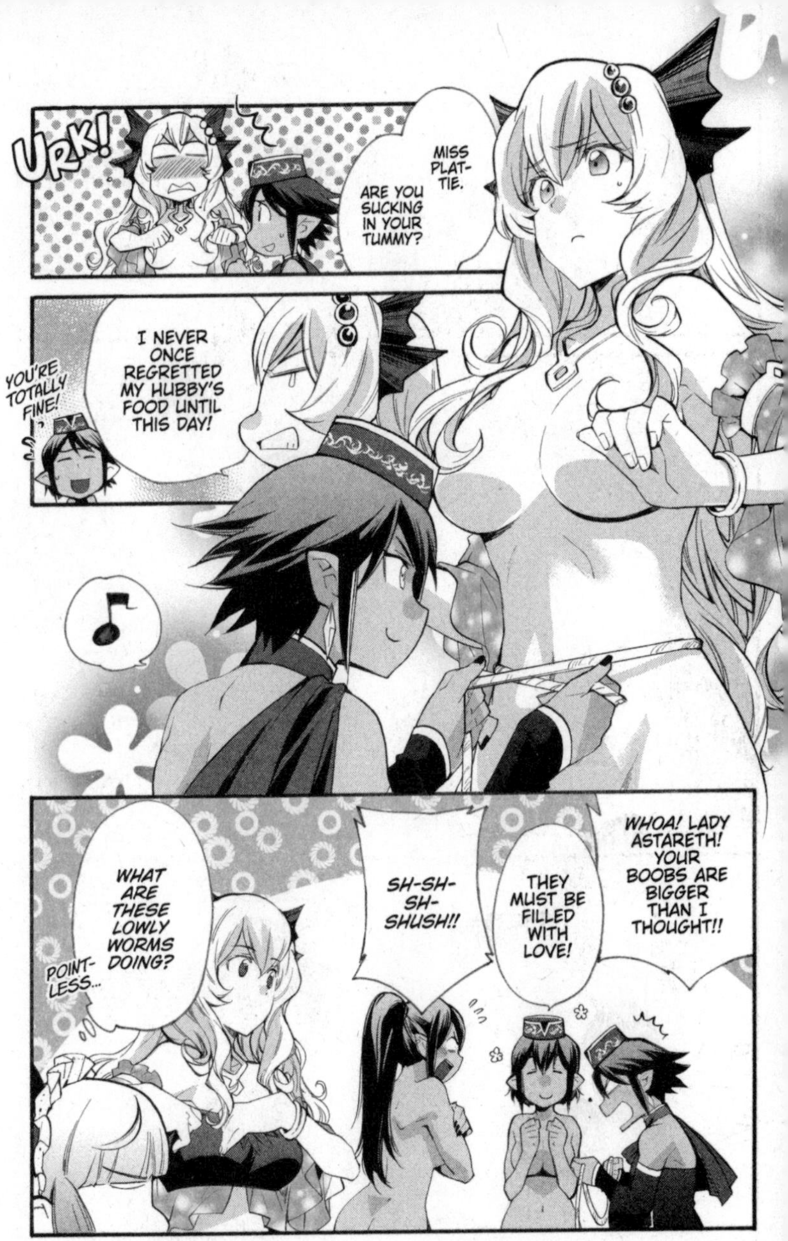
MISS PLAT-TIE.
ARE YOU SUCKING IN YOUR TUMMY?
URK!
I NEVER ONCE REGRETTED MY HUBBY'S FOOD UNTIL THIS DAY!
YOU'RE TOTALLY FINE!
WHOA! LADY ASTARETH! YOUR BOOBS ARE BIGGER THAN I THOUGHT!!
THEY MUST BE FILLED WITH LOVE!
SH-SH-SH-SHUSH!!
WHAT ARE THESE LOWLY WORMS DOING?
POINT-LESS...

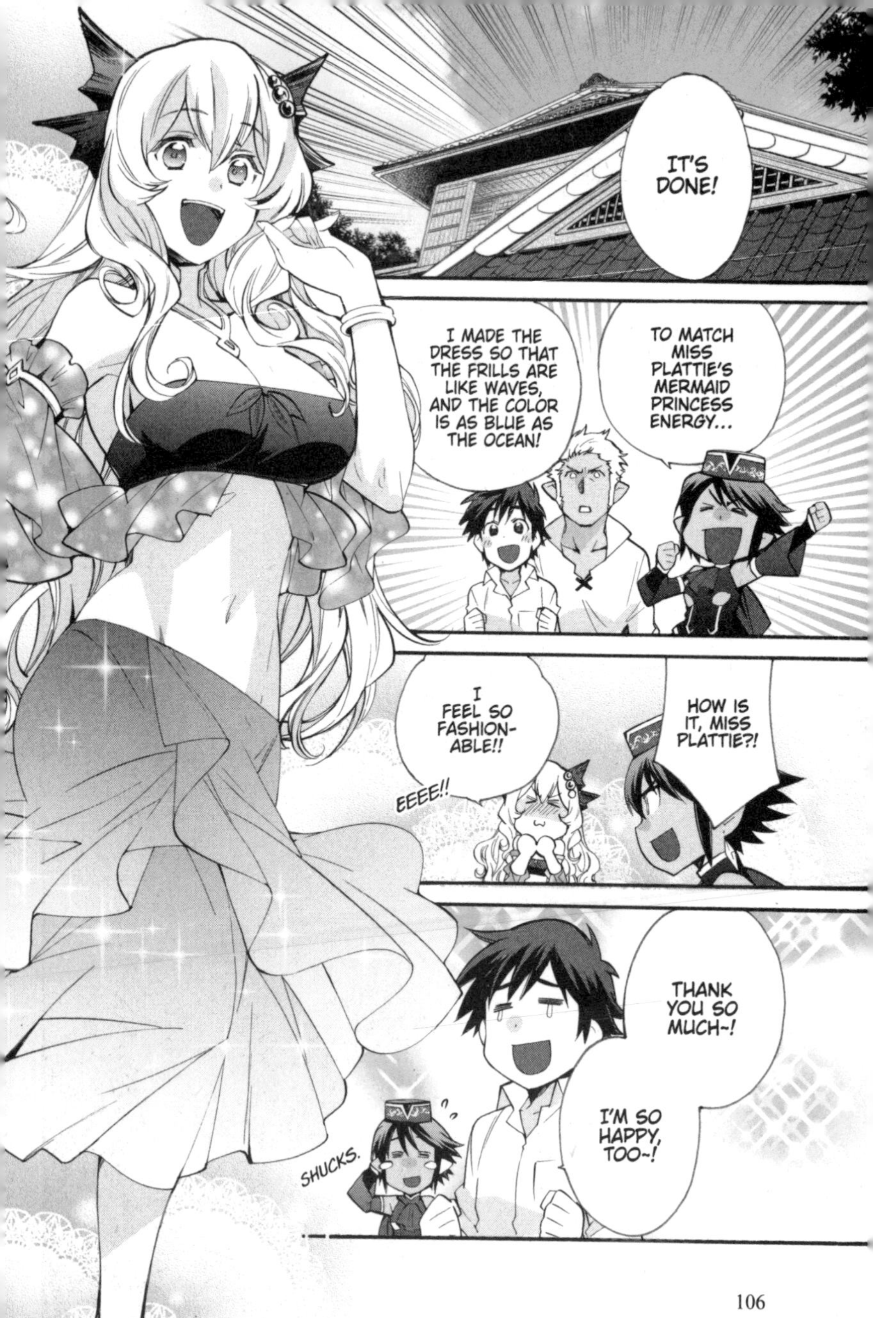
IT'S DONE!
TO MATCH MISS PLATTIE'S MERMAID PRINCESS ENERGY...
I MADE THE DRESS SO THAT THE FRILLS ARE LIKE WAVES, AND THE COLOR IS AS BLUE AS THE OCEAN!
HOW IS IT, MISS PLATTIE?!
I FEEL SO FASHION-ABLE!!
EEEE!!
THANK YOU SO MUCH~!
I'M SO HAPPY, TOO~!
SHUCKS.

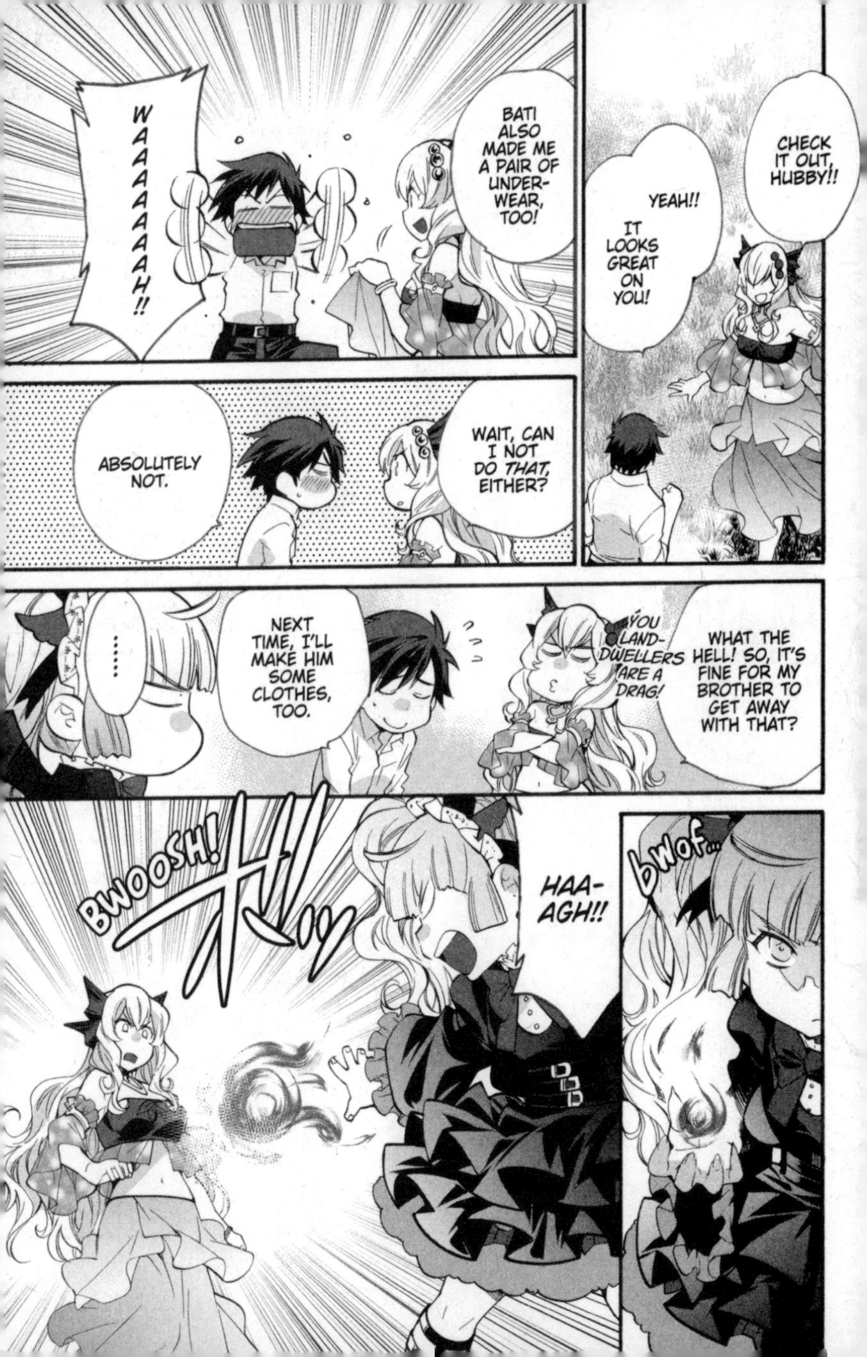
CHECK IT OUT, HUBBY!!
YEAH!!
IT LOOKS GREAT ON YOU!
BATI ALSO MADE ME A PAIR OF UNDER-WEAR, TOO!
WAAAAAAAAH!!
WAIT, CAN I NOT DO *THAT*, EITHER?
ABSOLUTELY NOT.
WHAT THE HELL! SO, IT'S FINE FOR MY BROTHER TO GET AWAY WITH THAT?
YOU LAND-DWELLERS ARE A DRAG!
NEXT TIME, I'LL MAKE HIM SOME CLOTHES, TOO.
......
bwof...
HAA-AGH!!
BWOOSH!!

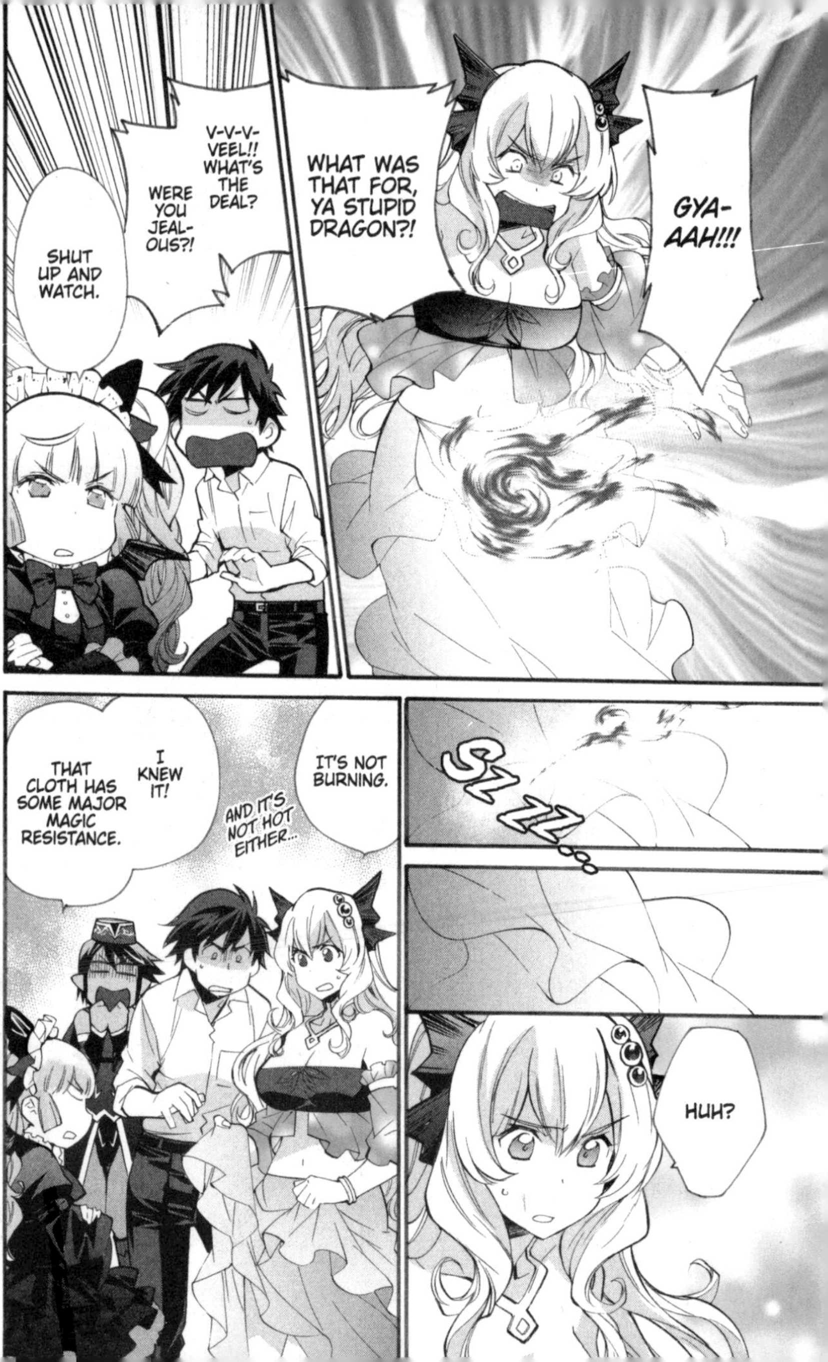
GYA-AAH!!!
WHAT WAS THAT FOR, YA STUPID DRAGON?!
V-V-V-VEEL!! WHAT'S THE DEAL?
WERE YOU JEAL-OUS?!
SHUT UP AND WATCH.
SIZZZ...
HUH?
IT'S NOT BURNING.
AND IT'S NOT HOT EITHER...
I KNEW IT!
THAT CLOTH HAS SOME MAJOR MAGIC RESISTANCE.

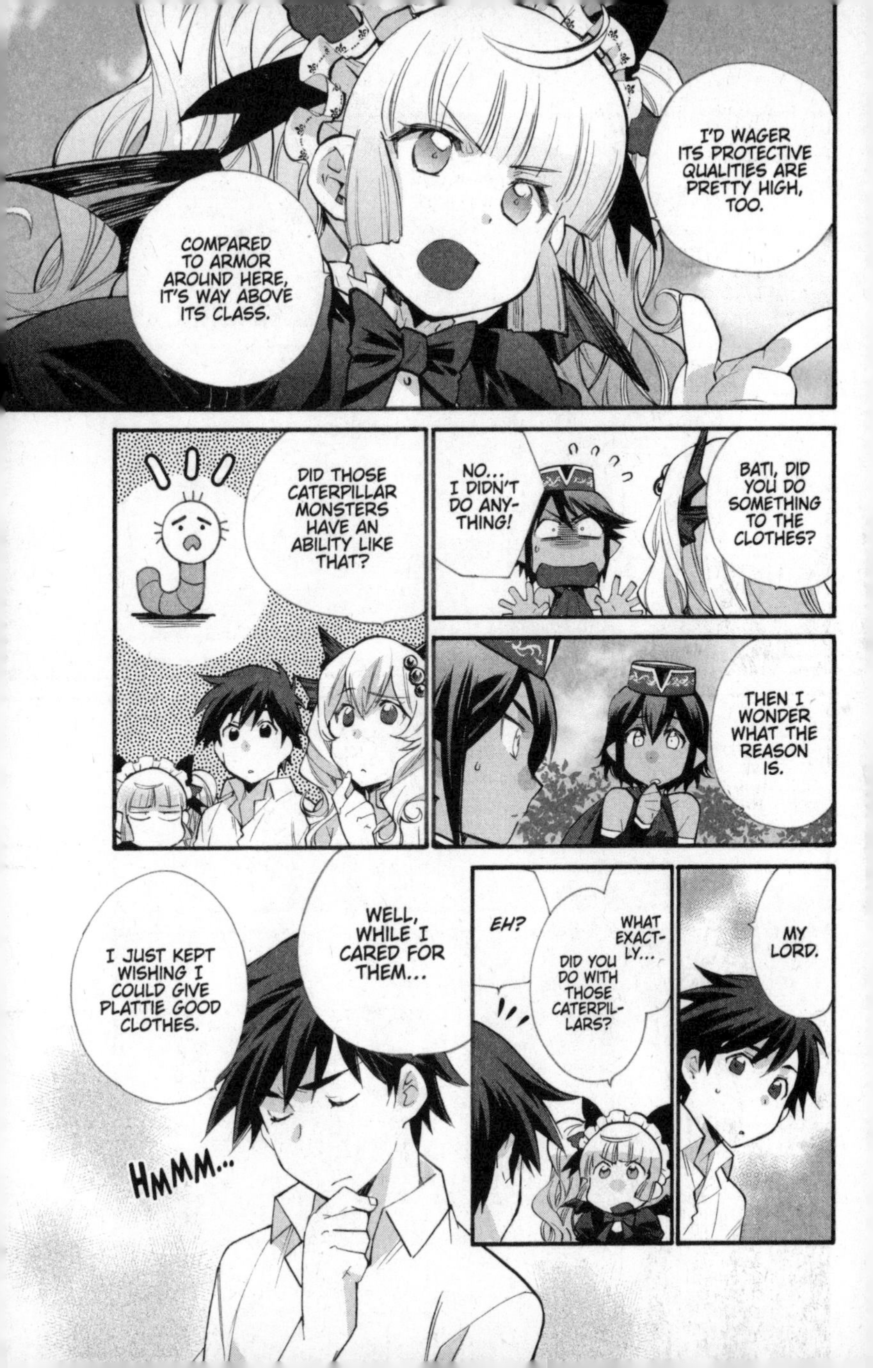
I'D WAGER ITS PROTECTIVE QUALITIES ARE PRETTY HIGH, TOO.
COMPARED TO ARMOR AROUND HERE, IT'S WAY ABOVE ITS CLASS.
BATI, DID YOU DO SOMETHING TO THE CLOTHES?
NO... I DIDN'T DO ANY-THING!
THEN I WONDER WHAT THE REASON IS.
DID THOSE CATERPILLAR MONSTERS HAVE AN ABILITY LIKE THAT?
MY LORD.
WHAT EXACT-LY... DID YOU DO WITH THOSE CATERPIL-LARS?
EH?
WELL, WHILE I CARED FOR THEM...
I JUST KEPT WISHING I COULD GIVE PLATTIE GOOD CLOTHES.
HMMM...

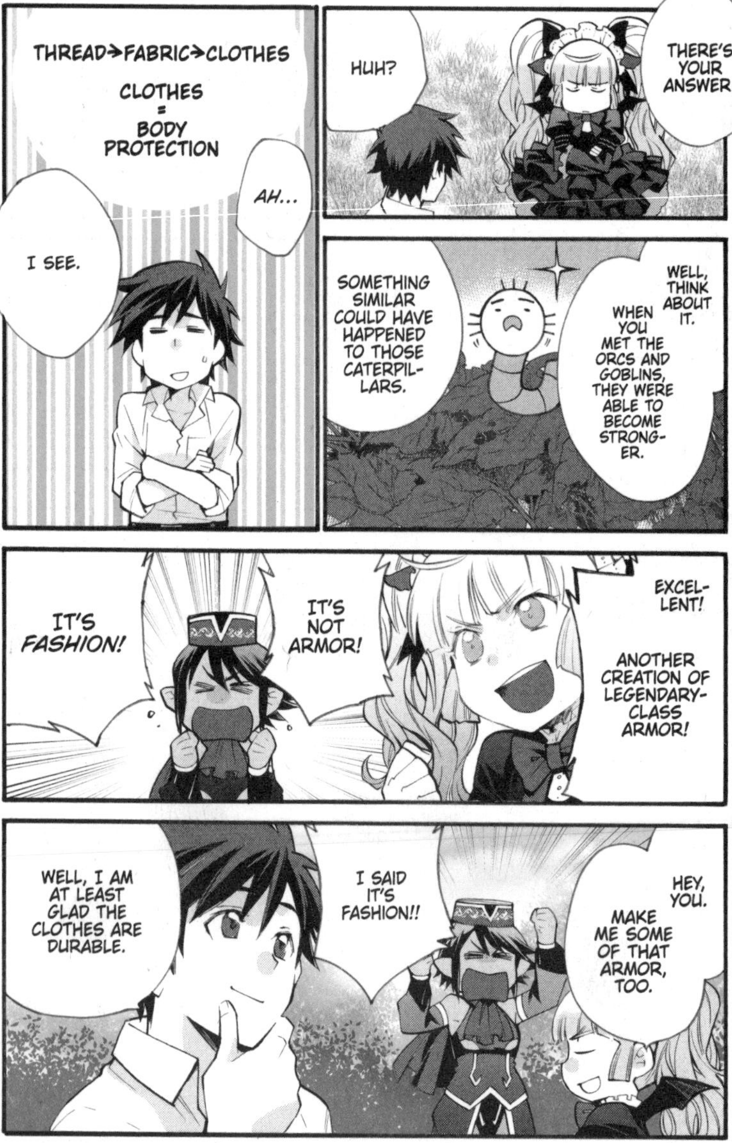
THERE'S YOUR ANSWER.
HUH?
WELL, THINK ABOUT IT.
WHEN YOU MET THE ORCS AND GOBLINS, THEY WERE ABLE TO BECOME STRONGER.
SOMETHING SIMILAR COULD HAVE HAPPENED TO THOSE CATERPILLARS.
THREAD→FABRIC→CLOTHES
CLOTHES = BODY PROTECTION
AH...
I SEE.
EXCELLENT!
ANOTHER CREATION OF LEGENDARY-CLASS ARMOR!
IT'S NOT ARMOR!
IT'S FASHION!
HEY, YOU.
MAKE ME SOME OF THAT ARMOR, TOO.
I SAID IT'S FASHION!!
WELL, I AM AT LEAST GLAD THE CLOTHES ARE DURABLE.

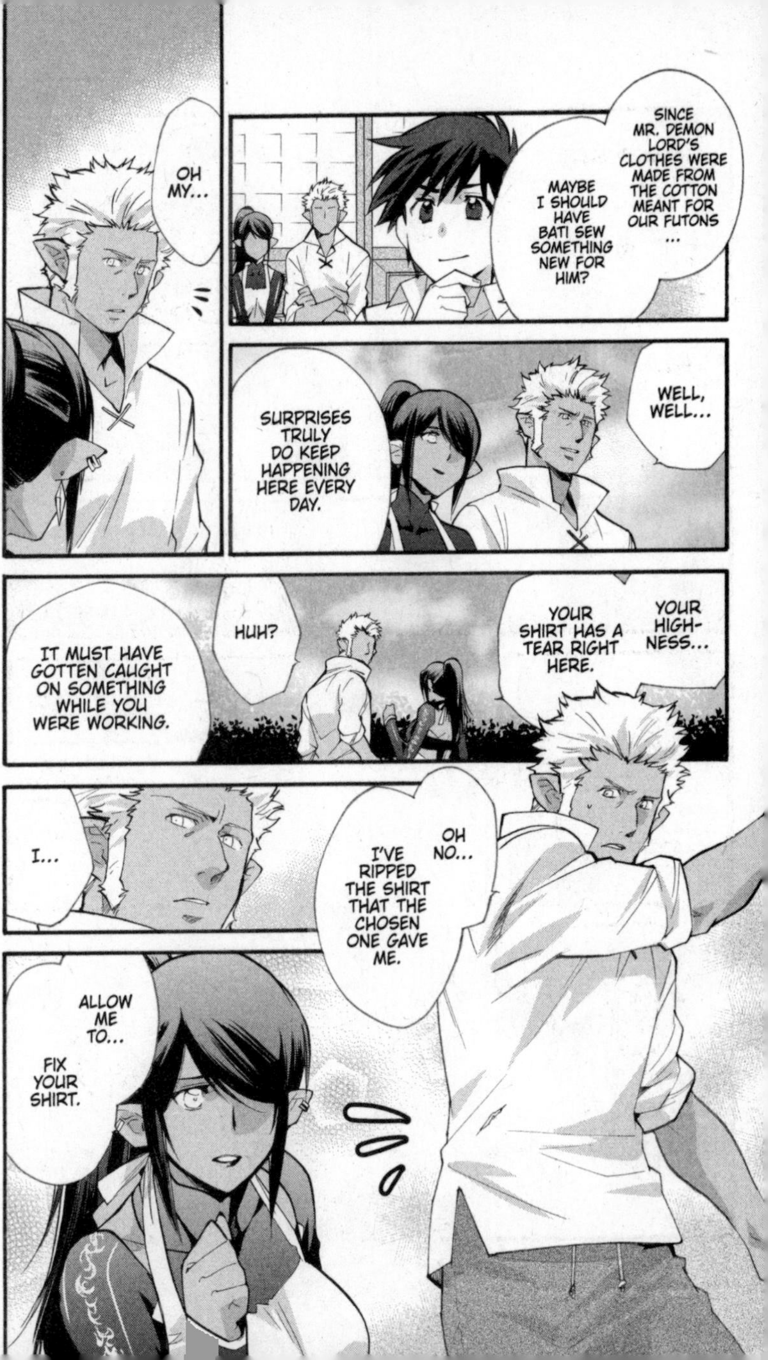
SINCE MR. DEMON LORD'S CLOTHES WERE MADE FROM THE COTTON MEANT FOR OUR FUTONS ...
MAYBE I SHOULD HAVE BATI SEW SOMETHING NEW FOR HIM?
WELL, WELL...
SURPRISES TRULY DO KEEP HAPPENING HERE EVERY DAY.
OH MY...
YOUR HIGH-NESS...
YOUR SHIRT HAS A TEAR RIGHT HERE.
HUH?
IT MUST HAVE GOTTEN CAUGHT ON SOMETHING WHILE YOU WERE WORKING.
OH NO...
I'VE RIPPED THE SHIRT THAT THE CHOSEN ONE GAVE ME.
I...
ALLOW ME TO...
FIX YOUR SHIRT.

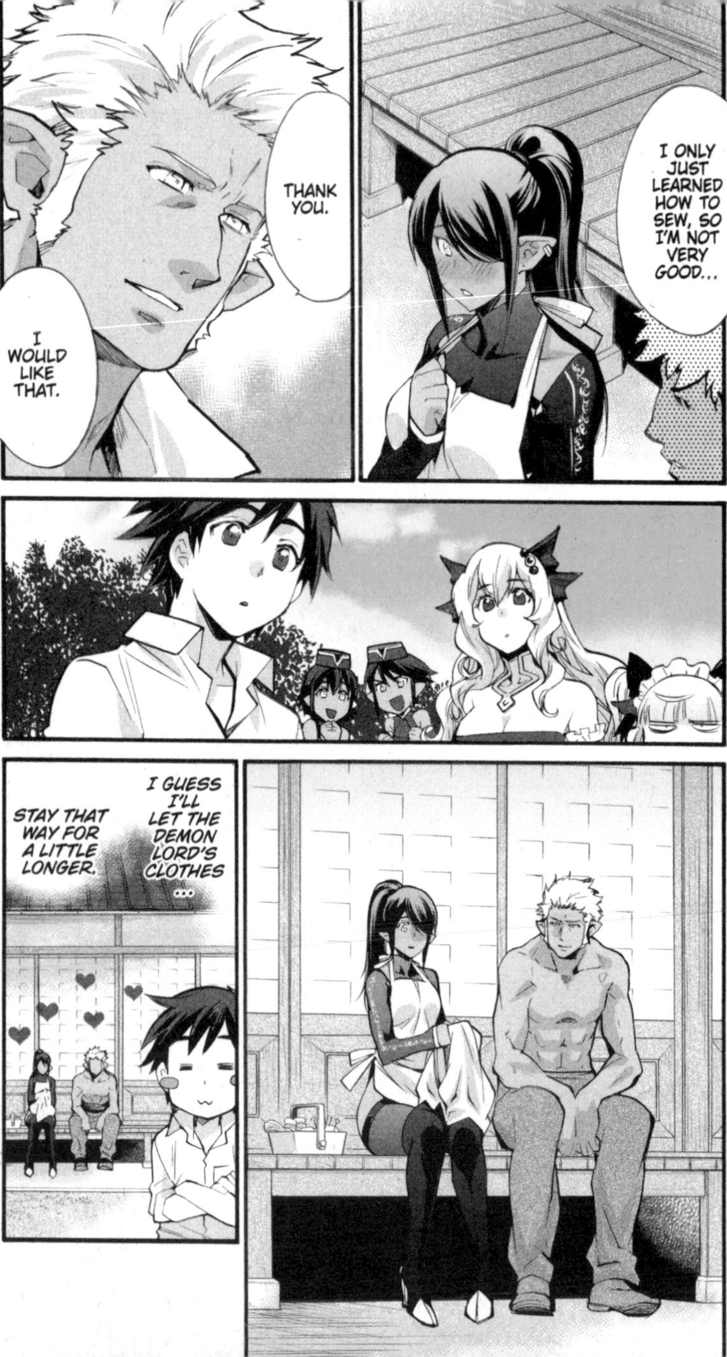
I ONLY JUST LEARNED HOW TO SEW, SO I'M NOT VERY GOOD...
THANK YOU.
I WOULD LIKE THAT.
I GUESS I'LL LET THE DEMON LORD'S CLOTHES...
STAY THAT WAY FOR A LITTLE LONGER.

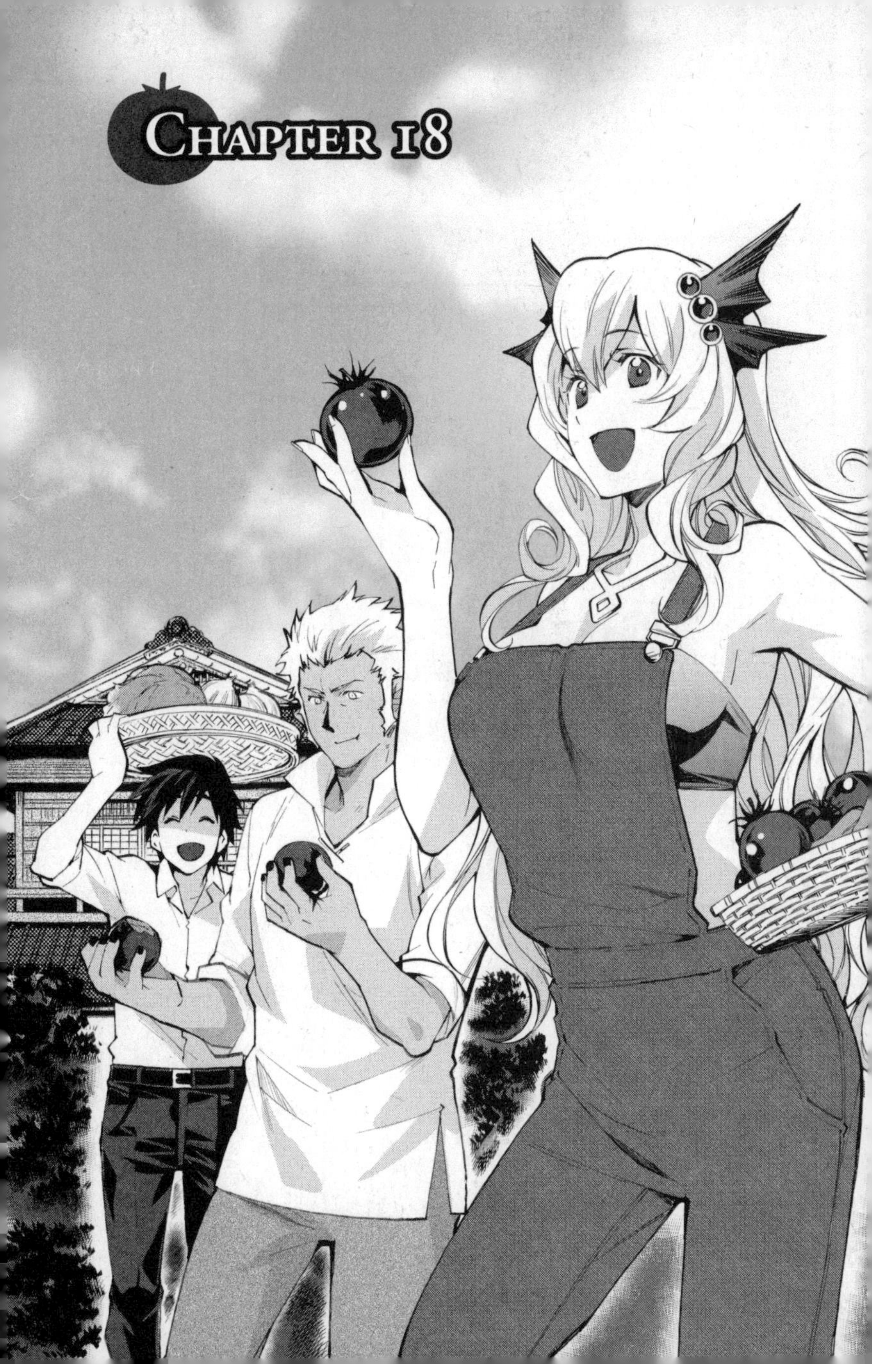
CHAPTER 18

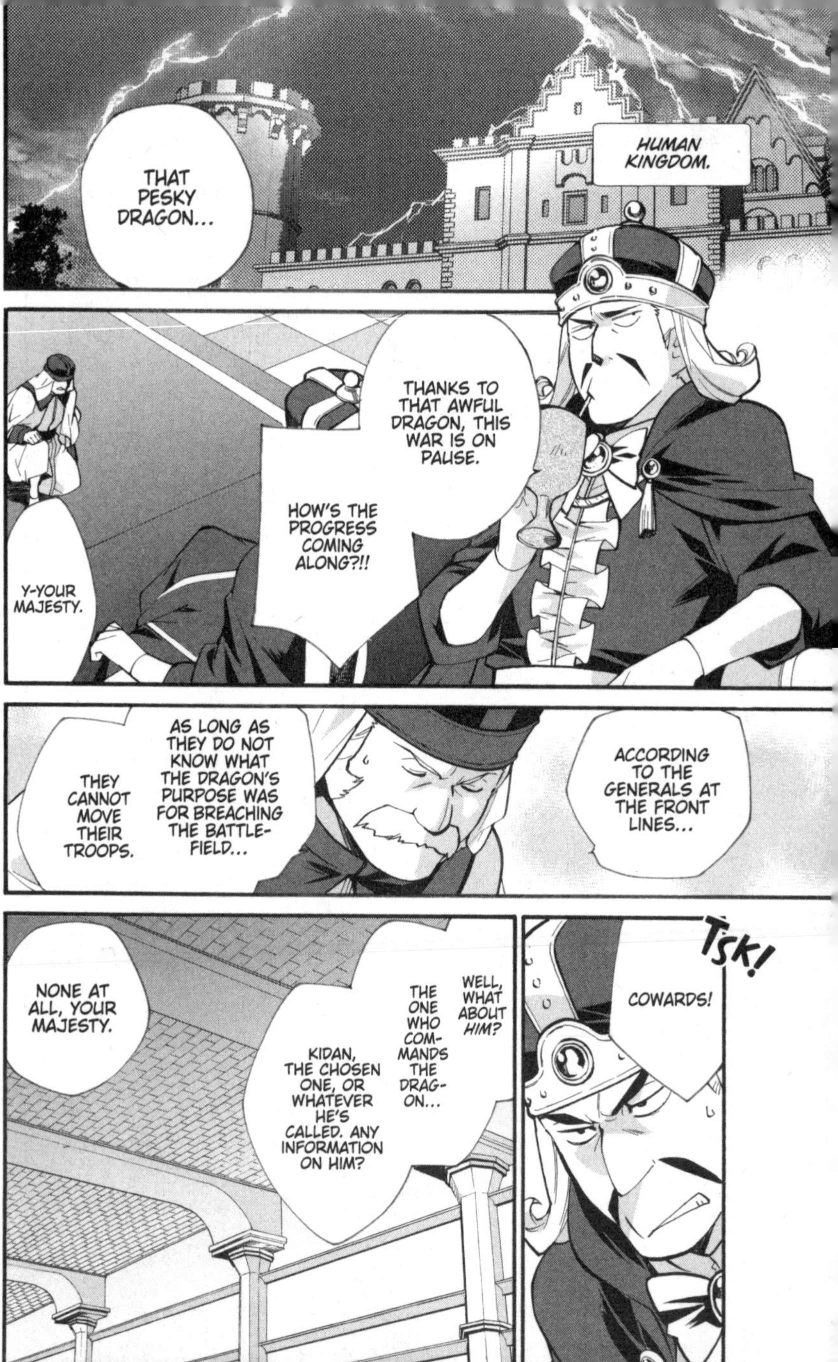
HUMAN KINGDOM.
THAT PESKY DRAGON…
THANKS TO THAT AWFUL DRAGON, THIS WAR IS ON PAUSE.
HOW'S THE PROGRESS COMING ALONG?!!
Y-YOUR MAJESTY.
ACCORDING TO THE GENERALS AT THE FRONT LINES…
AS LONG AS THEY DO NOT KNOW WHAT THE DRAGON'S PURPOSE WAS FOR BREACHING THE BATTLE-FIELD…
THEY CANNOT MOVE THEIR TROOPS.
TSK!
COWARDS!
WELL, WHAT ABOUT HIM?
THE ONE WHO COM-MANDS THE DRAG-ON…
KIDAN, THE CHOSEN ONE, OR WHATEVER HE'S CALLED. ANY INFORMATION ON HIM?
NONE AT ALL, YOUR MAJESTY.

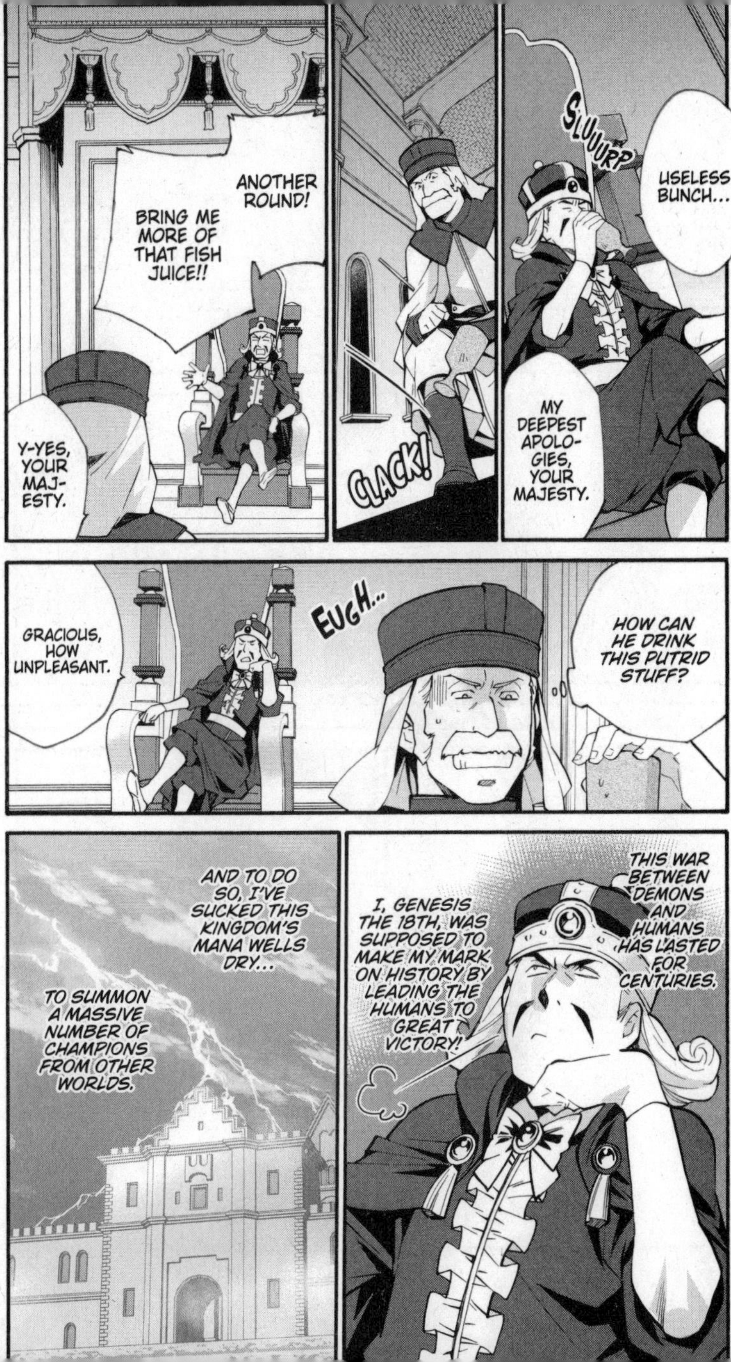
USELESS BUNCH…
SLUUURP
MY DEEPEST APOLOGIES, YOUR MAJESTY.
CLACK!
ANOTHER ROUND!
BRING ME MORE OF THAT FISH JUICE!!
Y-YES, YOUR MAJESTY.
HOW CAN HE DRINK THIS PUTRID STUFF?
EUGH…
GRACIOUS, HOW UNPLEASANT.
THIS WAR BETWEEN DEMONS AND HUMANS HAS LASTED FOR CENTURIES.
I, GENESIS THE 18TH, WAS SUPPOSED TO MAKE MY MARK ON HISTORY BY LEADING THE HUMANS TO GREAT VICTORY!
AND TO DO SO, I'VE SUCKED THIS KINGDOM'S MANA WELLS DRY…
TO SUMMON A MASSIVE NUMBER OF CHAMPIONS FROM OTHER WORLDS.

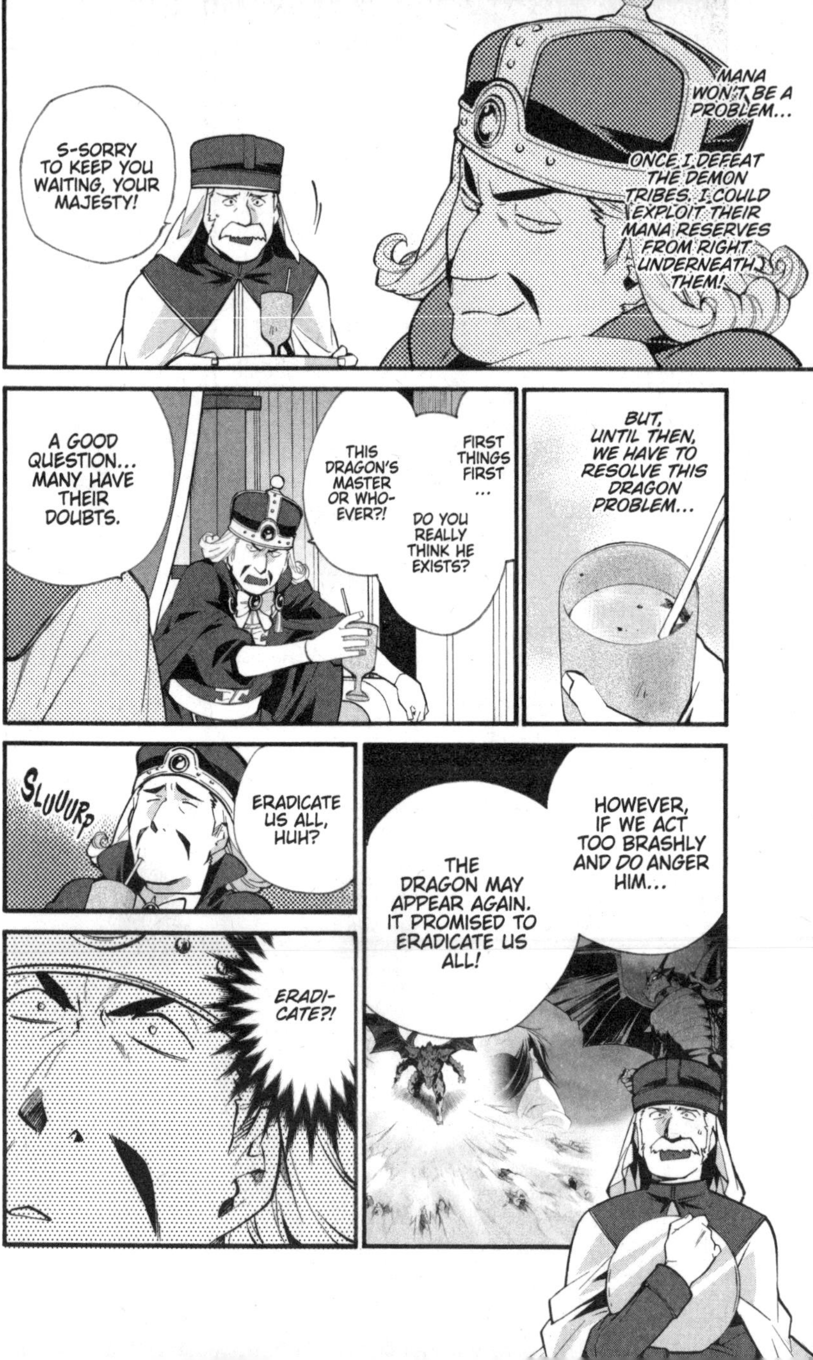
MANA WON'T BE A PROBLEM...
ONCE I DEFEAT THE DEMON TRIBES, I COULD EXPLOIT THEIR MANA RESERVES FROM RIGHT UNDERNEATH THEM!
S-SORRY TO KEEP YOU WAITING, YOUR MAJESTY!
BUT, UNTIL THEN, WE HAVE TO RESOLVE THIS DRAGON PROBLEM...
FIRST THINGS FIRST...
THIS DRAGON'S MASTER OR WHO-EVER?!
DO YOU REALLY THINK HE EXISTS?
A GOOD QUESTION... MANY HAVE THEIR DOUBTS.
HOWEVER, IF WE ACT TOO BRASHLY AND DO ANGER HIM...
THE DRAGON MAY APPEAR AGAIN. IT PROMISED TO ERADICATE US ALL!
SLUUURP
ERADICATE US ALL, HUH?
ERADI-CATE?!

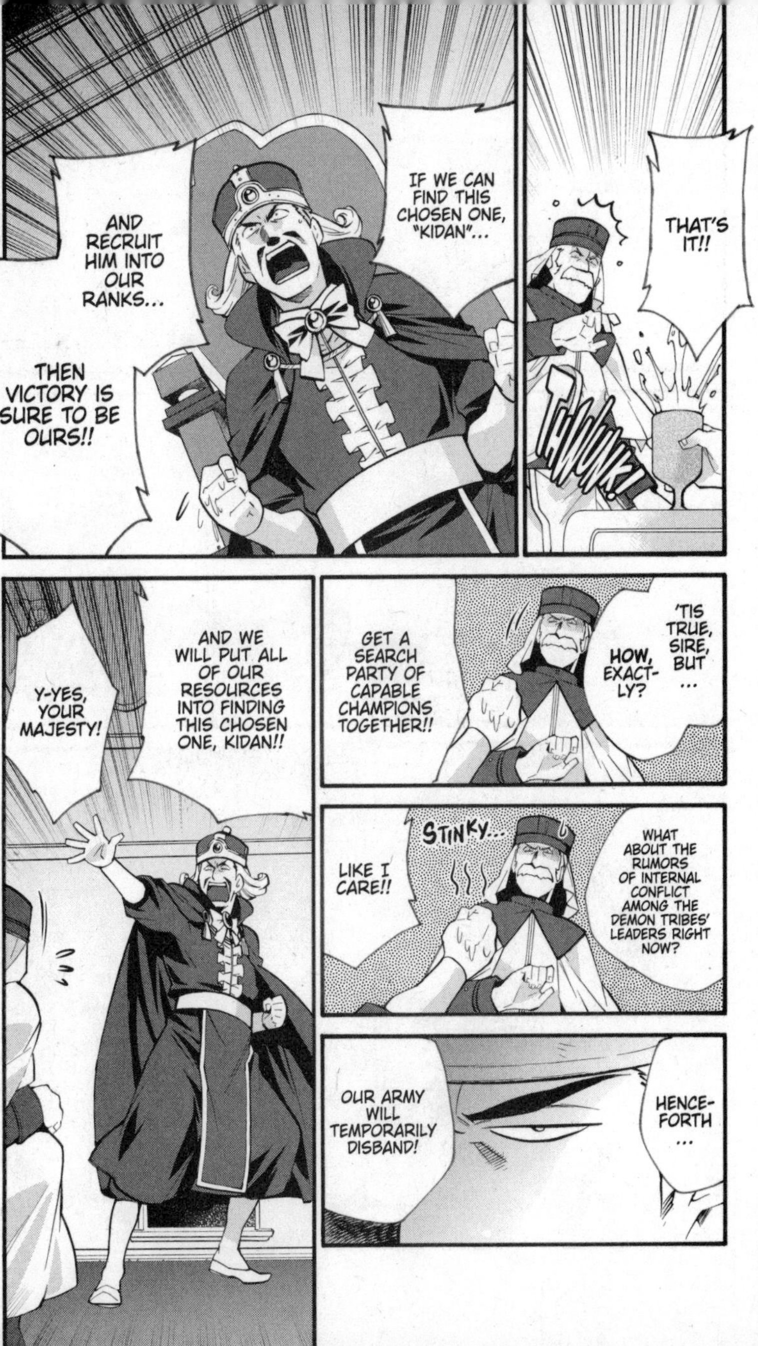
THAT'S IT!!
THWUNK!
IF WE CAN FIND THIS CHOSEN ONE, "KIDAN"...
AND RECRUIT HIM INTO OUR RANKS...
THEN VICTORY IS SURE TO BE OURS!!
'TIS TRUE, SIRE, BUT ...
HOW, EXACTLY?
GET A SEARCH PARTY OF CAPABLE CHAMPIONS TOGETHER!!
WHAT ABOUT THE RUMORS OF INTERNAL CONFLICT AMONG THE DEMON TRIBES' LEADERS RIGHT NOW?
STINKY...
LIKE I CARE!!
HENCEFORTH ...
OUR ARMY WILL TEMPORARILY DISBAND!
AND WE WILL PUT ALL OF OUR RESOURCES INTO FINDING THIS CHOSEN ONE, KIDAN!!
Y-YES, YOUR MAJESTY!

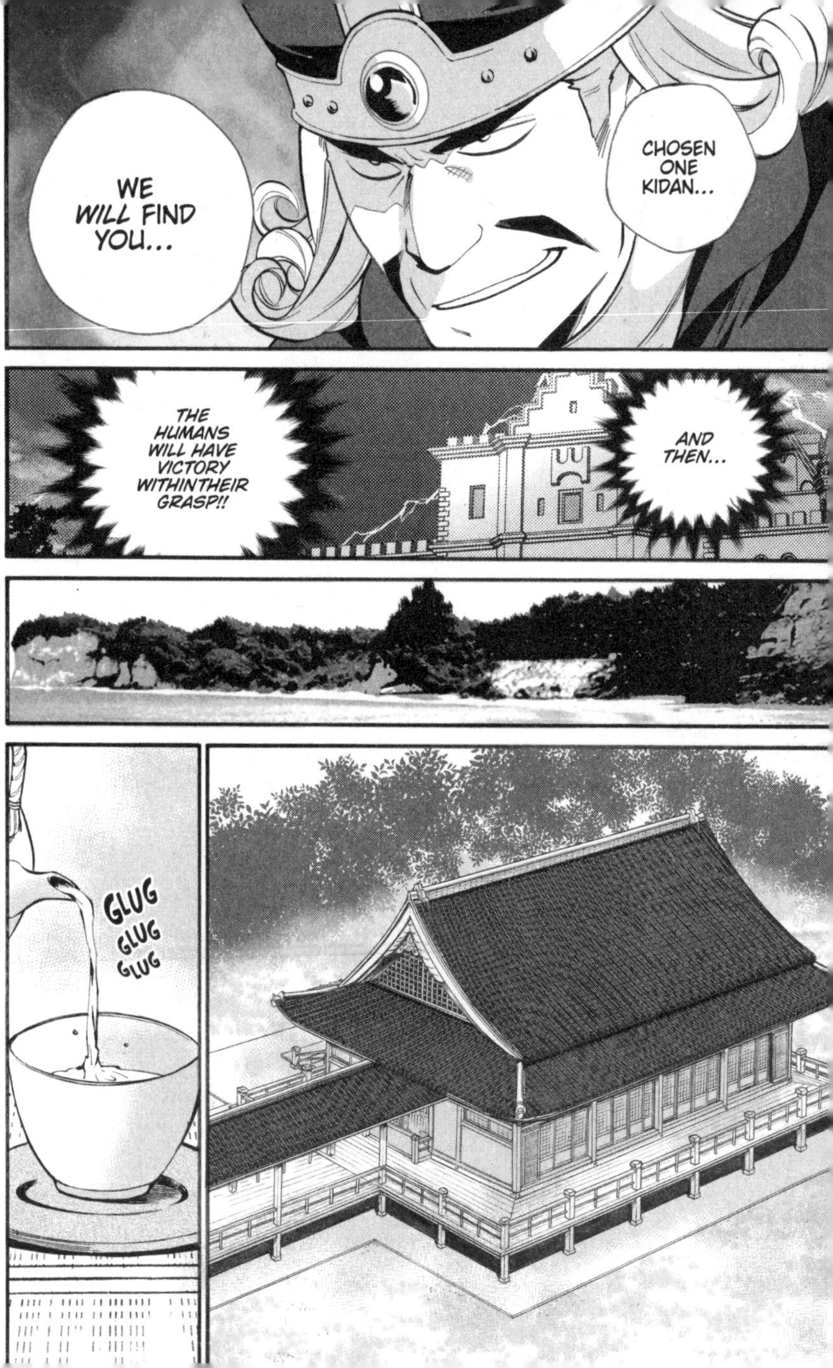
CHOSEN ONE KIDAN...
WE WILL FIND YOU...
AND THEN...
THE HUMANS WILL HAVE VICTORY WITHINTHEIR GRASP!!
GLUG GLUG GLUG

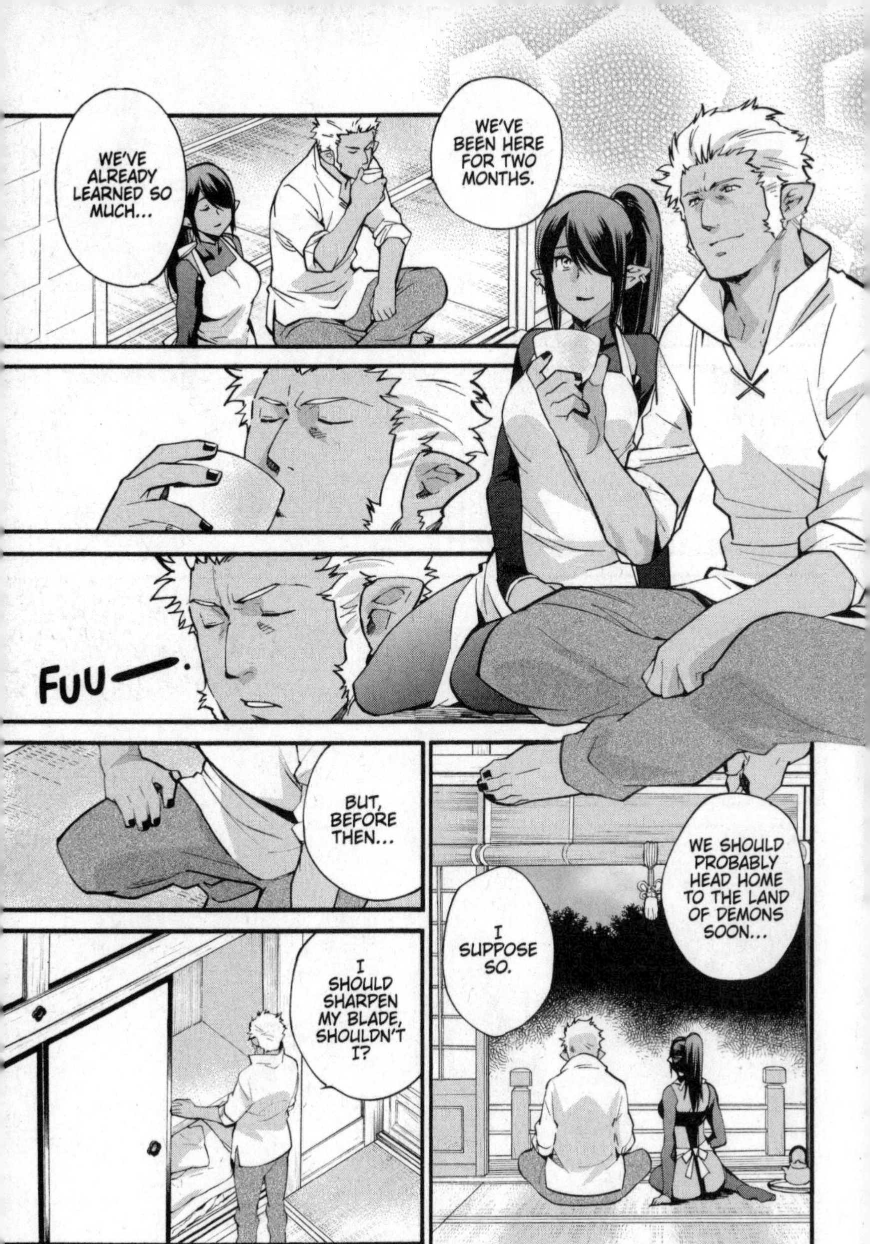
WE'VE BEEN HERE FOR TWO MONTHS.
WE'VE ALREADY LEARNED SO MUCH...
FUU—.
WE SHOULD PROBABLY HEAD HOME TO THE LAND OF DEMONS SOON...
I SUPPOSE SO.
BUT, BEFORE THEN...
I SHOULD SHARPEN MY BLADE, SHOULDN'T I?

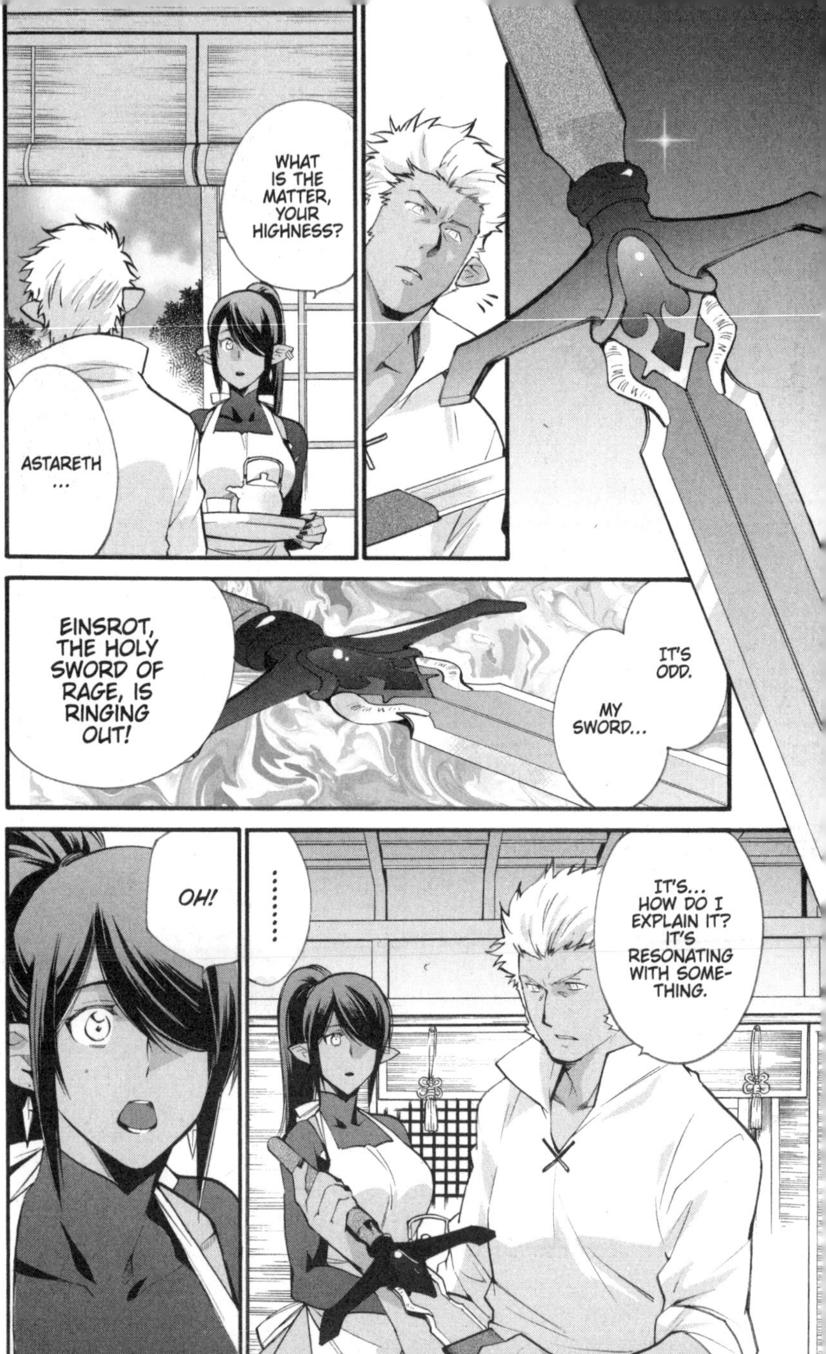
WHAT IS THE MATTER, YOUR HIGHNESS?
ASTARETH...
IT'S ODD.
MY SWORD...
EINSROT, THE HOLY SWORD OF RAGE, IS RINGING OUT!
IT'S... HOW DO I EXPLAIN IT? IT'S RESONATING WITH SOME-THING.
....
OH!

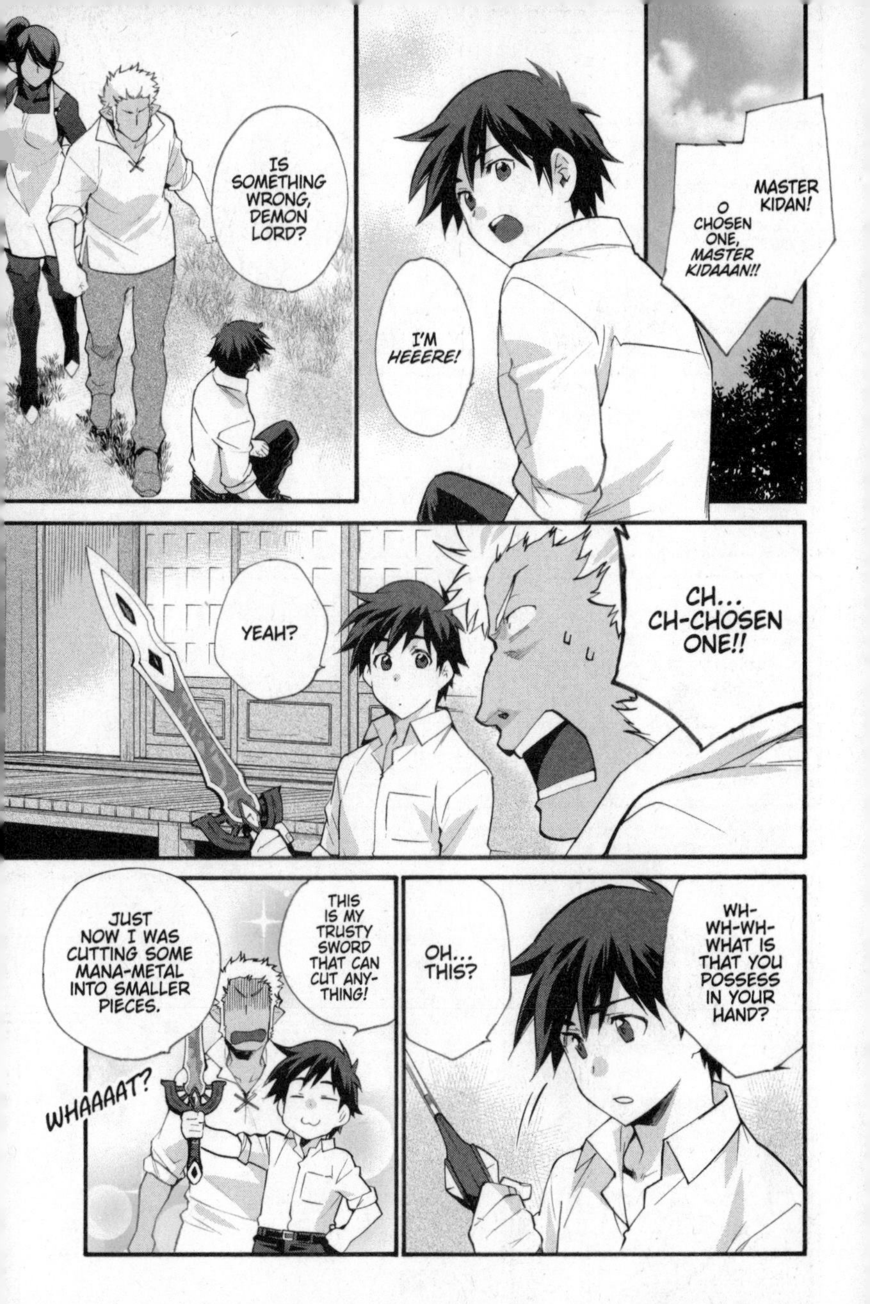
MASTER KIDAN!
O CHOSEN ONE, MASTER KIDAAAN!!
I'M HEEERE!
IS SOMETHING WRONG, DEMON LORD?
CH... CH-CHOSEN ONE!!
YEAH?
WH-WH-WH-WHAT IS THAT YOU POSSESS IN YOUR HAND?
OH... THIS?
THIS IS MY TRUSTY SWORD THAT CAN CUT ANYTHING!
JUST NOW I WAS CUTTING SOME MANA-METAL INTO SMALLER PIECES.
WHAAAAT?

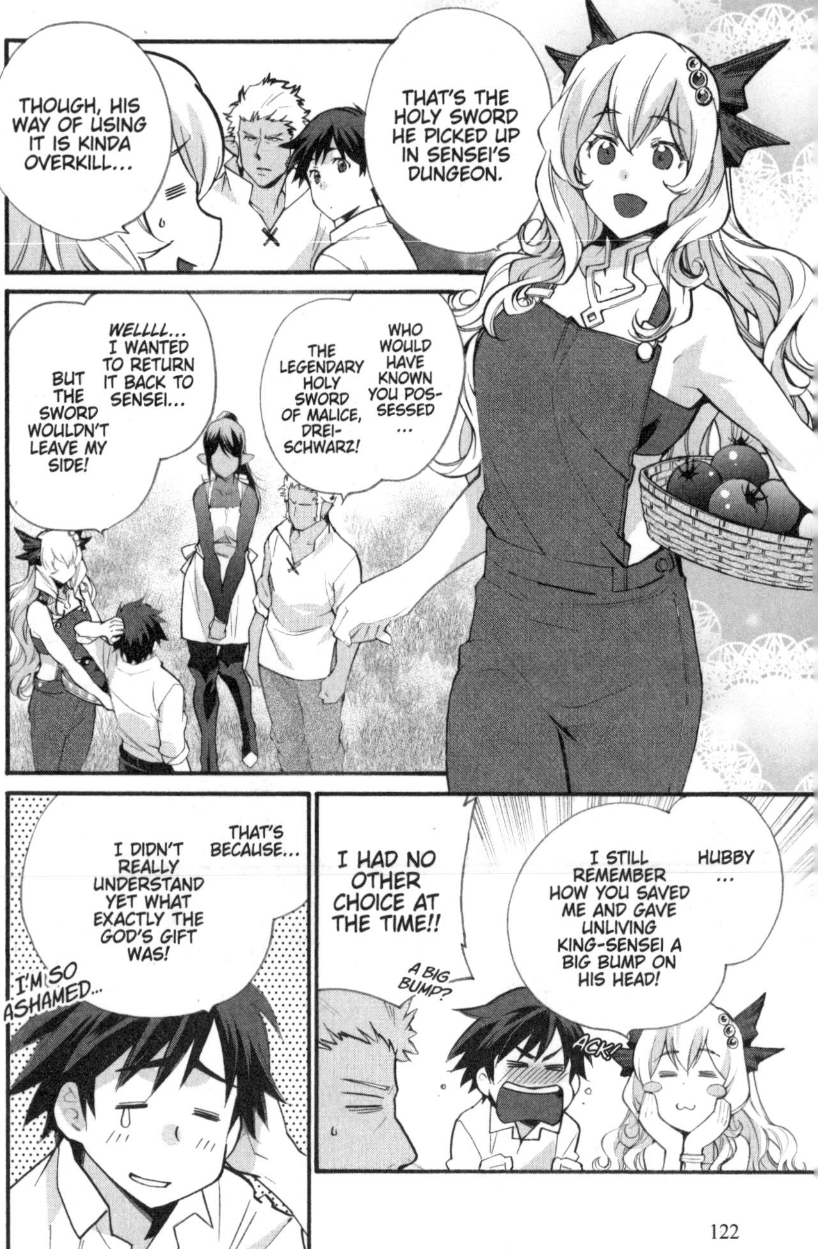
THAT'S THE HOLY SWORD HE PICKED UP IN SENSEI'S DUNGEON.
THOUGH, HIS WAY OF USING IT IS KINDA OVERKILL...
WHO WOULD HAVE KNOWN YOU POS-SESSED...
THE LEGENDARY HOLY SWORD OF MALICE, DREI-SCHWARZ!
WELLLL... I WANTED TO RETURN IT BACK TO SENSEI...
BUT THE SWORD WOULDN'T LEAVE MY SIDE!
HUBBY...
I STILL REMEMBER HOW YOU SAVED ME AND GAVE UNLIVING KING-SENSEI A BIG BUMP ON HIS HEAD!
A BIG BUMP?
ACK!
I HAD NO OTHER CHOICE AT THE TIME!!
THAT'S BECAUSE...
I DIDN'T REALLY UNDERSTAND YET WHAT EXACTLY THE GOD'S GIFT WAS!
I'M SO ASHAMED...

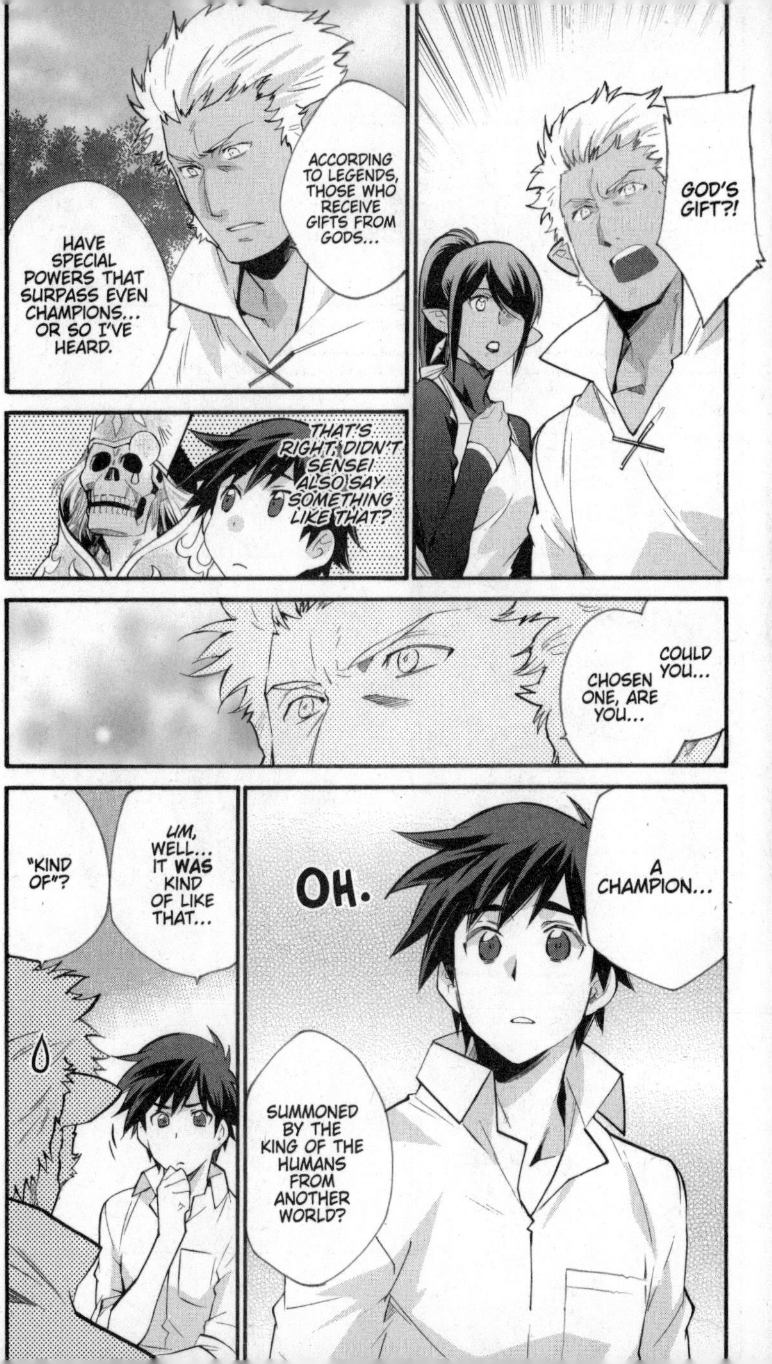
GOD'S GIFT?!
ACCORDING TO LEGENDS, THOSE WHO RECEIVE GIFTS FROM GODS...
HAVE SPECIAL POWERS THAT SURPASS EVEN CHAMPIONS... OR SO I'VE HEARD.
THAT'S RIGHT, DIDN'T SENSEI ALSO SAY SOMETHING LIKE THAT?
COULD YOU...
CHOSEN ONE, ARE YOU...
A CHAMPION...
OH.
SUMMONED BY THE KING OF THE HUMANS FROM ANOTHER WORLD?
UM, WELL... IT WAS KIND OF LIKE THAT...
"KIND OF"?

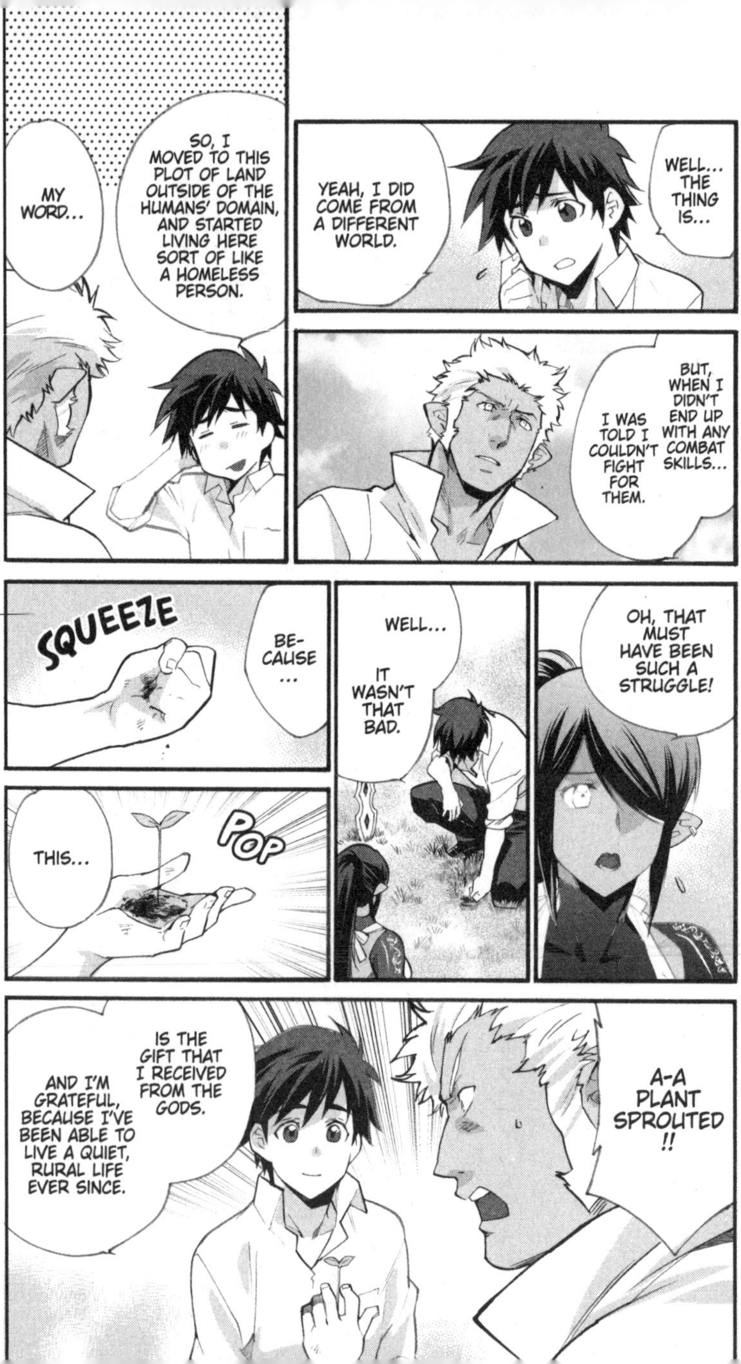

WELL... THE THING IS...
YEAH, I DID COME FROM A DIFFERENT WORLD.
BUT, WHEN I DIDN'T END UP WITH ANY COMBAT SKILLS...
I WAS TOLD I COULDN'T FIGHT FOR THEM.
SO, I MOVED TO THIS PLOT OF LAND OUTSIDE OF THE HUMANS' DOMAIN, AND STARTED LIVING HERE SORT OF LIKE A HOMELESS PERSON.
MY WORD...
OH, THAT MUST HAVE BEEN SUCH A STRUGGLE!
WELL...
IT WASN'T THAT BAD.
BE-CAUSE...
SQUEEZE
THIS...
POP
A-A PLANT SPROUTED!!
IS THE GIFT THAT I RECEIVED FROM THE GODS.
AND I'M GRATEFUL, BECAUSE I'VE BEEN ABLE TO LIVE A QUIET, RURAL LIFE EVER SINCE.

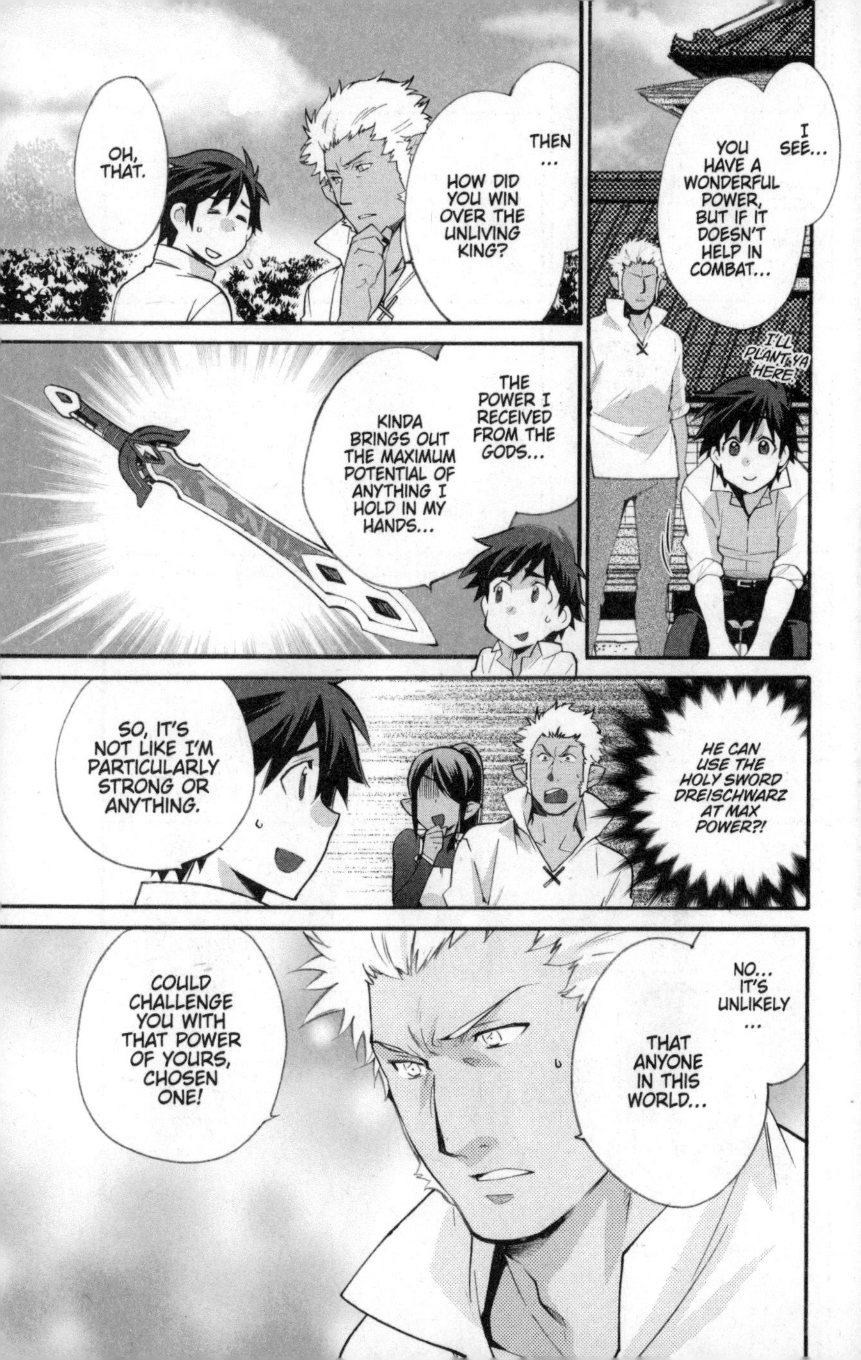
I SEE...
YOU HAVE A WONDERFUL POWER, BUT IF IT DOESN'T HELP IN COMBAT...
I'LL PLANT YA HERE.
THEN...
HOW DID YOU WIN OVER THE UNLIVING KING?
OH, THAT.
THE POWER I RECEIVED FROM THE GODS...
KINDA BRINGS OUT THE MAXIMUM POTENTIAL OF ANYTHING I HOLD IN MY HANDS...
HE CAN USE THE HOLY SWORD DREISCHWARZ AT MAX POWER?!
SO, IT'S NOT LIKE I'M PARTICULARLY STRONG OR ANYTHING.
NO... IT'S UNLIKELY...
THAT ANYONE IN THIS WORLD...
COULD CHALLENGE YOU WITH THAT POWER OF YOURS, CHOSEN ONE!

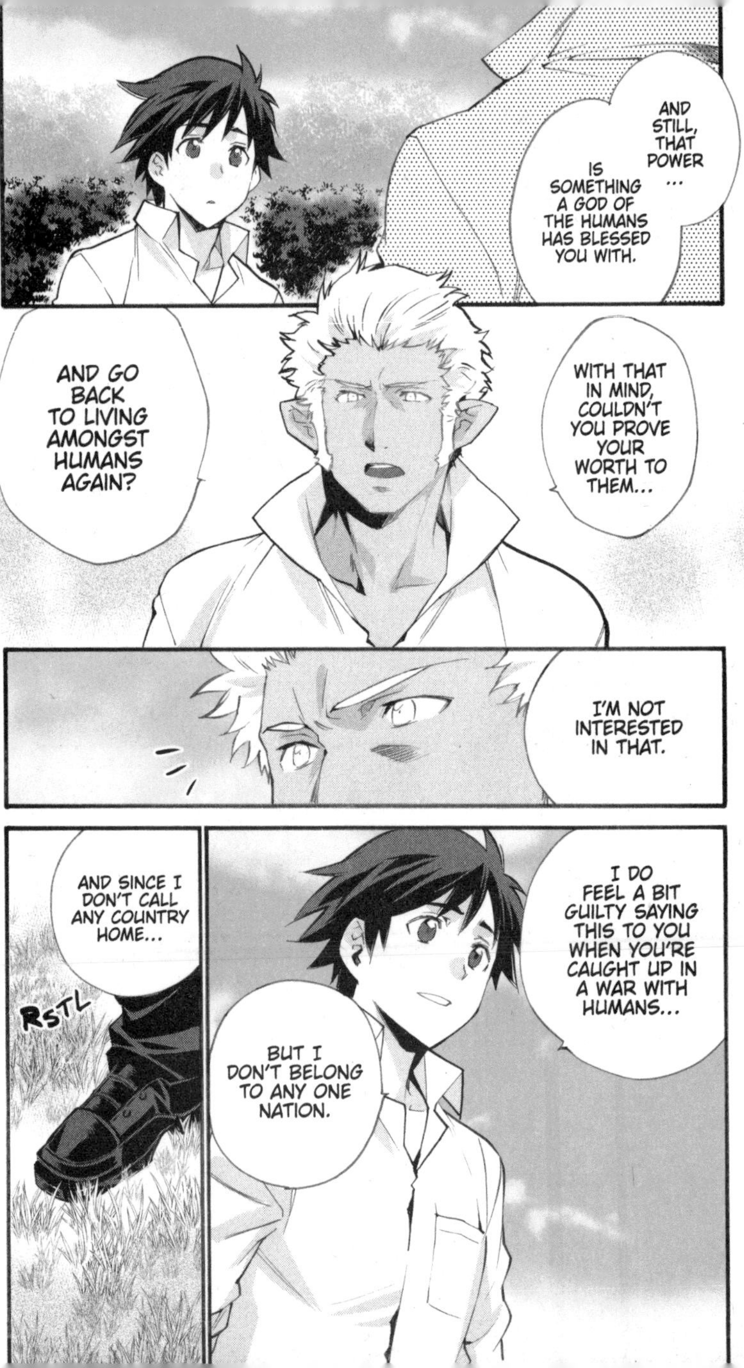
AND STILL, THAT POWER... IS SOMETHING A GOD OF THE HUMANS HAS BLESSED YOU WITH.
WITH THAT IN MIND, COULDN'T YOU PROVE YOUR WORTH TO THEM...
AND GO BACK TO LIVING AMONGST HUMANS AGAIN?
I'M NOT INTERESTED IN THAT.
I DO FEEL A BIT GUILTY SAYING THIS TO YOU WHEN YOU'RE CAUGHT UP IN A WAR WITH HUMANS...
BUT I DON'T BELONG TO ANY ONE NATION.
AND SINCE I DON'T CALL ANY COUNTRY HOME...
RSTL

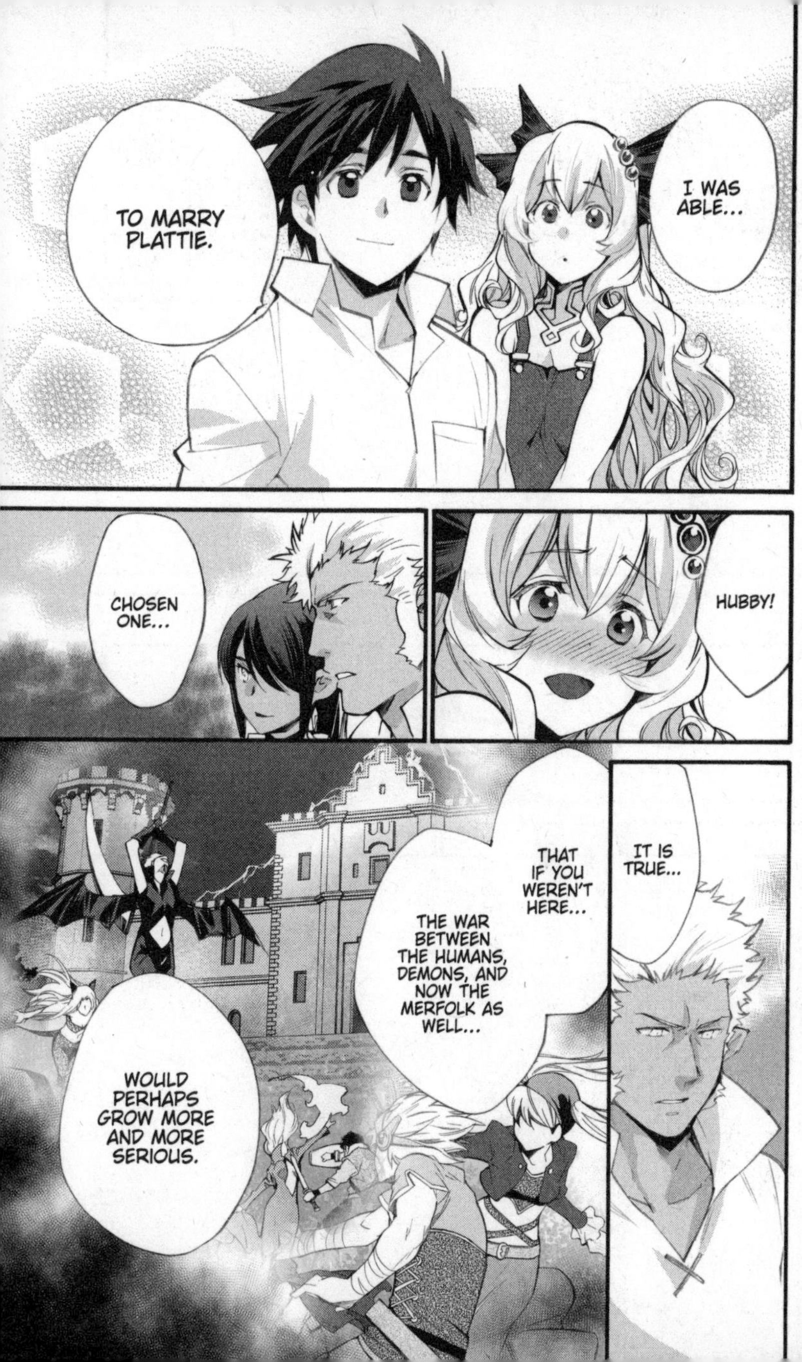
I WAS ABLE...
TO MARRY PLATTIE.
HUBBY!
CHOSEN ONE...
IT IS TRUE...
THAT IF YOU WEREN'T HERE...
THE WAR BETWEEN THE HUMANS, DEMONS, AND NOW THE MERFOLK AS WELL...
WOULD PERHAPS GROW MORE AND MORE SERIOUS.

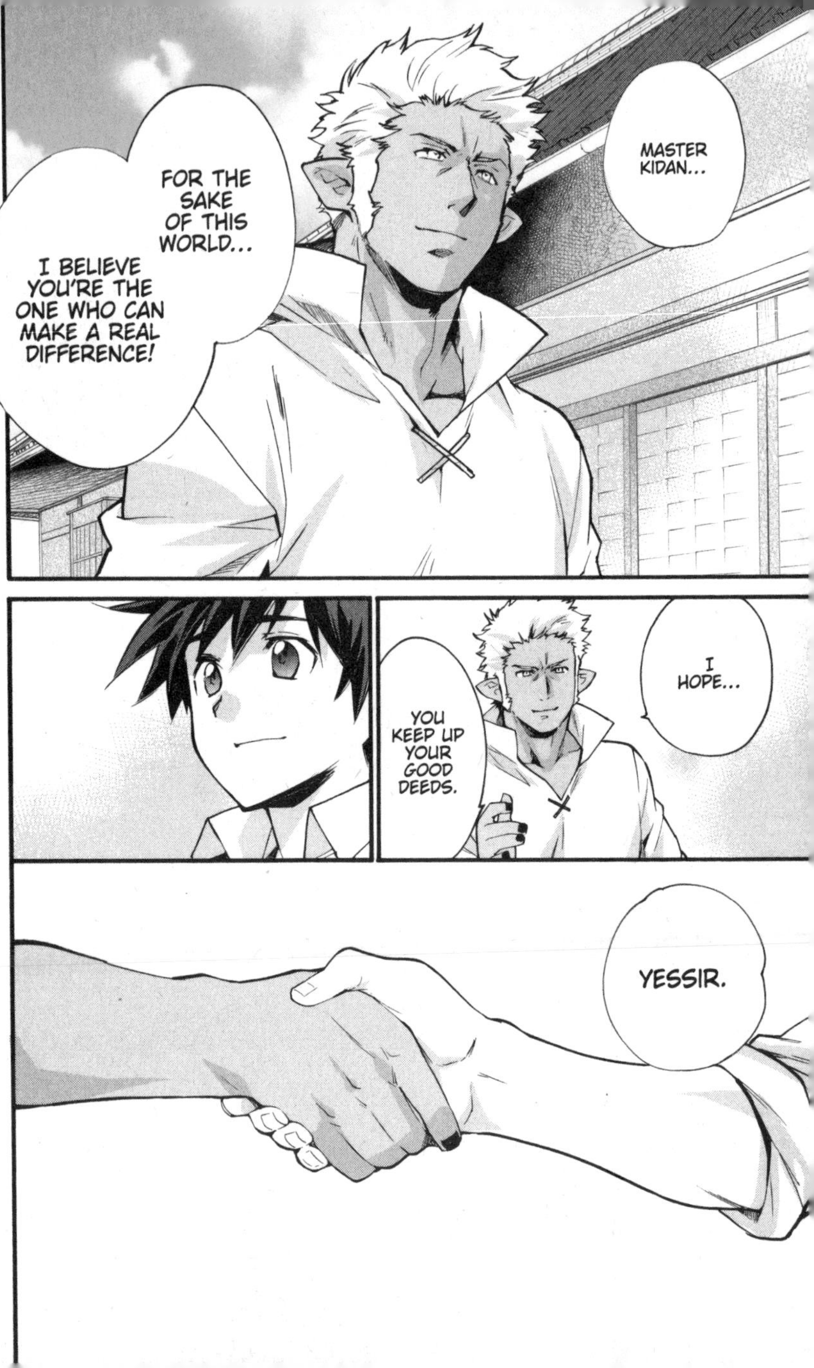
MASTER KIDAN...
FOR THE SAKE OF THIS WORLD... I BELIEVE YOU'RE THE ONE WHO CAN MAKE A REAL DIFFERENCE!
I HOPE...
YOU KEEP UP YOUR GOOD DEEDS.
YESSIR.

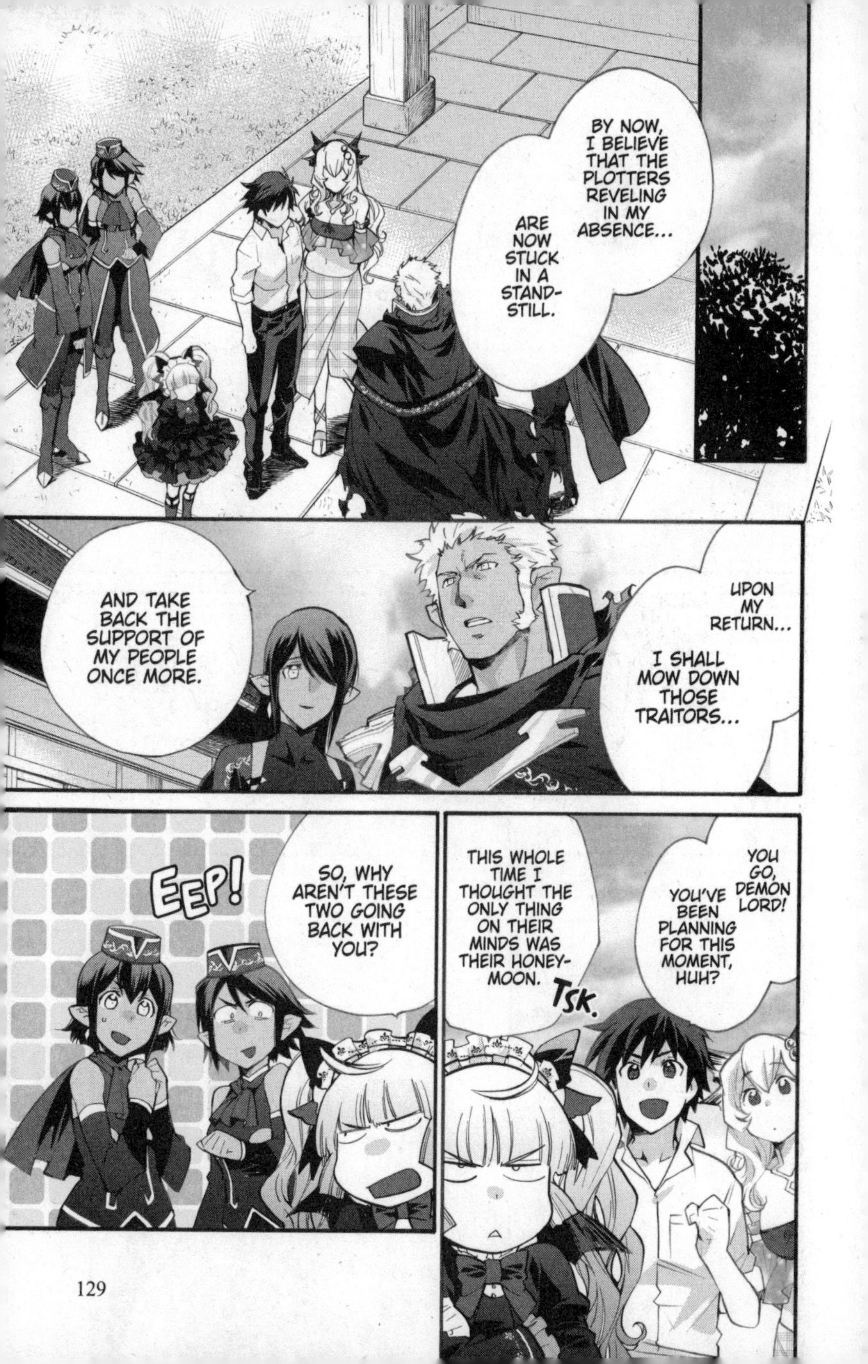
BY NOW, I BELIEVE THAT THE PLOTTERS REVELING IN MY ABSENCE...
ARE NOW STUCK IN A STAND-STILL.
UPON MY RETURN...
I SHALL MOW DOWN THOSE TRAITORS...
AND TAKE BACK THE SUPPORT OF MY PEOPLE ONCE MORE.
YOU GO, DEMON LORD!
YOU'VE BEEN PLANNING FOR THIS MOMENT, HUH?
THIS WHOLE TIME I THOUGHT THE ONLY THING ON THEIR MINDS WAS THEIR HONEY-MOON.
TSK.
SO, WHY AREN'T THESE TWO GOING BACK WITH YOU?
EEP!

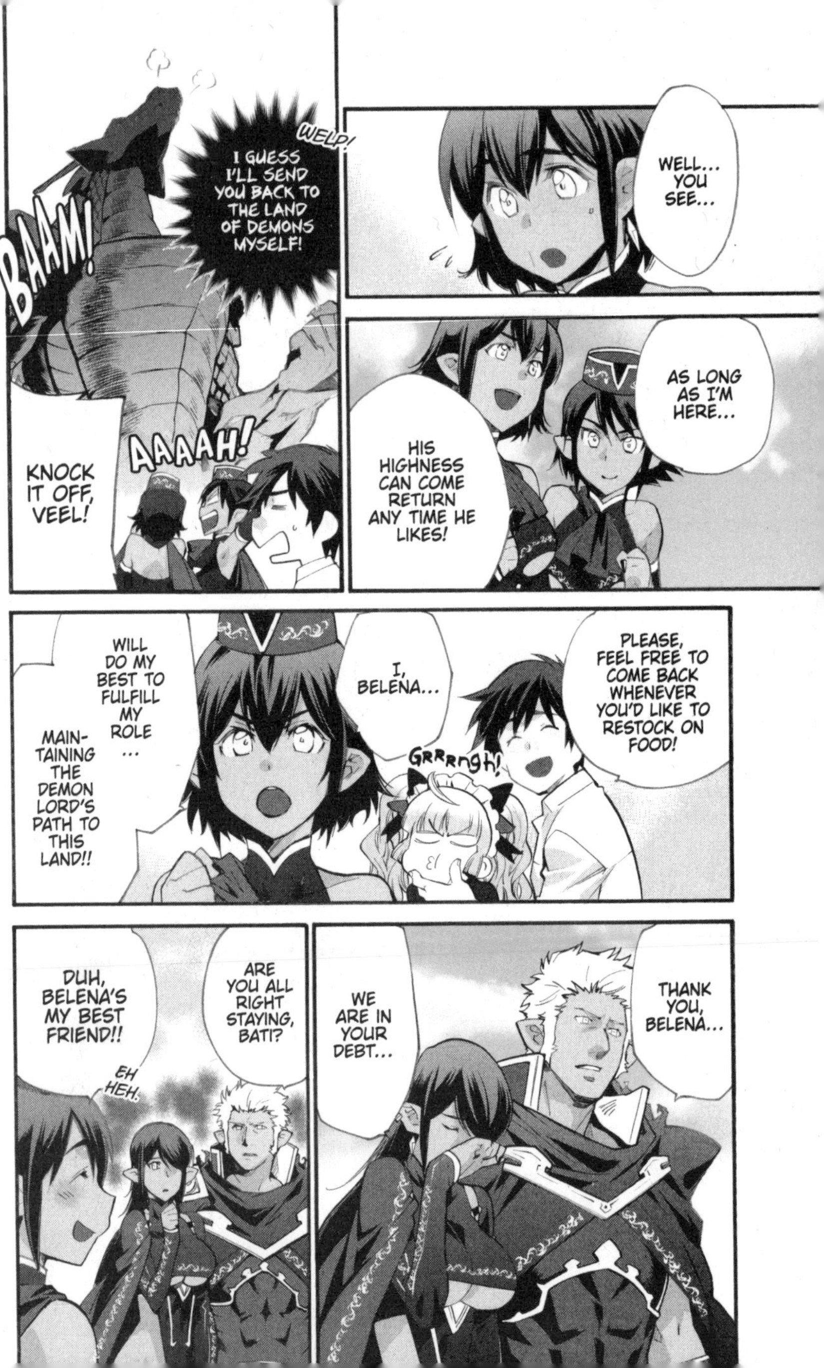
WELL... YOU SEE...
AS LONG AS I'M HERE...
HIS HIGHNESS CAN COME RETURN ANY TIME HE LIKES!
WELP!
I GUESS I'LL SEND YOU BACK TO THE LAND OF DEMONS MYSELF!
BAAM!
AAAAH!
KNOCK IT OFF, VEEL!
PLEASE, FEEL FREE TO COME BACK WHENEVER YOU'D LIKE TO RESTOCK ON FOOD!
GRRRNGH!
I, BELENA...
WILL DO MY BEST TO FULFILL MY ROLE...
MAIN-TAINING THE DEMON LORD'S PATH TO THIS LAND!!
THANK YOU, BELENA...
WE ARE IN YOUR DEBT...
ARE YOU ALL RIGHT STAYING, BATI?
DUH, BELENA'S MY BEST FRIEND!!
EH HEH.

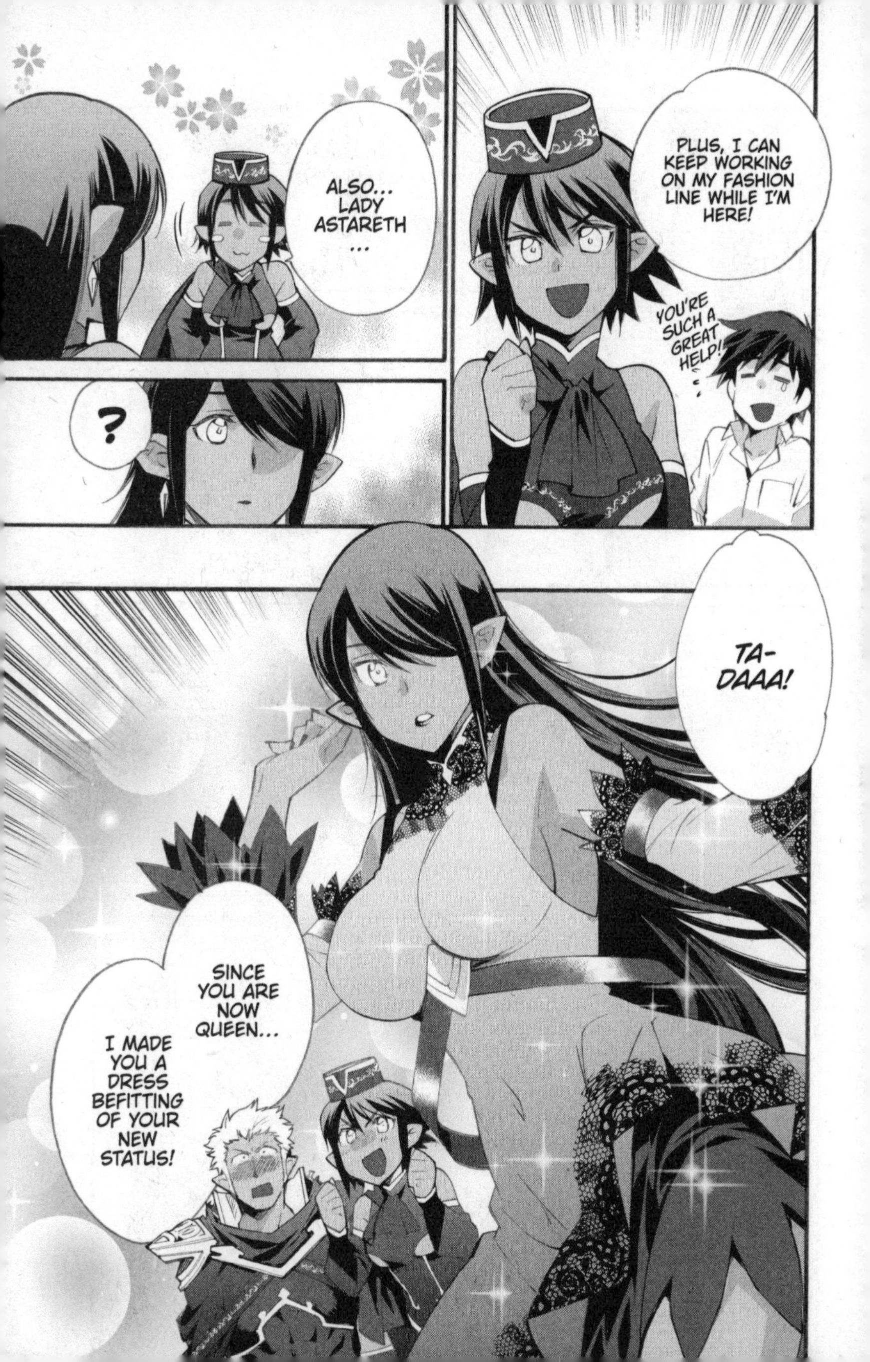
PLUS, I CAN KEEP WORKING ON MY FASHION LINE WHILE I'M HERE!
YOU'RE SUCH A GREAT HELP!
ALSO... LADY ASTARETH ...
?
TA-DAAA!
SINCE YOU ARE NOW QUEEN...
I MADE YOU A DRESS BEFITTING OF YOUR NEW STATUS!

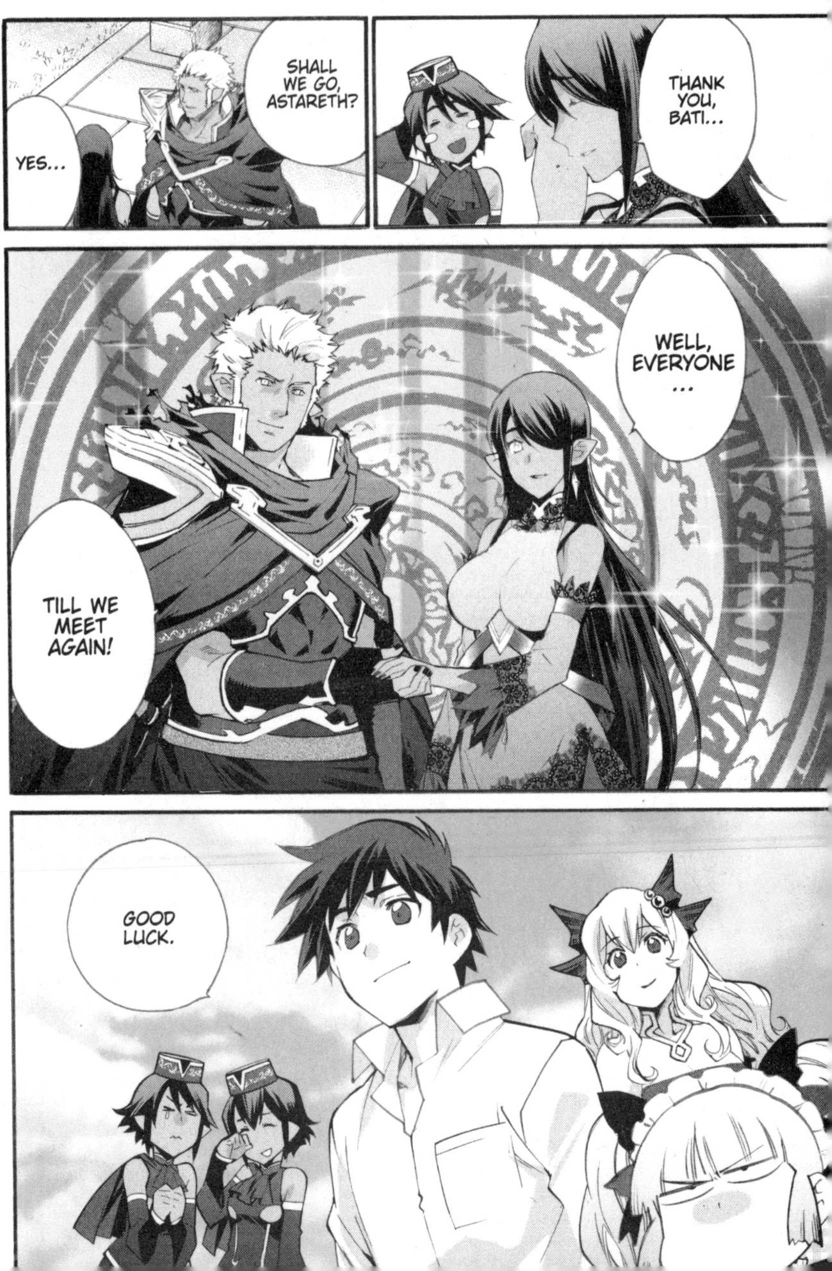
THANK YOU, BATI...
SHALL WE GO, ASTARETH?
YES...
WELL, EVERYONE ...
TILL WE MEET AGAIN!
GOOD LUCK.

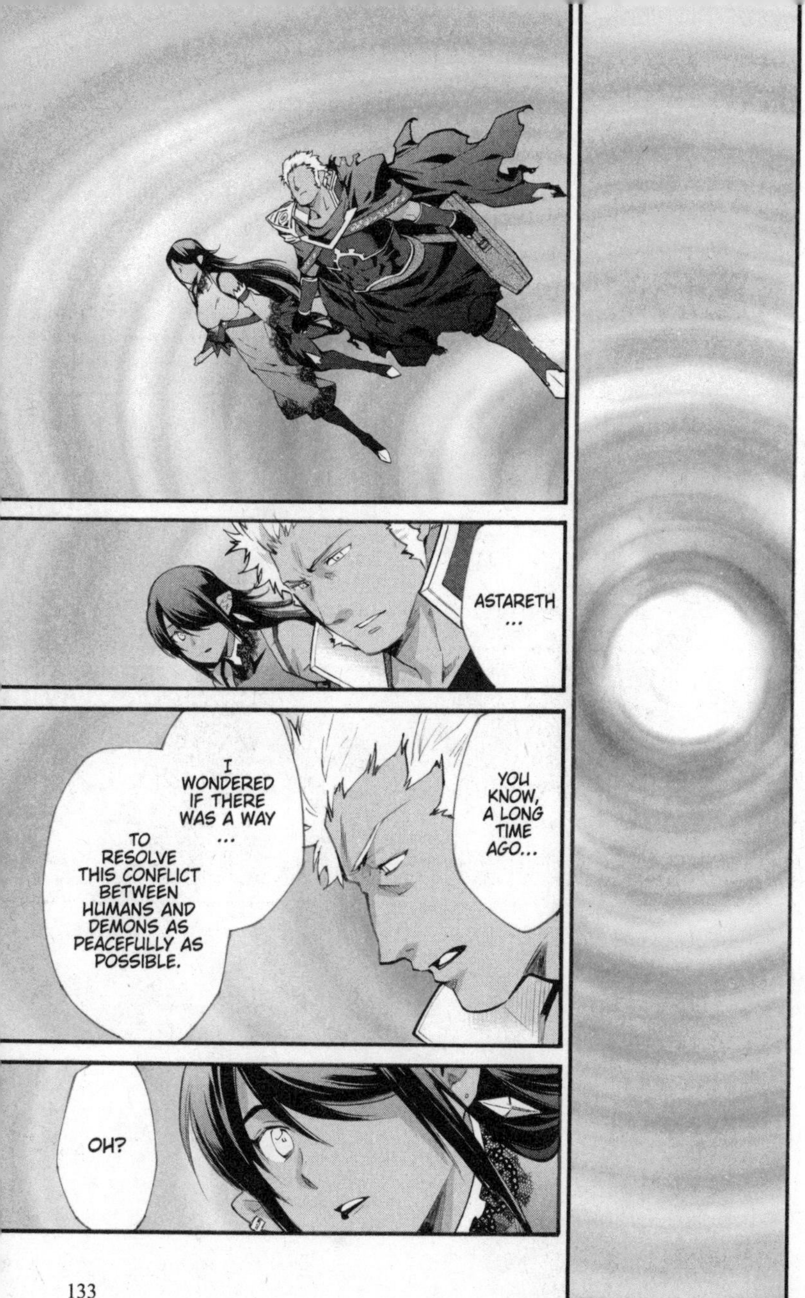

ASTARETH ...
YOU KNOW, A LONG TIME AGO...
I WONDERED IF THERE WAS A WAY ...
TO RESOLVE THIS CONFLICT BETWEEN HUMANS AND DEMONS AS PEACEFULLY AS POSSIBLE.
OH?

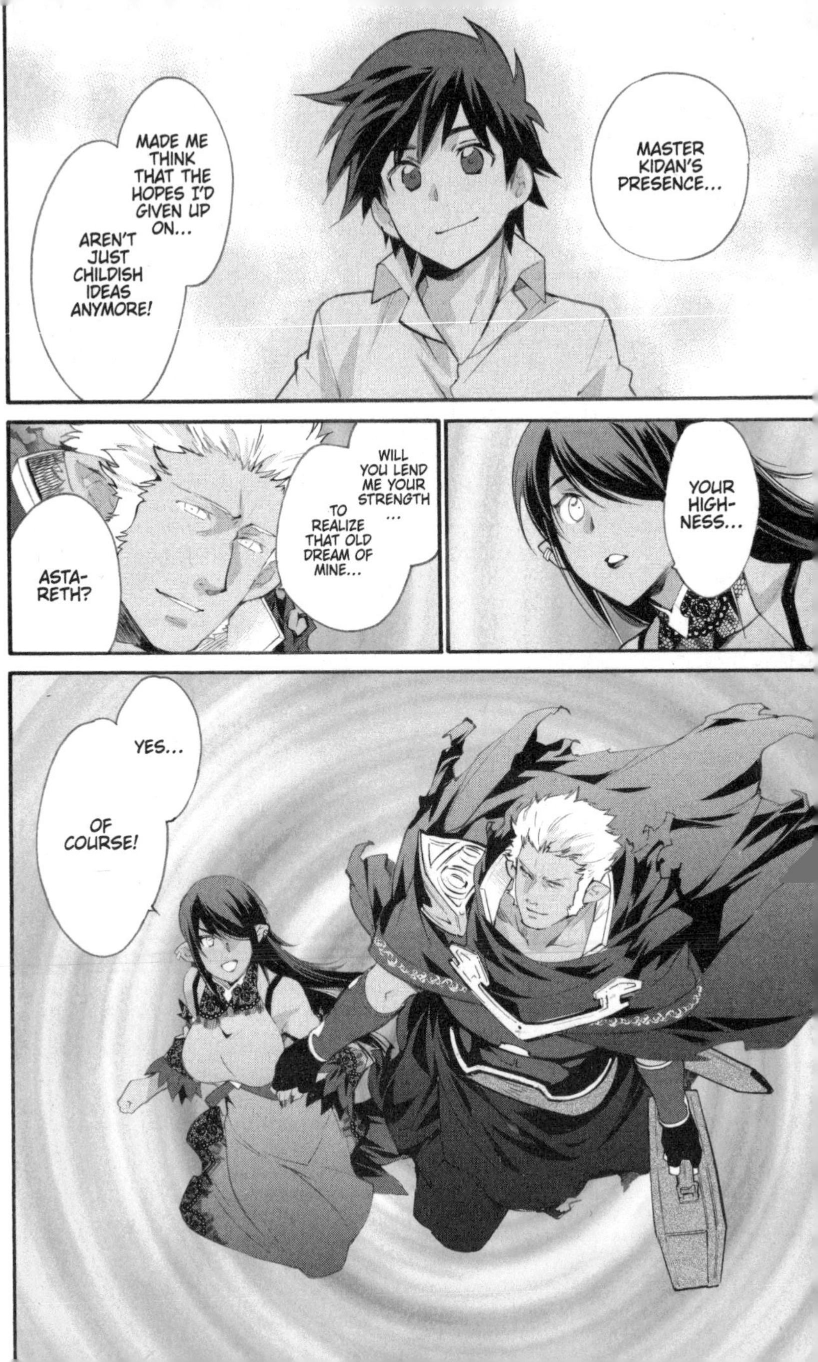
MASTER KIDAN'S PRESENCE...
MADE ME THINK THAT THE HOPES I'D GIVEN UP ON...
AREN'T JUST CHILDISH IDEAS ANYMORE!
YOUR HIGH-NESS...
WILL YOU LEND ME YOUR STRENGTH...
TO REALIZE THAT OLD DREAM OF MINE...
ASTA-RETH?
YES...
OF COURSE!

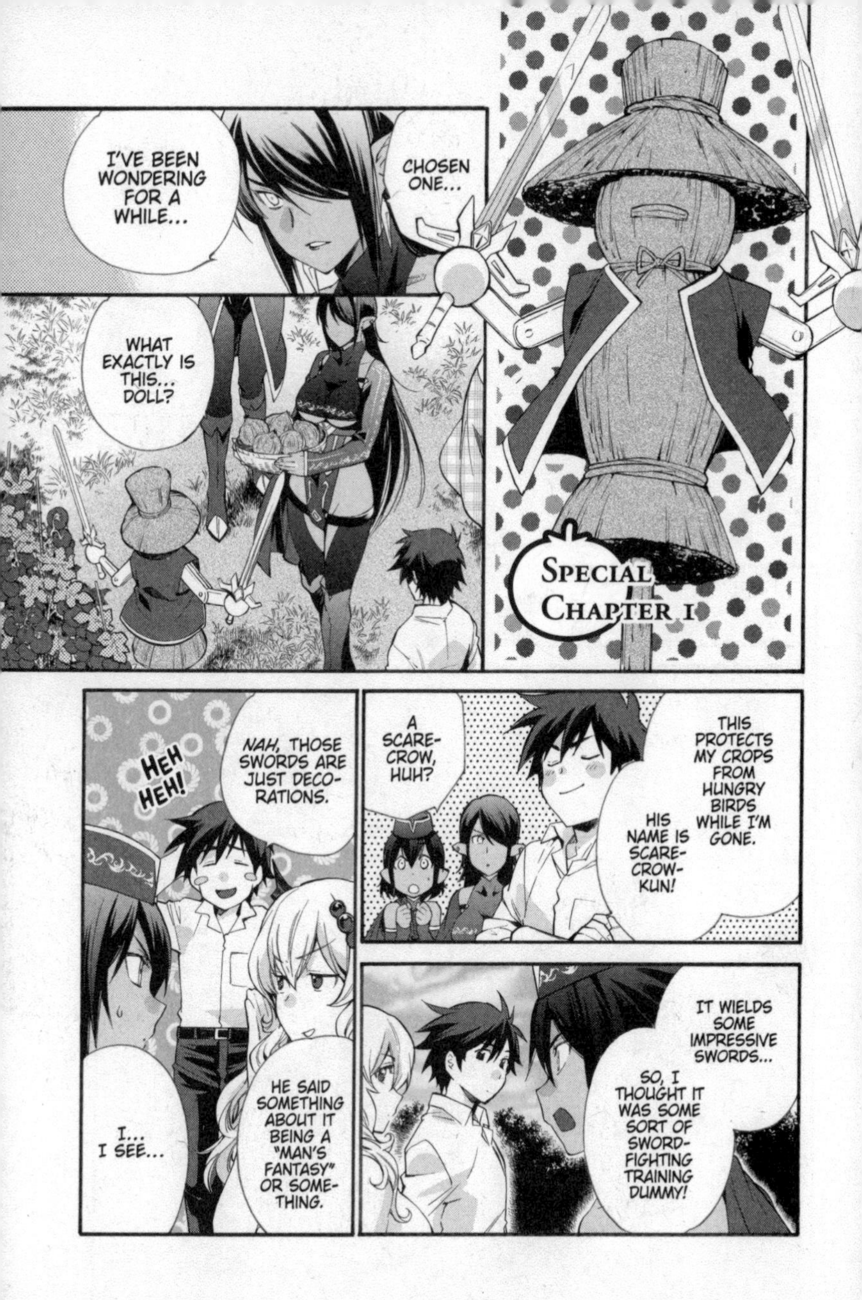
SPECIAL CHAPTER 1
CHOSEN ONE...
I'VE BEEN WONDERING FOR A WHILE...
WHAT EXACTLY IS THIS... DOLL?
THIS PROTECTS MY CROPS FROM HUNGRY BIRDS WHILE I'M GONE.
HIS NAME IS SCARE-CROW-KUN!
A SCARE-CROW, HUH?
IT WIELDS SOME IMPRESSIVE SWORDS...
SO, I THOUGHT IT WAS SOME SORT OF SWORD-FIGHTING TRAINING DUMMY!
NAH, THOSE SWORDS ARE JUST DECO-RATIONS.
HEH HEH!
HE SAID SOMETHING ABOUT IT BEING A "MAN'S FANTASY" OR SOME-THING.
I... I SEE...

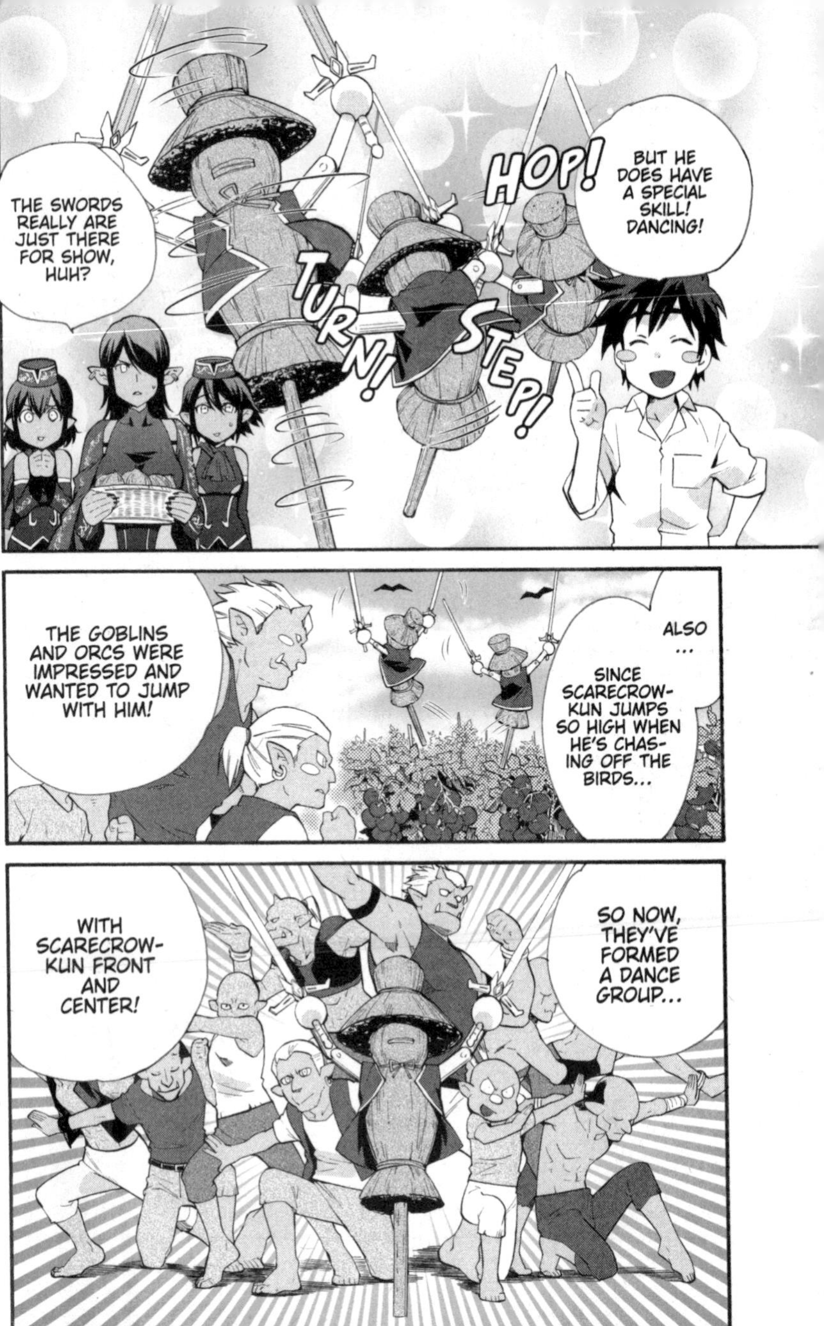
BUT HE DOES HAVE A SPECIAL SKILL! DANCING!
HOP!
STEP!
TURN!
THE SWORDS REALLY ARE JUST THERE FOR SHOW, HUH?
ALSO... SINCE SCARECROW-KUN JUMPS SO HIGH WHEN HE'S CHASING OFF THE BIRDS...
THE GOBLINS AND ORCS WERE IMPRESSED AND WANTED TO JUMP WITH HIM!
SO NOW, THEY'VE FORMED A DANCE GROUP...
WITH SCARECROW-KUN FRONT AND CENTER!

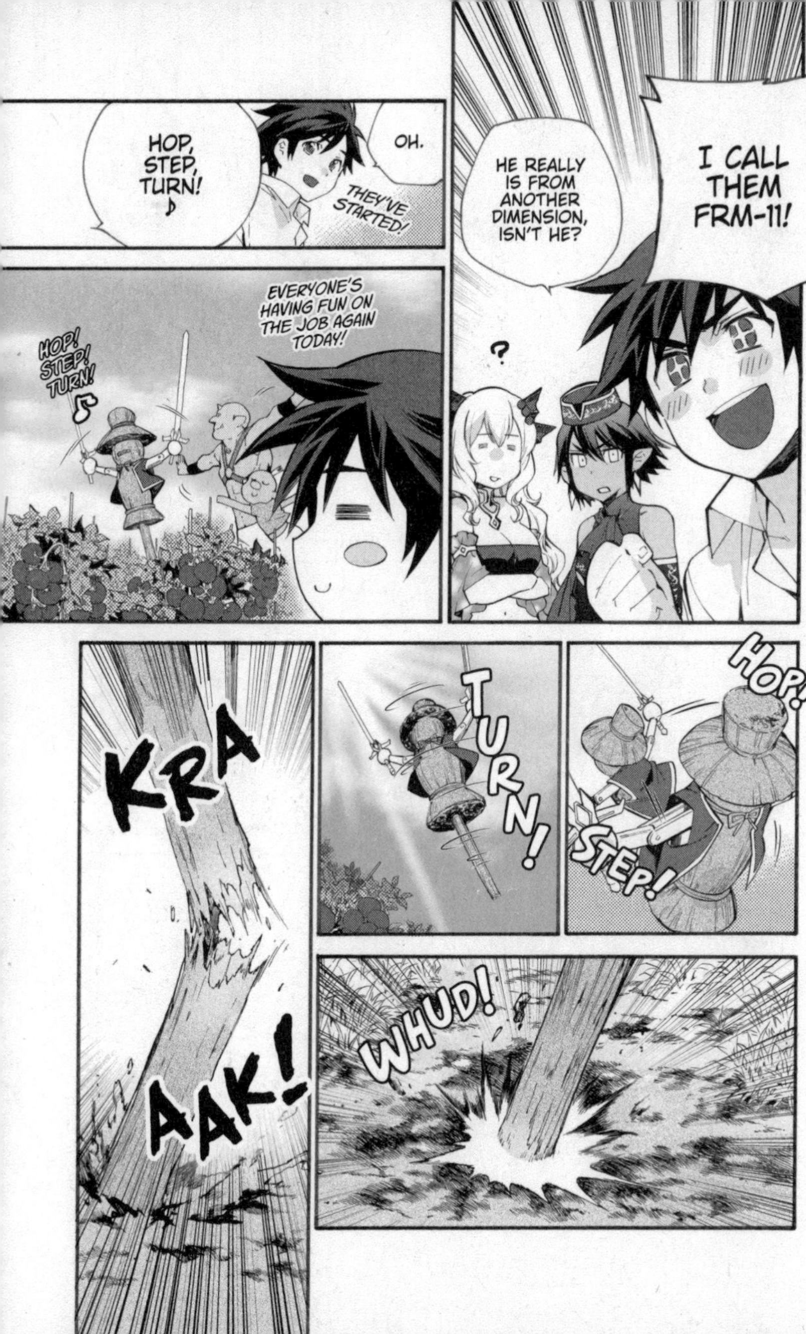
I CALL THEM FRM-11!
HE REALLY IS FROM ANOTHER DIMENSION, ISN'T HE?
?
OH.
THEY'VE STARTED!
HOP, STEP, TURN! ♪
EVERYONE'S HAVING FUN ON THE JOB AGAIN TODAY!
HOP! STEP! TURN! ♪
HOP!
STEP!
TURN!
WHUD!
KRAAAK!

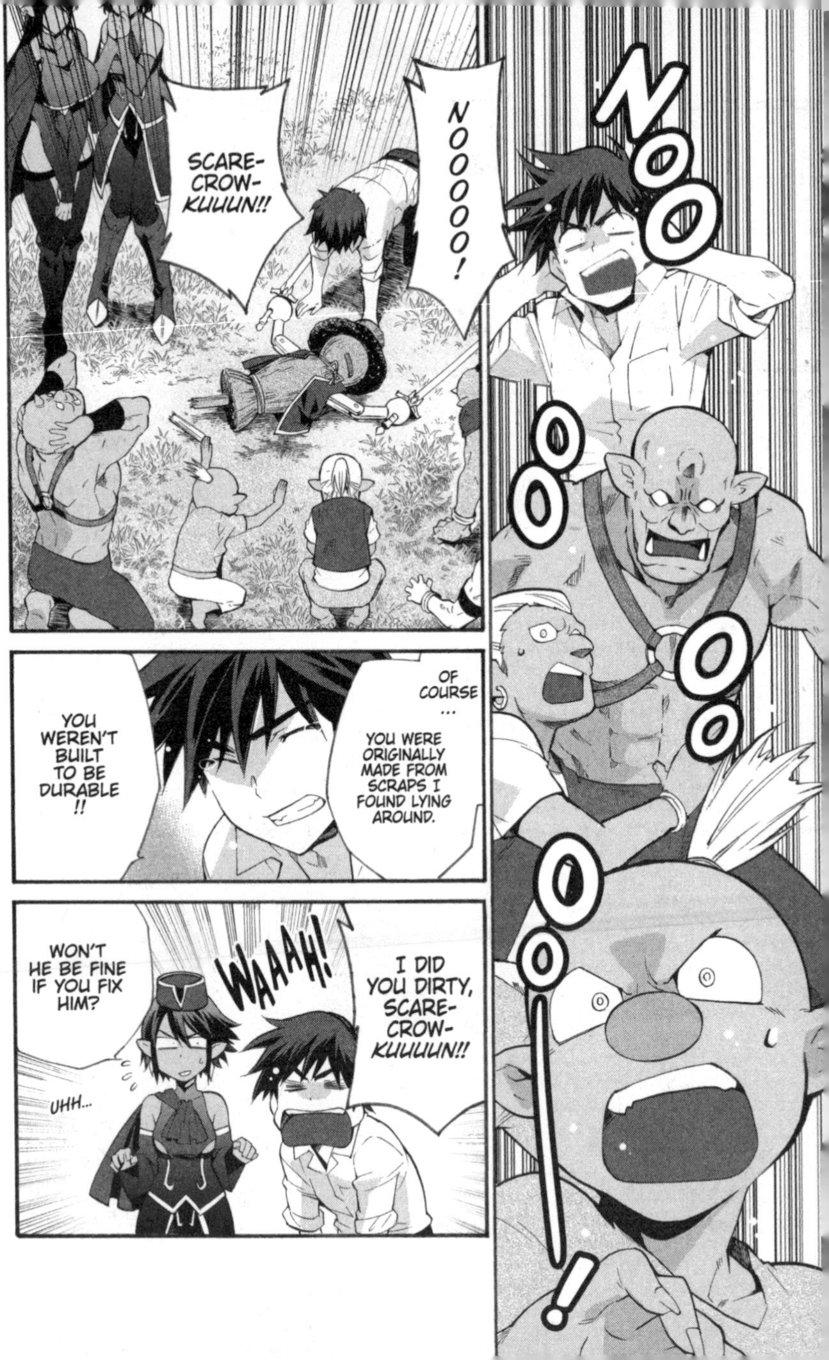
NOOOOOOOOOO—!
NOOOOOO!
SCARE-CROW-KUUUN!!
OF COURSE...
YOU WERE ORIGINALLY MADE FROM SCRAPS I FOUND LYING AROUND.
YOU WEREN'T BUILT TO BE DURABLE!!
I DID YOU DIRTY, SCARE-CROW-KUUUUN!!
WAAAH!
WON'T HE BE FINE IF YOU FIX HIM?
UHH...

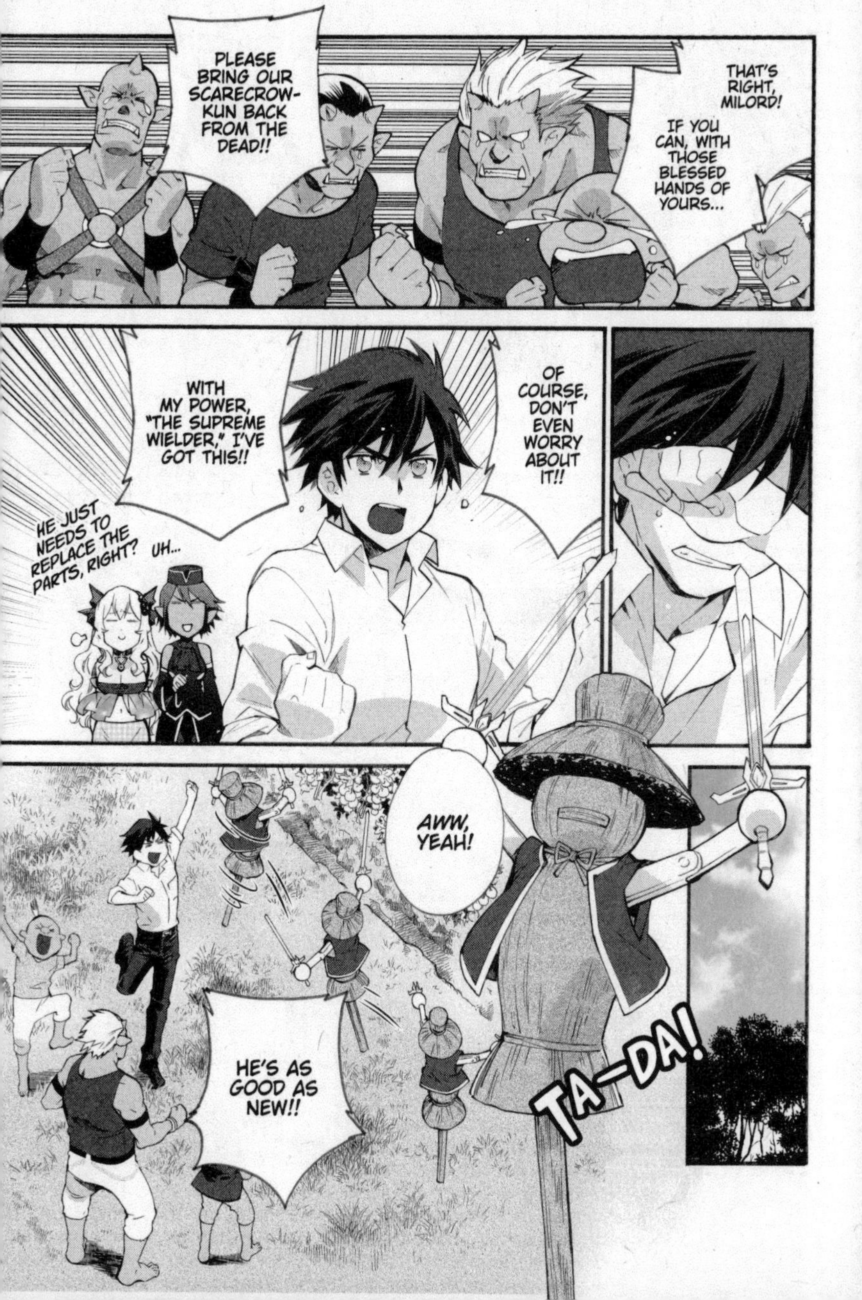
THAT'S RIGHT, MILORD!
IF YOU CAN, WITH THOSE BLESSED HANDS OF YOURS...
PLEASE BRING OUR SCARECROW-KUN BACK FROM THE DEAD!!
OF COURSE, DON'T EVEN WORRY ABOUT IT!!
WITH MY POWER, "THE SUPREME WIELDER," I'VE GOT THIS!!
HE JUST NEEDS TO REPLACE THE PARTS, RIGHT?
UH...
TA-DA!
AWW, YEAH!
HE'S AS GOOD AS NEW!!

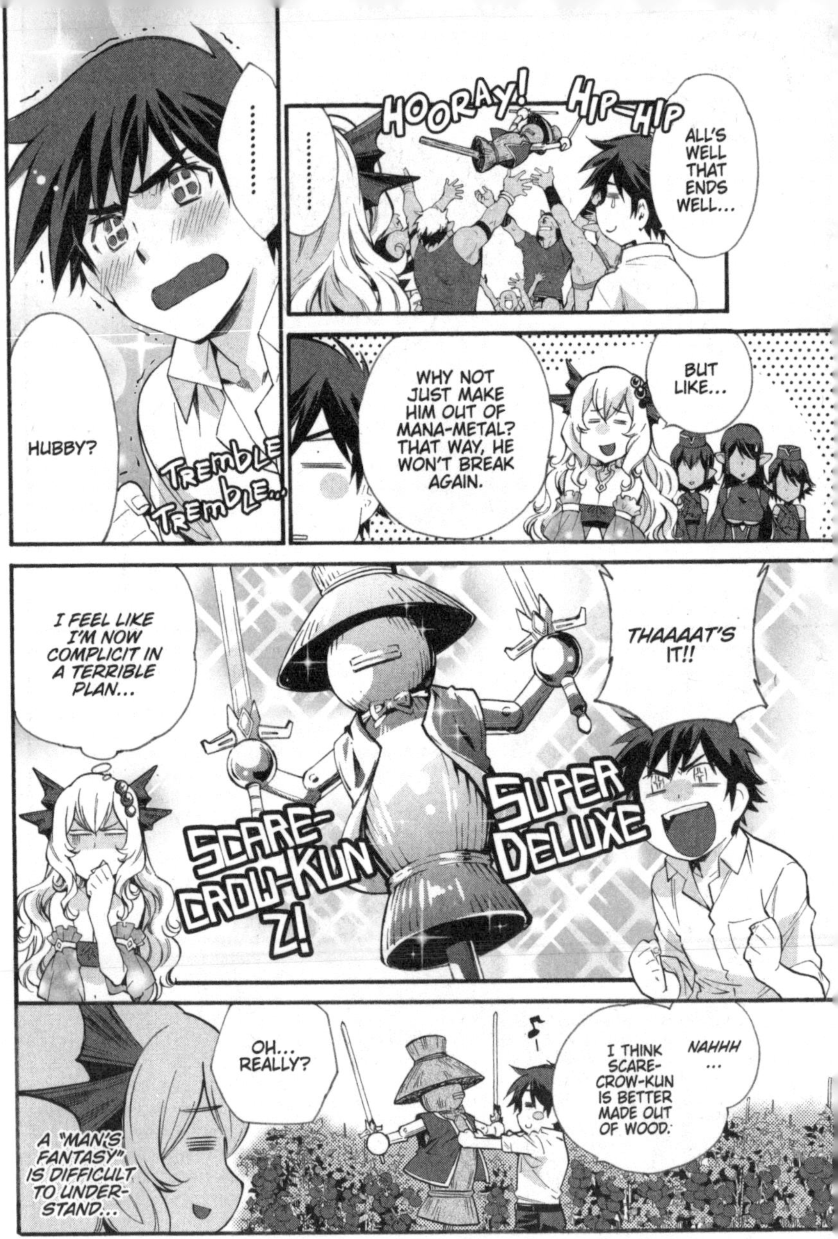
ALL'S WELL THAT ENDS WELL...
HIP-HIP HOORAY!
......
BUT LIKE...
WHY NOT JUST MAKE HIM OUT OF MANA-METAL? THAT WAY, HE WON'T BREAK AGAIN.
......
HUBBY?
TREMBLE TREMBLE...
THAAAAT'S IT!!
SUPER DELUXE
SCARE-CROW-KUN Z!
I FEEL LIKE I'M NOW COMPLICIT IN A TERRIBLE PLAN...
NAHHH...
I THINK SCARE-CROW-KUN IS BETTER MADE OUT OF WOOD.
OH... REALLY?
A "MAN'S FANTASY" IS DIFFICULT TO UNDER-STAND...

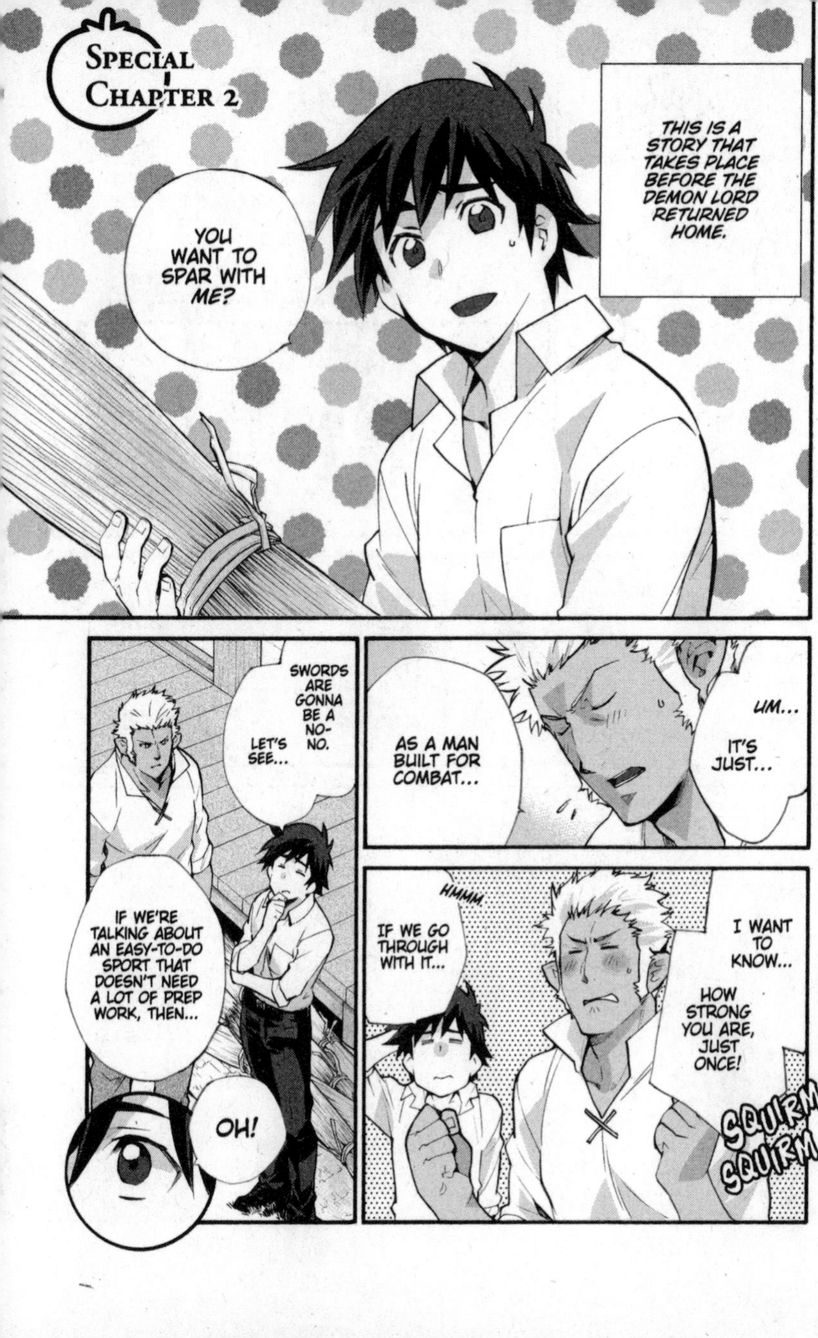
SPECIAL CHAPTER 2
THIS IS A STORY THAT TAKES PLACE BEFORE THE DEMON LORD RETURNED HOME.
YOU WANT TO SPAR WITH ME?
UM... IT'S JUST...
AS A MAN BUILT FOR COMBAT...
I WANT TO KNOW... HOW STRONG YOU ARE, JUST ONCE!
SQUIRM SQUIRM
HMMM
IF WE GO THROUGH WITH IT...
SWORDS ARE GONNA BE A NO-NO.
LET'S SEE...
IF WE'RE TALKING ABOUT AN EASY-TO-DO SPORT THAT DOESN'T NEED A LOT OF PREP WORK, THEN...
OH!

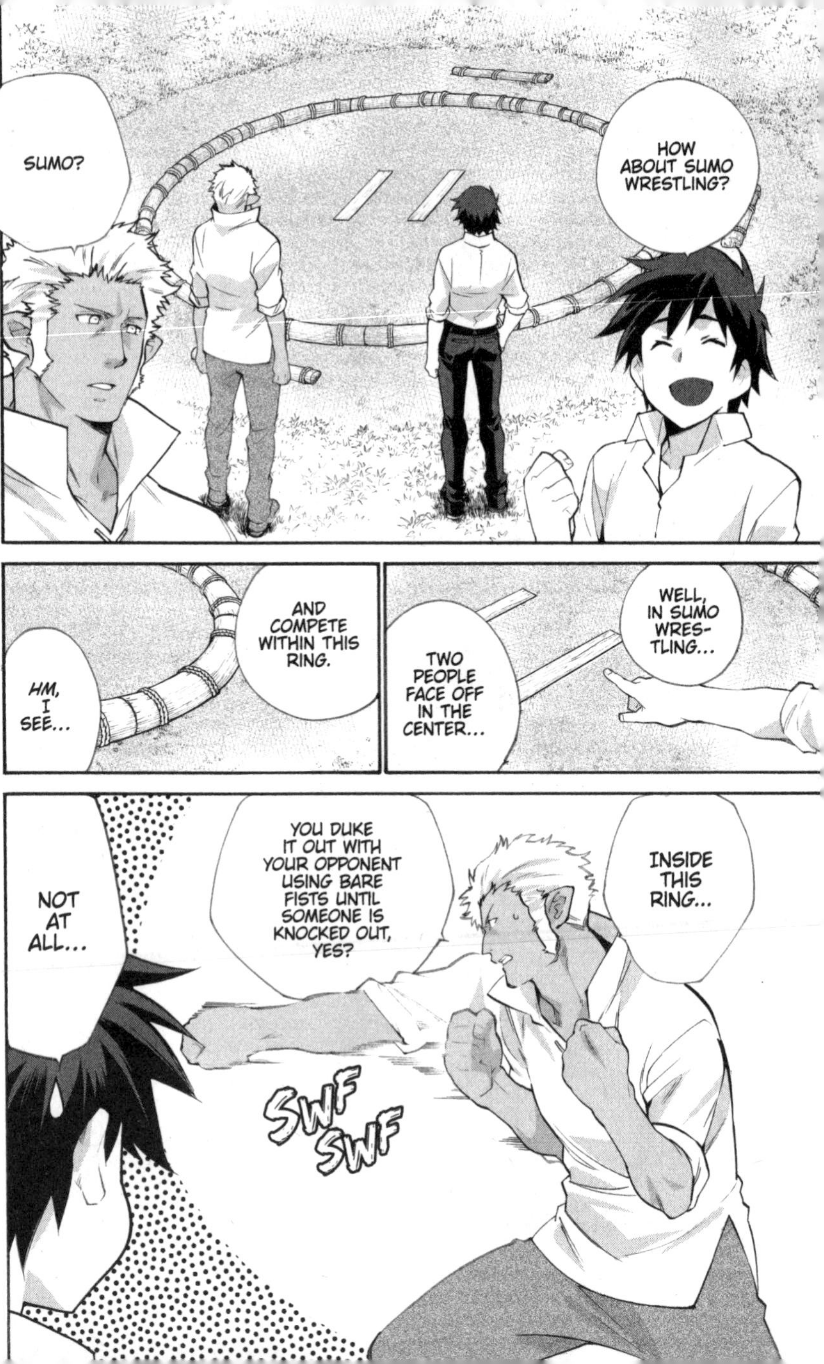
HOW ABOUT SUMO WRESTLING?
SUMO?
WELL, IN SUMO WRES-TLING...
TWO PEOPLE FACE OFF IN THE CENTER...
AND COMPETE WITHIN THIS RING.
HM, I SEE...
INSIDE THIS RING...
YOU DUKE IT OUT WITH YOUR OPPONENT USING BARE FISTS UNTIL SOMEONE IS KNOCKED OUT, YES?
SWF SWF
NOT AT ALL...

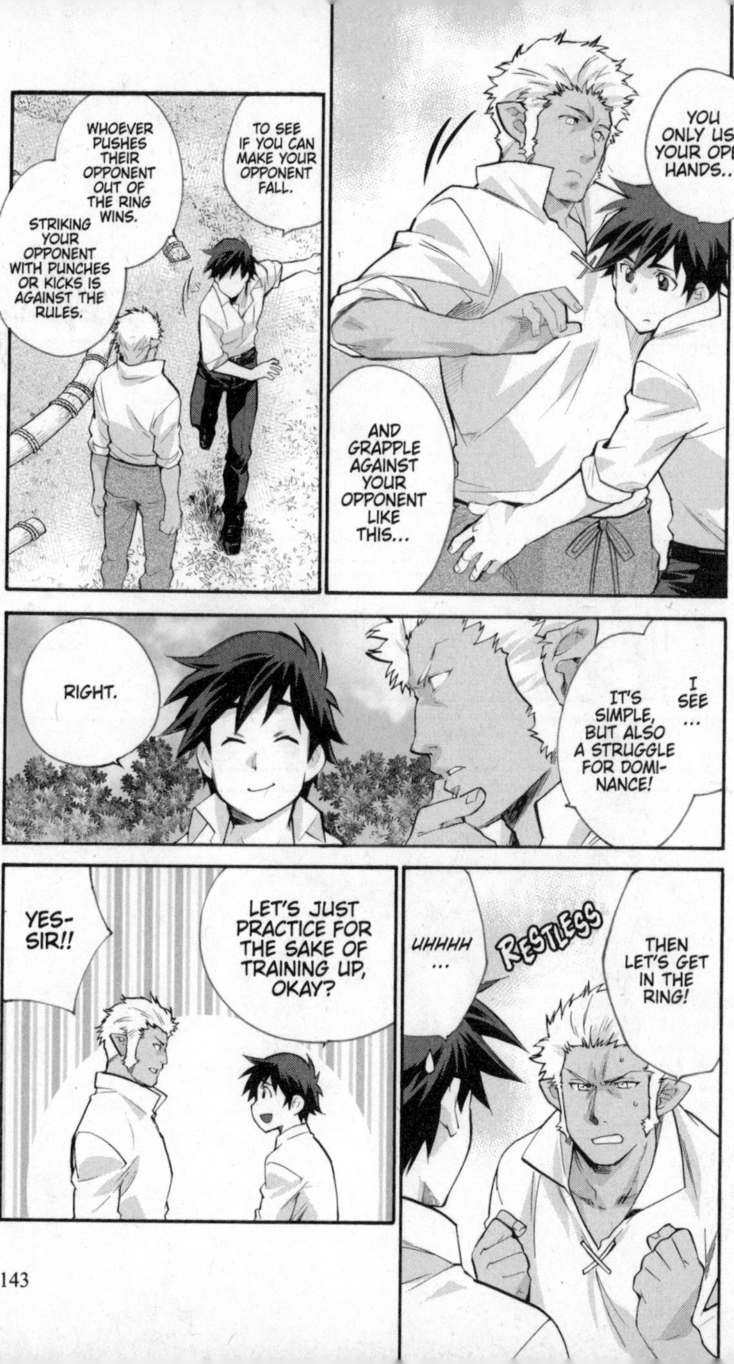
YOU ONLY USE YOUR OPEN HANDS...
AND GRAPPLE AGAINST YOUR OPPONENT LIKE THIS...
TO SEE IF YOU CAN MAKE YOUR OPPONENT FALL.
WHOEVER PUSHES THEIR OPPONENT OUT OF THE RING WINS.
STRIKING YOUR OPPONENT WITH PUNCHES OR KICKS IS AGAINST THE RULES.
I SEE...
IT'S SIMPLE, BUT ALSO A STRUGGLE FOR DOMINANCE!
RIGHT.
THEN LET'S GET IN THE RING!
RESTLESS
UHHHH...
LET'S JUST PRACTICE FOR THE SAKE OF TRAINING UP, OKAY?
YES-SIR!!

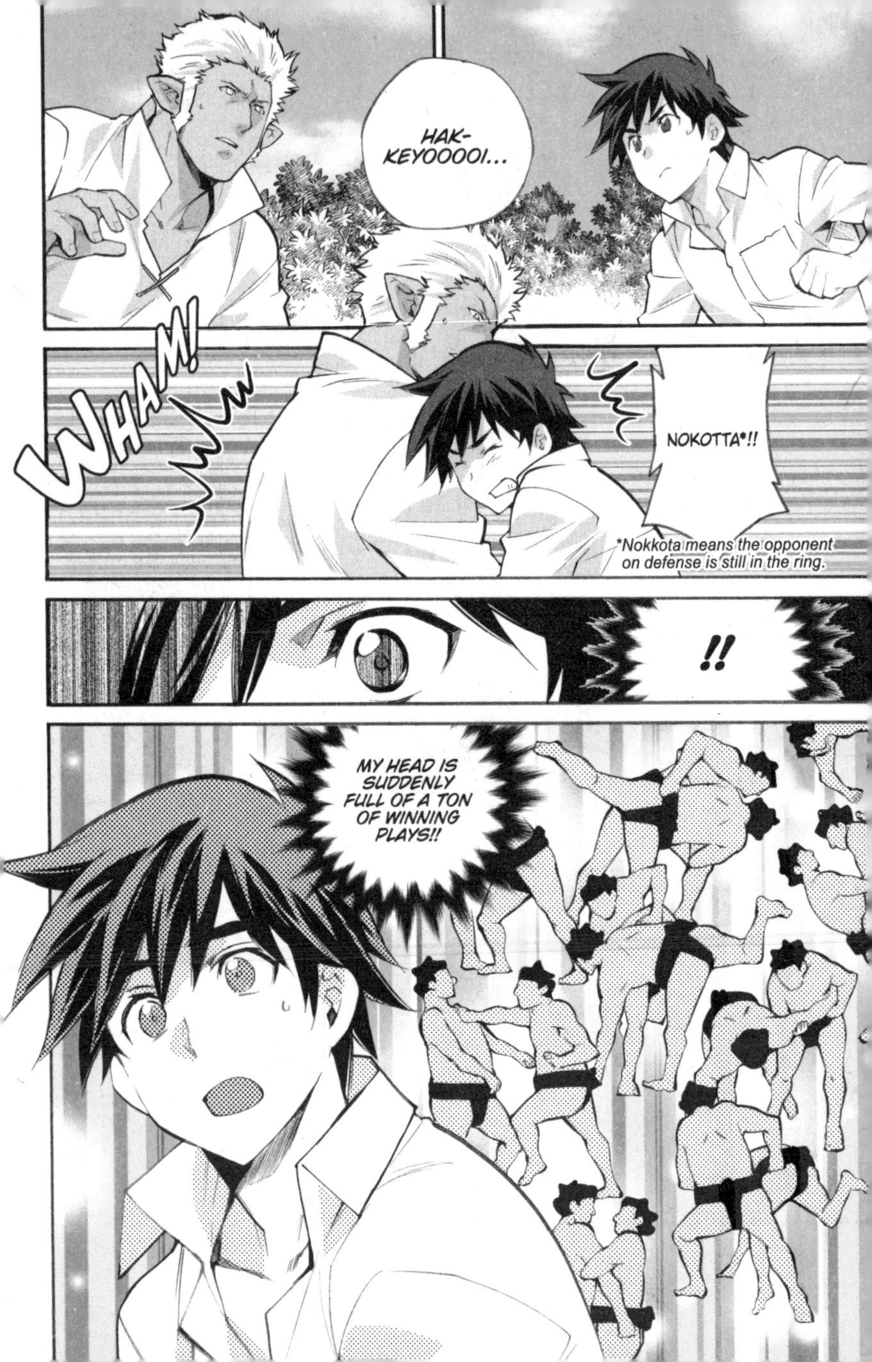
HAK-KEYOOOOI...
NOKOTTA*!!
WHAM!
*Nokkota means the opponent on defense is still in the ring.
!!
MY HEAD IS SUDDENLY FULL OF A TON OF WINNING PLAYS!!

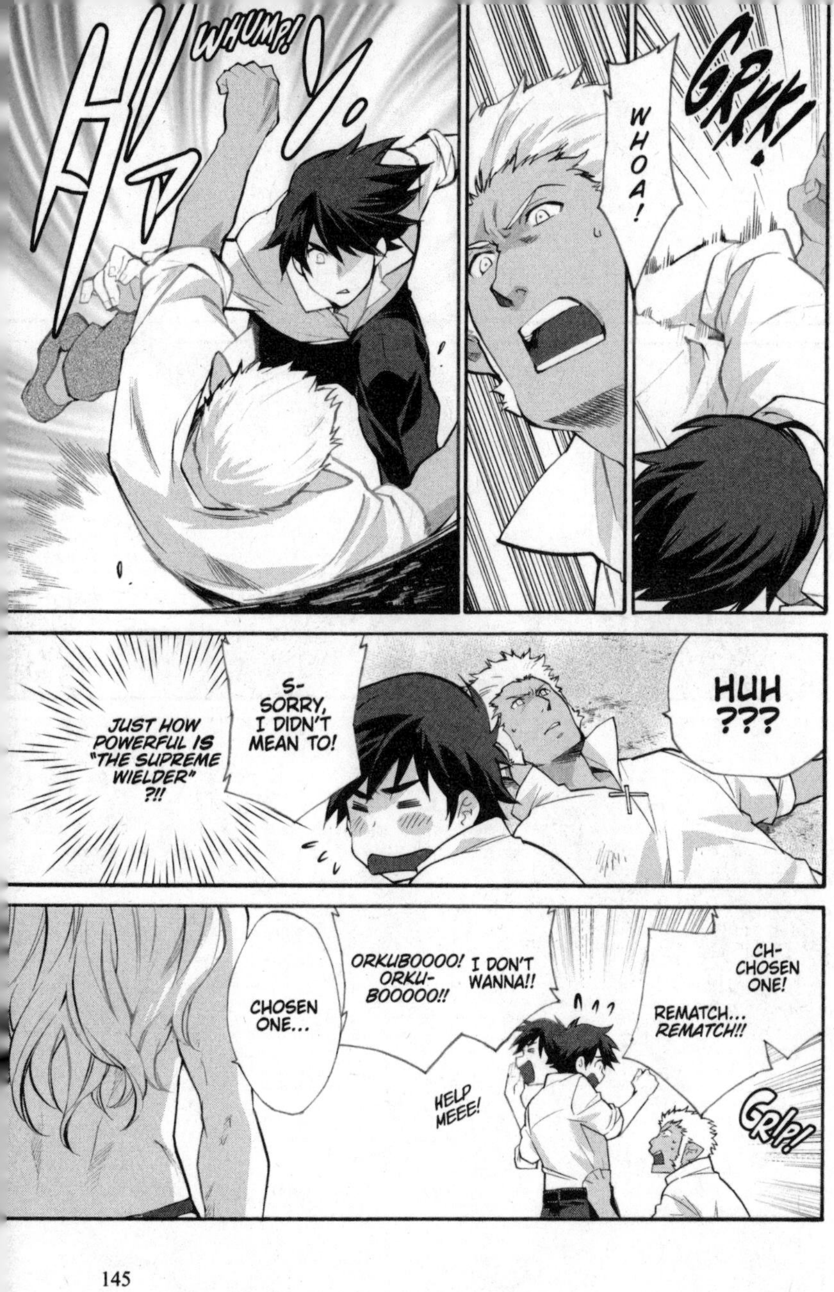
GRK!
WHOA!
WHUMP!
HUH ???
S-SORRY, I DIDN'T MEAN TO!
JUST HOW POWERFUL IS "THE SUPREME WIELDER" ?!!
CH-CHOSEN ONE!
REMATCH... REMATCH!!
GRIP!
I DON'T WANNA!!
HELP MEEE!
ORKUBOOOO! ORKU-BOOOOO!!
CHOSEN ONE...

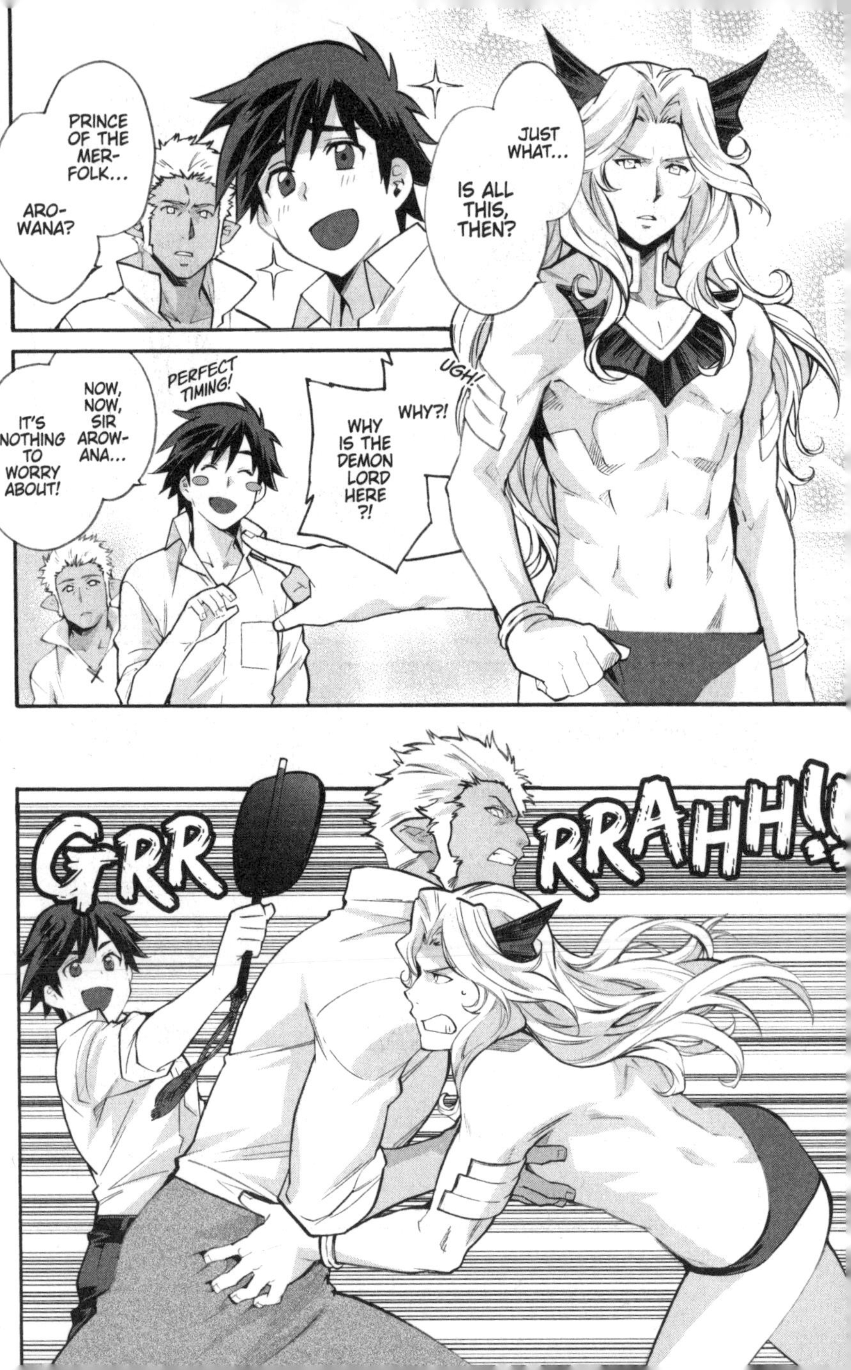
JUST WHAT... IS ALL THIS, THEN?
PRINCE OF THE MERFOLK... ARO-WANA?
UGH!
WHY?!
WHY IS THE DEMON LORD HERE?!
PERFECT TIMING!
NOW, NOW, SIR AROW-ANA...
IT'S NOTHING TO WORRY ABOUT!
GRR RRAHH!!

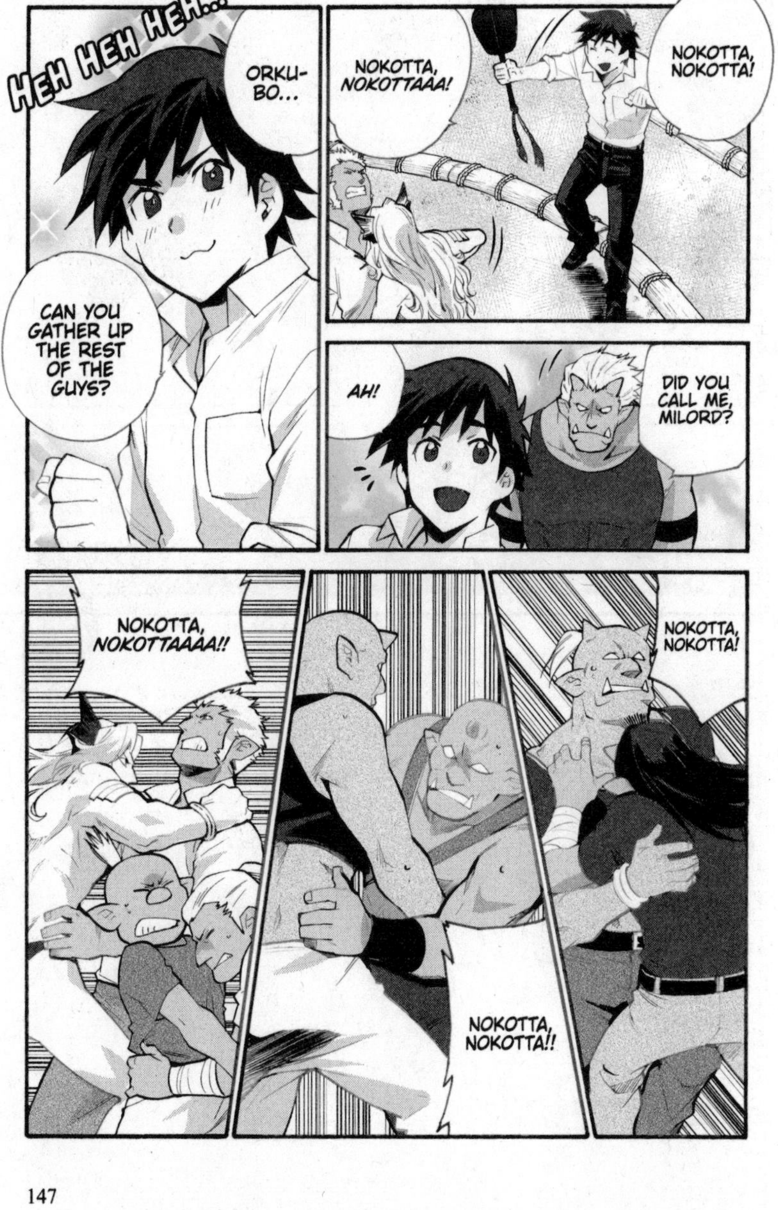
NOKOTTA, NOKOTTA!
NOKOTTA, NOKOTTAAA!
DID YOU CALL ME, MILORD?
AH!
HEH HEH HEH...
ORKU-BO...
CAN YOU GATHER UP THE REST OF THE GUYS?
NOKOTTA, NOKOTTA!
NOKOTTA, NOKOTTA!!
NOKOTTA, NOKOTTAAAA!!

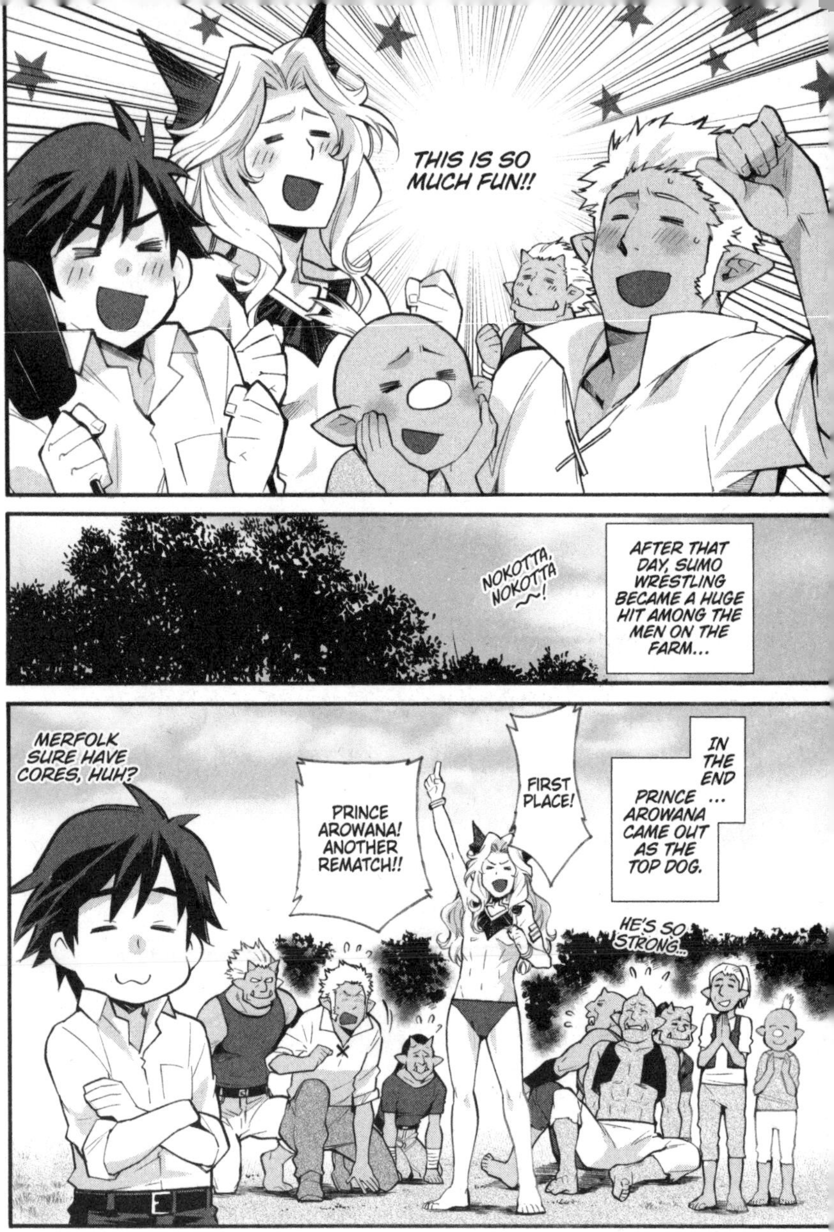
THIS IS SO MUCH FUN!!
AFTER THAT DAY, SUMO WRESTLING BECAME A HUGE HIT AMONG THE MEN ON THE FARM...
NOKOTTA, NOKOTTA ~!
IN THE END... PRINCE AROWANA CAME OUT AS THE TOP DOG.
FIRST PLACE!
PRINCE AROWANA! ANOTHER REMATCH!!
MERFOLK SURE HAVE CORES, HUH?
HE'S SO STRONG...

to be continued

LET'S BUY THE LAND and CULTIVATE IT IN A DIFFERENT WORLD

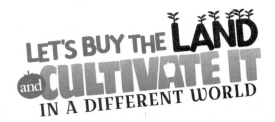

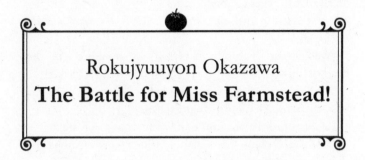

Rokujyuuyon Okazawa
The Battle for Miss Farmstead!

"Being born female means that you should always aim to be the strongest in the world," Veel said, blurting out that previously unheard-of phrase out of nowhere.

I was heading out to work in the fields, until her shouting this stopped me at the door.

"Things have been getting too rowdy here lately. You're fine, of course, my lord, but all these new monsters and demons have been loitering everywhere...and I don't feel good with this mob of creatures crowding my space. So..."

Veel looked at me decisively. "Why don't you choose?"

"Choose what?"

"Who's the strongest one here, that's what!"

The hell was she going on about? I wondered.

"A group can only find order under an obvious alpha!

The leader of a pack needs to be strong! That's the requirement! So, you gotta make it clear who's the strongest of all of us!" Veel continued.

I was really confused. *Seriously, what in the world was she talking about?*

"Well, I started this farm myself, so shouldn't I be the head of this farm? Am I not a qualified leader?" I asked.

"Oh, no, no, no, no! That's not what I meant! You're the best, my lord! That's not what I mean…!"

Veel was pretty cute stumbling over what to say next.

"It's like…I think it is worth figuring out who should be the leader of the women! You know, the matriarch!"

How does she even know that word?

Though it was true; the longer I lived on this farm, the more people have gradually settled here with me. First there was me, then Plattie elbowed her way in, and after I got to know Sensei, I met Veel.

Not long after, we were joined by Miss Astareth, Bati, Belena, then all the orcs and goblins, and finally the Demon Lord. The farm really has sprung to life, hasn't it?

It might just be her dragon instincts talking, but it seemed like whenever Veel integrated into a group, she wouldn't rest until there was a strong pecking order.

"So, let's decide who's the strongest chick here by battling it out! You can't survive if you're not ready to fight!"

Veel slyly limited the competition to women. With men disqualified, not only couldn't I participate, but neither could Sensei. The result of this was the fact that there weren't a lot of people left on the farm who could take on Veel. She was a dragon, after all.

"Let's not! Let's not!"

"Yeah, there's no way we can win against a dragon! Just let Veel have her victory!"

Bati and Belena cried out in protest from the girls' side.

Well, yeah. If you fought Veel, you were just going to die in the worst way possible. I'd be desperately finding any reason to not fight her, too...

"Don't worry! I don't wanna fight a battle where there aren't any stakes, so I'll give myself a handicap! I'll fight you in my current form!"

Her current form...? Oh, she means the human form she was currently taking.

Being a huge dragon was pretty inconvenient, so while on the farm Veel usually used magic to stay in the form of a cute little girl.

"If she's in that form, then maybe...?!"

"But...how much does her human form even limit her powers?"

To Bati and Belena's questions, Veel replied, "It doesn't change much at all. Even in my human form, I can blast away a whole mountain if I feel like it."

"Then that's not a handicap at all!"

Bati and Belena burst into tears, convinced they were absolutely going to hell. I really wanted to protest and stop this event altogether, but before I could...

"Ha ha...! Well, doesn't this sound interesting."

Someone suddenly showed up very eager to join the party: my mermaid wife, Plattie.

"I love these kinds of events. Who is the strongest woman? Doesn't everyone wanna know?"

My wife was way more eager to pick a fight than I expected.

"As a previous member of the Demon Lord's Four Heavenly Kings, I cannot turn down any challenge that comes my way."

Even Miss Astareth was going along with it.

So, we had Veel, Plattie, and Miss Astareth, versus Bati and Belena. Since there were five women on the farm, three to two voted in favor of the battle of the fittest.

May the gods bless their souls. I thought with a tinge of amusement.

"*Noooo*! I don't wanna *dieeee*! I still have my dream to open my own *stooore*!" Bati cried.

"'Here lies a fool who died fighting a dragon' will be carved upon my gravestone!" Belena, too, cried.

If they were so against it, they could just forfeit the fight…but then I remembered that they served under Miss Astareth. I heard it said that those who desert in the face of an enemy have no value as a warrior, and are destined to be executed. That explained why the two of them had no choice but to fight, even if they were in tears.

And so, the skirmish began. It took the form of a battle royale, where all the participants would fight all at once. A tournament or a round-robin would have been fine, but today was a normal work day for the farm, so I wanted this distraction to be over.

In short, I just wanted this to end as soon as possible.

"Astareth! Demonstrate your spotless record from the Demon Army! Don't break your winning streak!" The Demon Lord cheered.

"Gu hu hu huh! You fools! I will give you another chance

to witness the strength of a dragon! Witness my heaven-thundering, land-shaking power, and tremble on the ground in fear!"

Well, in most people's minds, Veel would be the obvious winner. It didn't matter if you were a Mermaid Princess or a demonic Heavenly King, even if you combined those forces and duplicated them a hundred times you had no chance of winning. The dragons were simply the most powerful mortal beings.

"Well...I'm sure you'd like to think that, but I, Plattie the Mermaid Princess, would be an idiot to stand in the ring without a chance of victory!"

Plattie brandished an unfazed smile.

"Let's begin the match! Duo of Honorable Defeat, come out!"

"I beg your pardon?!" Bati and Belena cried as they skipped their way out.

"Veel-sama! Feast your eyes on *this*!" the demons said in unison, while holding up a...

"What is *thaaaaat*?!" Veel yelled in shock. "Is that...the meat of a bird monster that protected my dungeon?! Hasn't that thigh meat been braising bone-in with soy sauce in a pot for hours till tender and savory?! It looks so *yummyyy*!"

Huh?! Aren't those yesterday's leftovers?! When did they swipe that?! I thought.

"If my lord made it, it must be *deliciousssss*! Gimme! Lemme eat it!"

In an instant, Veel rushed over, forgetting about everything except the piece of thigh meat dangling in front of her. She charged at full speed.

"Ugyaaaah!! She's coming right at us!"

"Belena, run! It's all over if she catches *youuuuu*!"

The two of them bolted away at full speed like madmen, still clutching the piece of thigh meat. I wondered what they were trying to even do, but with one look, their objective was clear.

"You're out! Veel, you lose."

"What?! Huh?!"

Veel's snapped out of it when she bit into the meat, but her senses returned too late.

That's right. I failed to mention this sooner, but we set up a boundary for this match. Plattie and the others who were at a disadvantage otherwise could have run into the forest for a chance to attack, guerilla-style, but that would have just prolonged the battle. *To think that they would use it to their advantage...* I thought, a bit surprised at their ingenuity.

Veel, with the piece of soy-braised meat clutched in her mouth, did not see where she was going and stepped out of bounds, defeated.

"Dammit! I can't believe these lowly mortals got me!"

"I guess your arrogance came out, huh?"

There was no doubt that Plattie came up with the plan, but the ones who made it happen were Bati and Belena. In order to lure their target, Veel, out of bounds, they also stepped over the line and lost...but I guess that was worth it. After all, what was important to them wasn't the glory, but surviving another day.

So, who remained now? Plattie and Miss Astareth. No one could have seen that coming. What? Those two are gonna fight each other?

"What a good opportunity. I've always wanted to see how strong one of the Four Heavenly Kings was with my own two hands."

"Originally, I came here to capture you, but that's now water under the bridge. Now I only want to see the skill of the most talented young woman in the Merfolk Kingdom."

Huh? What? What's with this serious competitive energy they're glowing with? Wasn't this battle supposed to end when Veel was eliminated? I had underestimated my wife's competitiveness again.

"Ufu fu... No matter how dedicated you were to your mission, I still don't think you could have captured me that easily. After all, I am one of the rare Merkingdom witches!"

"Then let me prove to you that my title as a Heavenly King is not simply for show!"

After that exchange of words, they leaped into action! The two were much more evenly matched than I imagined, going point for point. We, the spectators, watched their intense battle with hands clenched, dripping in sweat. Both the Demon Lord and I cheered for our wives until our voices grew raspy, and with each cheer, Plattie and Astareth fought masterfully. Magic potions flew in every direction, and swords flashed, until a strip of the farm was in left in a state of carnage.

Finally, the fight ended at a draw when the two were drained of all their energy, and collapsed simultaneously from exhaustion. It was tie.

The match that began from Veel's spontaneous idea blew up and finished bigger than I could have ever saw coming.

***

"Ugyaaaah!! She's coming right at us!"

"Belena, run! It's all over if she catches *youuuuu!*"

The two of them bolted away at full speed like madmen, still clutching the piece of thigh meat. I wondered what they were trying to even do, but with one look, their objective was clear.

"You're out! Veel, you lose."

"What?! Huh?!"

Veel snapped out of it when she bit into the meat, but her senses returned too late.

That's right. I failed to mention this sooner, but we set up a boundary for this match. Plattie and the others who were at a disadvantage otherwise could have run into the forest for a chance to attack, guerrilla-style, but that would have just prolonged the battle. *To think that they would use it to their advantage...* I thought, a bit surprised at their ingenuity.

Veel, with the piece of soy-braised meat clutched in her mouth, did not see where she was going and stepped out of bounds, defeated.

"Dammit! I can't believe these lowly mortals got me!"

"I guess your arrogance came out, huh?"

There was no doubt that Plattie came up with the plan, but the ones who made it happen were Bati and Belena. In order to lure their target, Veel, out of bounds, they also stepped over the line and lost...but I guess that was worth it. After all, what was important to them wasn't the glory, but surviving another day.

So, who remained now? Plattie and Miss Astareth. No one could have seen that coming. What? Those two are gonna fight each other?

"What a good opportunity. I've always wanted to see how strong one of the Four Heavenly Kings was with my own two hands."

"Originally, I came here to capture you, but that's now water under the bridge. Now I only want to see the skill of the most talented young woman in the Merfolk Kingdom."

Huh? What? What's with this serious competitive energy they're glowing with? Wasn't this battle supposed to end when Veel was eliminated? I had underestimated my wife's competitiveness again.

"Ufu fu... No matter how dedicated you were to your mission, I still don't think you could have captured me that easily. After all, I am one of the rare Merkingdom witches!"

"Then let me prove to you that my title as a Heavenly King is not simply for show!"

After that exchange of words, they leaped into action! The two were much more evenly matched than I imagined, going point for point. We, the spectators, watched their intense battle with hands clenched, dripping in sweat. Both the Demon Lord and I cheered for our wives until our voices grew raspy, and with each cheer, Plattie and Astareth fought masterfully. Magic potions flew in every direction, and swords flashed, until a strip of the farm was in left in a state of carnage.

Finally, the fight ended at a draw when the two were drained of all their energy, and collapsed simultaneously from exhaustion. It was a tie.

The match that began from Veel's spontaneous idea blew up and finished bigger than I could have ever seen coming.

***

SEVEN SEAS ENTERTAINMENT PRESENTS

LET'S BUY THE LAND and CULTIVATE IT
IN A DIFFERENT WORLD
VOLUME 3

story by ROKUJUUYON OKAZAWA   art by JUN SASAMEYUKI   character designs by YUICHI MURAKAMI

TRANSLATION
Jess Leif

ADAPTATION
Amanda Lafrenais

LETTERING
Isabell Struble

LOGO DESIGN
George Panella

COVER DESIGN
Nicky Lim

PROOFREADER
Leighanna DeRouen

EDITOR
Abby Lehrke

COPY EDITOR
B. Lillian Martin

PRODUCTION DESIGNER
Eve Grandt

PRODUCTION MANAGER
Lissa Pattillo

PREPRESS TECHNICIAN
Melanie Ujimori
Jules Valera

EDITOR-IN-CHIEF
Julie Davis

ASSOCIATE PUBLISHER
Adam Arnold

PUBLISHER
Jason DeAngelis

Isekai de Tochi wo katte Noujou wo tsukurou volume 3
© OKAZAWA ROKUJUUYON, SASAMEYUKI JUN/OVERLAP,
GENTOSHA COMICS 2020
Originally published in Japan in 2020 by GENTOSHA COMICS INC., Tokyo.
English translation rights arranged with GENTOSHA COMICS INC., Tokyo.
through TOHAN CORPORATION, Tokyo.

Seven Seas press and purchase enquiries can be sent to Marketing Manager Lianne
Sentar at press@gomanga.com. Information regarding the distribution and purchase of
digital editions is available from Digital Manager CK Russell at digital@gomanga.com.

Seven Seas and the Seven Seas logo are trademarks of
Seven Seas Entertainment. All rights reserved.

ISBN: 978-1-68579-492-7
Printed in Canada
First Printing: April 2023
10 9 8 7 6 5 4 3 2 1

READING DIRECTIONS

This book reads from *right to left*,
Japanese style. If this is your first time
reading manga, you start reading from
the top right panel on each page and
take it from there. If you get lost, just
follow the numbered diagram here.
It may seem backwards at first,
but you'll get the hang of it! Have fun!!

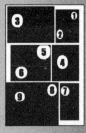

Follow us online: www.SevenSeasEntertainment.com